The Distorted World of Soviet-Type Economies

JAN WINIECKI

University of Pittsburgh Press

Series in Russian and East European Studies No. 8
Published in Great Britain by Croom Helm Ltd.
Published in the USA by the University of Pittsburgh Press, Pittsburgh
    Pa., 15260
Copyright © 1988, Jan Winiecki
Printed and bound in Great Britain

Library of Congress Cataloging-in-Publication Data

Winiecki, Jan.
    The distorted world of Soviet type economies / Jan Winiecki.
        p.   cm. — (Russian and East European studies)
    Bibliography: p.
    ISBN 0-8229-1149-3
    1. Central planning — Europe, Eastern. 2. Europe, Eastern —
Economic conditions — 1945- 3. Europe, Eastern — Economic policy.
I. Title. II. Series: Russian and East European studies
(Pittsburgh, Pa.)
HC244.W573   1988
338.947-dc19   87-25193

Contents

Abbreviations

CMEA	Alternative abbreviation for COMECON
COMECON	Council for Mutual Economic Assistance
CPE	Centrally planned economy
CPI	Consumer price index
CPSS	Communist Party of the Soviet Union
ECE	Economic Commission for Europe (UN)
FYP	Five-year plan
GDP	Gross domestic product
GNP	Gross national product
ISIC	International Standard Industrial Classification
LDC	Less developed country
MDC	'Middle' developed country
ME	Market economy
NMP	Net material product
PIG	Physical-indicators (global) methodology
R and D	Research and development
SD	Standard deviation
STE	Soviet-type economy
SYP	Seven-year plan
YP	Yearly plan

Introduction

The need for a book on system-specific economic distortions and their impact on economic performance of the Soviet-type economies was, not for the first time, strongly felt by me in the spring of 1983 in a Warsaw ice-cream parlor, while I discussed the latest developments in the area with an American friend, an expert on Eastern Europe. The friend, looking at the quite crowded place, remarked casually: 'I can imagine how crowded it will be after office hours.' 'Wrong', I said: 'After office hours, it will become half empty, since most people will go home or, more probably, go queueing somewhere.' Since there was so much to discuss, my friend saw for himself the place getting emptier and emptier as 4 p.m. approached.

I then realised once again that it was something more than a case of the misunderstanding of labour supply reactions in the Soviet-type economy.[1] It also furnished anecdotal evidence of the fact — and the umpteenth case of it — that even Western experts tend to take for granted the normality and, consequently, the universality of behavioural patterns grounded in the rationality of the Western system. Behind each piece of such anecdotal evidence of the misunderstanding by Western experts of one or another facet of the Soviet system was usually the underlying belief in a common rationality for both the market-type and the Soviet-type economies — a largely mistaken view.

Consequently, deviations from what may be regarded as behavioural normality in Western eyes seemed desirable as a focus of analysis for Soviet-type economies. Moreover, since behavioural deviations tend to translate themselves into economic distortions, in the sense of lasting adverse effects upon economic performance, it has been important to point out the links between deviations from Western rationality at the behavioural level and resultant economic losses — or gains forgone — at the aggregate level. Thus, the behaviour of economic agents in the Soviet system is rational at the micro level, but this rationality is clearly different from that of agents in the market system; and, what is more, there is no concordance between micro and macro rationality in the former, as there is in the latter. On the contrary, it is precisely the contradictions between the two that generate fundamental economic distortions.

A few comments about the book itself are in order. To begin with the readership, this is a researcher's book, and as such, it was written with other researchers in mind. I hope that at least some of them find enough new and provocative material herein to stimulate further discussion on the distortionary world of Soviet-type economies. However, given its non-mathematical presentational style, this is also a book for other readers as well — for scholars who are non-specialists in comparative economic studies and/or East European area studies, but are nonetheless interested in the subject; for officials dealing with East–West issues; and — last but not least — for business men involved in or envisaging trade or other deals with Eastern European institutions or enterprises. Readers from each group may find in this study answers to some vexing questions which are unanswerable on the basis of the rationality governing the behaviour of the economic agents in the system with which they are familiar.[2]

As to the style, the material in this book is presented in a largely non-mathematical fashion. This has not been done merely to attract the wider readership that I had in mind: for much of the theory — if not most of it — of the Soviet-type economy ought to take into account the distinctively different institutional and behavioural features of the system, such that its formal modelling in the tradition of modern Western economic theory would become a very precarious exercise.[3]

Readers will themselves be able to judge to what extent the presentational style has indeed become lighter as a result of the scattering throughout the pages of the book of the 'system-specific' jokes heard in Eastern Europe. However, the occasional joke was not only intended to give the reader a 'laughing space', but also to offer a joke *as a shortcut to understanding*. In addition, anecdotal evidence is sometimes presented along similar lines, since — in the words of a 1981 Polish cabaret song — life in the Soviet system surpassed anything cabaret writers could invent. An example would be the story of an enterprising Pole who took advantage of irrational relative prices and bought bottles of sorrel soup, poured the soup into the nearby streams, cleaned the bottles there, and sold empty bottles to salvage storehouses, with a profit rate of 150 per cent (less the cost of cleaning and transportation).[4] Or another story, this time from the long list of Potemkin village-type cases: a new Soviet factory was reported to be completed and a document putting it into commission was signed — although it existed only on paper! (*Pravda*, quoted in Dyker, 1982).

As regards the terminology, this author concurs with the view that Soviet-type economies (or STEs) represent a distinctive type of economic system and the term used reflects their most important feature (Clarke, 1983). Another term, 'centrally planned economies' (or CPEs) was more widely used in the past, but some countries (e.g. Hungary) claimed that they had shed the institutional characteristics of CPEs. Regardless of the validity of that claim, Hungary continues to be an STE since it retains the linkages between the political and economic system, both formal and informal, characteristic for the Soviet system as a whole.

On the other hand, the term 'Eastern Europe' (or East for short) has a distinctive usage in this book. The term covers both the Soviet Union *and* six smaller STEs: Bulgaria, Czechoslovakia, East Germany (GDR), Hungary, Poland, and Romania. The exclusion of the Soviet Union from 'Eastern Europe' found in many studies is not justified, because it is precisely the fact that they are within the Soviet sphere that makes the six smaller STEs *Eastern* European countries. After all, in earlier (and happier) times, the same area was called Central Europe . . .[5] Finally, the terms, STEs and East European countries are used with respect to *countries*, while the terms the Soviet-type economy, the Soviet system and central planning are used interchangeably with reference to *the economic system* dominant in Eastern Europe.

The content of this book and its order of presentation reflect the author's ideas concerning the fundamental distortions generated by STEs, as well as the linkages among them. Thus, the book is divided into three parts. The first part deals with the dynamics of the system, i.e. distortions affecting economic growth and price changes; the second with the structure of national economies as influenced by the dynamics of the system and the policies pursued (with special regard to the distortionary role of Soviet-type industrialisation); and the third with the impact of the dynamics and structure upon foreign trade performance and technology imports.

Some of the issues taken up in this book have already been studied extensively, as is the case with the so-called macroeconomics of central planning, i.e. aggregate quantity and price changes. What I have added to the picture is a behaviourally grounded clarification of the investment cycle concept, as well as the empirical evidence of the distortionary and inherently wasteful nature of the said phenomenon. Uncertainty has also been put into sharper focus. Another novel feature is a disaggregation of hidden inflation on the basis of establishing who is hiding it from whom, i.e. inflation hidden by the centre, by the public (meaning the enterprises) and half-hidden by both at the same time. Another classification of hidden inflation, according to whether hidden price change appears in the guise of quantity change or is hidden price change pure and simple, contributes in my view to the clarification of the somewhat muddled perception of the STE distortions existing in the price-quantity area.

If the first part of the book is mainly reinterpreting, reclassifying and empirically verifying concepts already in use in the literature on the subject, the second is different due to the presentation and later empirical verification of my own concepts. This change has been necessitated by the dearth of studies examining structural change and the inexorable structural distortions under central planning. Here I was venturing upon almost untouched ground. I used in particular the concept of twofold underspecialisation — at the level of a national economy and at that of an enterprise — to explain the empirically established distortions in the structure of production and employment of STEs that increasingly set them apart from the rest of the world in this respect. The concept may be seen as an intermediate explanation, since underspecialisation is itself caused by the dynamics of the Soviet system and that of its inward-oriented policy formation. The distortionary role of industry — or, more specifically, of the socialist industrialisation process — is a central theme of this second part of the study.

The third part of the book concentrates upon the foreign trade performance of the Soviet-type economies. Many thorough empirical studies in the literature on the subject freed me from the necessity of repeating my approach in the second part, where the evidence had to be built from scratch. Rather, I tried to link the characteristics of the dynamics and structure of STEs to their (poor) performance on the world market. Both the evolving theory of the STE and the received Western theory were useful in this exercise. In addition, my own theoretical considerations suggested why STEs failed in their attempt to reduce the developmental gap with the West through the import of technology and capital (contrary to what one would expect from the latter theory grounded in Western economic rationality).

In my conclusions, I restate the fundamental problems, i.e. the distortions generated in the areas of dynamics, structure and foreign trade, as well as stress the linkages between them and their mutually reinforcing character. Since distortions are increasingly costly, I also highlight the stagnation and decline facing the distorted world of the STEs.

Many of the chapters are based on or adapted from previously published articles. Thus Chapter 1 appeared in condensed form in

Banca Nazionale del Lavoro Quarterly Review, no. 157, 1986. Chapter 2 is an adapted version of an article in *Rivista Internazionale di Scienze Economiche e Commerciali*, nos. 10–11, 1986. Chapter 4 appeared in extended form in *Studies in Comparative and International Development*, vol. 23, 1988. Chapter 5 is an extended and rewritten article that appeared in *Economic Notes* of the Monte dei Paschi di Siena, no. 2, 1985. Chapter 6 is an adapted version of an article in *Technovation* vol. 6, 1987. The several publishers allowed me to integrate and elaborate upon these materials in this book, for which I express my appreciation. Also, I would like to thank MAW Publishers, Warsaw, for allowing the editors to use a cartoon published by them on the cover of this book.

NOTES

1. Quite a common occurrence for some economists: see the critique of Portes *et al.* in Winiecki (1985b).
2. For example, business men may find herein reasons for the failure of, or disagreement over, many licence-related deals (called 'industrial co-operation' in the official bureaucratic parlance).
3. For a critique by this author of disequilibrium modelling as applied to Soviet-type economies, see Kemme and Winiecki (1984) and Winiecki (1985b). See also Nove (1985).
4. At approximately the same time, a second entrepreneur bought bottles straight from the glass factory and sold them to salvage store-houses for a fat profit, given the large price differential in favour of price established for used bottles (in theory, to encourage recycling). The former found his profits taken away by *ad hoc* confiscatory taxes, and the later finished up in prison.
5. Or more rarely, East Central Europe.

Part One

The Distorted Macroeconomics of Central Planning

1

Quantities

1.1. PERMANENCE OF EXCESS DEMAND: A STATIC VIEW

The pitfalls awaiting analysts of Soviet-type economies (STEs) using a coherent framework have often been underestimated. These pitfalls are generally of two kinds: firstly, difficulties in explaining macro-economic relationships in terms of the received theory (whether neoclassical or Keynesian); and secondly, difficulties in using the distorted official data. Both sets of problems stem from the same sources. It is system-specific features which make the characteristic macro effects under central planning — excess demand, shortage, uncertainty — mean something somewhat different from those terms as they are understood by many Western economists (which is, by the way, an important source of misunderstanding). Moreover, the same features generate quantity and price distortions that again make STE statistics different from those in market economies (or MEs).

The author has tried to avoid both types of pitfalls. System-specific terminology and theoretical concepts that make otherwise valuable Eastern European contributions incomprehensible for the Western reader have either been eliminated or explained in under-standable terms. On the other hand, the author has also rejected as no less unsatisfactory, simplistic applications of Western disequi-librium theory to a different institutional setting.

In my view, the starting point for the analysis of the distorted dynamics of STEs is the perennial excess demand and shortage plaguing these economies. Both problems appeared in STEs almost from the start, and have become a permanent feature ever since. Over the years writings accumulated in both the East and in the West that tried to explain their sources and concomitants. To an extent we may even talk about a kind of consensus explanation, especially with

3

respect to the incentive structure that generates excess demand.[1] In a condensed form it runs as follows. There exist certain system-specific features that result in what Kornai (1971, 1972, 1979, 1980) has called 'rush growth' and a group of Polish economists centred at one time around Wakar[2], less well known than Kornai in the West, dubbed 'expansive formulas of management'. According to these authors, enterprises in STEs have from the start felt the impact of the structure of incentives that motivated them to expand production almost at any cost. In other words, incentives to execute and exceed plan targets were positively correlated with volume or value of production, but were not at the same time negatively correlated with production costs. This structure of incentives did not change substantially and has been dominant under both traditional (command-type) and modified (mixed command/parametric-type) policy instruments.

Central planners, in their fundamentally autarkic approach, usually react to perceived needs in only one way — i.e. by trying to increase production of goods in short supply. Thus, plans are drawn up, which with respect to aggregate economic growth and the production structure (especially the latter!) cannot be executed due to the shortage of resources. There may be many simultaneously existing causes for this shortage. The first may be that the resources are not there because *the quantities reported earlier by enterprises were* — to some degree — *fictitious*. It is a perennial problem in STEs where everybody at the enterprise level, from manager to worker, is interested in showing doctored performance figures.[3] This 'imaginative reporting' may take the form of pure fiction, i.e. reporting higher output volume than the actual one. Possibilities of such imaginative reporting are enormous. According to A. Shitov, first deputy chairman of the USSR Committee for National Control, 'to a greater or smaller extent additions [to the actual output figures] and other distortions were discovered in every third enterprise' (*Planovoye Khozyaistvo,* no. 11, 1981).

Doctored reports may concern everything from sophisticated machinery (again, see Shitov, ibid.) to homogeneous commodities, like coal or cotton, as was the case some years ago with respect to the former in Poland and Romania, and in Uzbekistan (USSR) with respect to the latter. Other methods of doctoring are probably much more numerous, i.e. reports of higher output volume when in fact only output value increased.[4] Thus, plan targets are executed or even exceeded, but a part of output — that constitutes input for other enterprises — exists only on paper.

The second reason for resource shortage may be that *the resources are not of the right quality*. To stay with the simple example of coal, enterprises, in their attempts at executing or exceeding plan targets, lower the quality of output (that is, coal's calorific content) by adding more non-coal ingredients. This not only plays havoc with the central planners' balancing activity, but also has further negative repercussions for domestic[5] coal users; and if downward quality shifts exist with respect to homogeneous goods like coal, they are all the greater with respect to differentiated ones.

The third reason may be that *the resources are not of the right type*. The suppliers are usually interested in producing as few types, grades, sizes, etc., as possible. Since enterprises in STEs cannot turn to another supplier, they either have an option of producing from, say, thicker steel plates and using more labour and capital inputs, more energy and — by definition — more costly material (steel), or that of not producing at all.[6] The inability of an enterprise in a STE to obtain the right type of inputs does not stem from the fact that it is tied to a specific supplier (because under the modified system of central planning it is not so tied), but because it knows that other domestic suppliers behave in the same way (this explains, *inter alia*, the permanent preference for imports, and, more specifically, for imports from the West.[7]

The fourth reason for resource shortage may be that the *resources are not there at the right time*. Even the most centralised planning cannot dream of allocating everything in detail, and such details are left to enterprises. And for an enterprise that was given a command to produce something, it makes a difference whether an input-producing enterprise ships a given input at the beginning, in the middle or at the end of a planning period (a month, quarter or a year). A command to supply inputs does not specify such details and it should not be forgotten that a supplier is itself coping with shortages of its own. Thus, delayed shipments may interrupt production schedules.

The fifth reason may be that the resources *are not given at the right place*. In the aggregate, there may be enough of a given input of the right quality and type to allocate among enterprises but there are general priorities (producer, i.e. intermediate and investment, goods), specific priorities (investment projects on a priority list) and *ad hoc* priorities (created by political interventions — see next section) which together result in the misallocation of inputs.

At this point it is worth noting that the first three causes outlined

5

above stress the existence of shortages due to the system-specific structure of incentives, while the last two highlight the other institutional and policy characteristics of a STE. They also imply the impossibility of proper plan-execution in the (theoretical) case of a plan that is feasible, i.e. in which the aggregate amount of inputs is exactly that needed for plan execution (on this point, see Ericson, 1983).

The above shortages interact, creating *the overall climate of shortage*. Shortage is further aggravated by the behaviour of enterprises which, being aware of shortages and trying to minimise the risk of non-execution of the plan stemming from shortages, demand excessive labour, spare parts for the equipment, and material inputs. As every enterprise behaves in this way — and everybody else knows that others behave thus — additional excess demand is generated (on hoarding and inventories, see, *inter alia*, Goldmann and Kouba, 1969; Kornai, 1980; Winiecki, 1982; and Porket, 1984). It should be noted that in a STE, shortage is a *relative* rather than an absolute phenomenon. The amount of inputs expended per unit of output is inordinately high in STEs. Table 1.1. illustrates this with respect to energy and steel.

It will be shown elsewhere that the excessive use of inputs is partly related to the overgrown industrial sector in STEs (see Chapter 3). However, the fact that the industrial sector, so large relative to that of MEs, is unable to eliminate persistent shortage is yet another indictment against central planning, not a justification of inordinately high input use. The same may be said with respect to the aggravating factor considered here, i.e. much higher inventories per unit of output in STEs than in market economies (in Hungary, for example, they are twice as high: Kornai, 1982).

It should not be surprising, then, that actual figures for inventories deviate from plan targets by more than those for other indicators: for example, in Poland during the three consecutive five-year plans (or FYPs), actual figures for inventories exceeded planned ones by between 23.5 and 48.8 per cent (Maciejewski and Zajchowski, 1982). Even if shortages are more relative than real, however, excess demand is very real, for indeed, there are no adequate resources of the right quality and type at the right time and place.[8]

The results are well known. An important one is *increased costs* of production in the rush when enterprises are striving to execute or exceed planned quality targets or they are trying to make up for the time lost due to late deliveries of material inputs. Another result is

Table 1.1: Resource intensity of East European STEs and industrialised West European MEs: the cases of energy and steel, 1979–80

Countries	Energy intensity in 1979 (in kg of coal equiv. consumption per 1000 US dollars[b] of GDP	Steel intensity in 1980 (in kg of steel consumption per 1000 US dollars[b] of GDP
East European STEs[a]		
Bulgaria	1464	87
Czechoslovakia	1290	132
Hungary	1058	88
GDR	1356	88
Poland	1515	135
Soviet Union	1490	135
Average, unweighted (6)	1362	111
West European MEs		
Austria	603	39
Belgium	618	36
Denmark	502	30
Finland	767	40
France	502	42
FRG	565	52
Italy	655	79
Norway	1114	38
Sweden	713	44
Switzerland	371	26
United Kingdom	820	38
Average, unweighted (11)	660	42

Notes: a. Except Romania
b. US$ of 1979
Sources: *World development report* (1981); *Yearbook of international statistics* (1981); own calculations.

the *decline in quality*, when enterprises decide not to wait for inputs of the right quality and use inputs of a sub-standard quality. In fact, lower quality is also a concomitant of 'rushed production'. Not only specific supply problems, but also the general climate of buyers' pressure for more output, imbues suppliers with a careless attitude towards cost and quality; and this, in turn, demoralises, to a varying extent, the labour force which in turn takes an equally careless attitude towards materials and equipment. (After all, both enterprises as goods suppliers and workers as labour suppliers perform on the seller's market!)

The results are cost overruns that are compensated at higher levels of the bureaucratic hierarchy by subsidies, lower taxes, price increases, and so on, with the tacit understanding that it is quantity — always in short supply — that counts most. In this way, 'hard' direct commands to produce are accompanied under central planning by 'soft' budget constraints (to use Kornai's (1979, 1980) term) with respect to input costs. Quantity performance becomes almost completely divorced from financial performance. This situation may continue almost indefinitely. Even in Hungary, with its modified system, the list of (pre-1968) largest loss-makers did not differ much from a similar list drawn a dozen years later before the next phase of systemic modifications in the early 1980s (Csaba, 1983b).

Enterprise demand is thus almost infinite under central planning. In order to put this unusual situation in terms of classical economics and illustrate it diagrammatically in the price-quantity space, demand of enterprises should be marked by a vertical, i.e. price-independent, demand line. At the same time, supply should also be marked by a vertical line, since production plans are fixed in advance and are also price- (and demand-) independent. In Figure 1.1, the Q_1Q_2 section of the abscissa determines the size of excess demand that is independent of the price level. Kornai (1979, 1980) is right in stating that excess demand may persist under stable, falling or rising prices. Incidentally, the situation presented on the diagram implies that with respect to producer goods, the official price index is irrelevant as a measure of excess demand (even if prices are allowed to fluctuate). They are not much more relevant with respect to consumer goods either, as will be shown in the next chapter.

Later, in the second and third parts of this book, it will be shown that years and decades of economic growth under central planning has built into the system lasting distortions that aggravate shortages even further and make excess demand much worse and more difficult to eliminate. Their inclusion at this point would not change the picture, however, because they are also system-specific. What has been shown so far is system-specific institutions and policies whose interactions reproduce excess demand independently of 'taut', 'mobilising' or simply over-optimistic plans decreed by central planners and their political masters. (On the endogeneity of shortages and excess demand, and their independence from this, much over-emphasised, feature of STEs, see Tamas Bauer, 1978; Kornai, 1979, 1980 and Winiecki, 1982).

We have so far been considering the producer goods market alone. This is a legitimate approach, for it is in the world of central

Figure 1.1: Vertical, i.e. price-independent, demand line, depicting unlimited demand of enterprises in STEs under conditions of soft budget constraint. The supply line is also vertical due to the rigidity of the plan and resultant demand-independence of supply. Excess demand, i.e. Q_1Q_2, will be the same under the existing price level (P_0), as well as under higher (P_2) or lower (P_3) price levels.

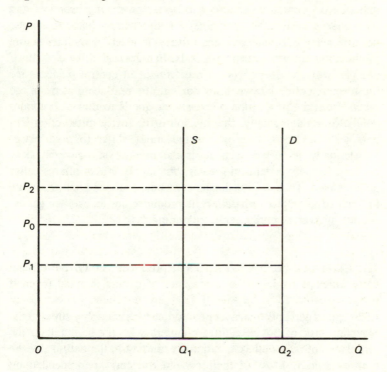

planners (here lumped together with the intermediate levels of bureaucratic hierarchy) and enterprises that most fundamental distortions arise. Nonetheless, their consequences spill over to the consumer goods market. We deal with some of them, i.e. various atypical inflationary phenomena in STEs, in the next chapter. Here, only some fundamentals are outlined in order to round off the picture of permanent excess demand.

Thus, higher production costs under the conditions of shortage described above spill over to the consumer goods market through labour hoarding and overtime, which together result in the exceeding of plan targets for wage-fund growth. In Poland over the period 1960–75, for example, the wage fund and the average monthly wage were amongst those indicators whose actual yearly figures deviated from planned yearly figures (YPs) by the largest percentage (Maciejewski and Zajchowski, 1982). Since increased incomes did not meet commensurate increases in consumer goods, excess has been created on the demand side.

Kornai (1979, 1980) strengthens the case by highlighting the fact that enterprises in both sectors (i.e. those producing producer and consumer goods) often compete for the same material inputs, because many of them may alternatively be used for the production of either producer or consumer goods. In a general climate of short-age and with the deeply rooted preferences of central planners for the former, policy interventions during YPs reallocate some of the inputs from the production of consumer goods to that of producer goods. Methodologically, the division of industrial production into two sectors allows such undetected input shifts to take place. Substantially, an inflationary gap is also created on the supply side, because not only is demand greater, but supply is also often smaller than planned. Thus, excess demands on both markets are inseparable in spite of attempted separation of producer and consumer goods-producing sectors under central planning.[9]

1.2. CENTRAL PLANNING AND UNCERTAINTY: THE TWIN BROTHERS

Long ago, a perceptive analyst of a Soviet-type economy stressed the Sisyphus task of Soviet central planners who try to maintain the semblance of balance in the national economy in the absence of the scarcity prices. Most of their time and effort are expended on substituting — very imperfectly — central planning for the most elementary accomplishments of the market system (Grossman, 1963). This view, shared by many, may be put in sharp focus in the light of our earlier considerations.

It is true that thousands of the so-called material balances drawn by planners at all levels of the bureaucratic hierarchy still leave a lot of room for uncertainty in the face of millions of products, final and intermediate, manufactured in STEs (for example, some 20 million in the Soviet Union).[10] This is what everyone points out when stressing the balancing problems of central planning. However, these size-equals-complexity views rest on two underlying assump-tions. The first assumption is that the data upon which material balances are based reflect reality, while the second equates the macroeconomic balance between supply and demand with the non-existence of shortages.

The preceding subsection enables us to understand why neither of these assumptions is true for STEs. The structure of incentives there is such that the reports on plan implementation include various overstatements as to quantity and/or quality that leave balancing activities on very shaky ground. What looks at the planning stage as a balance may quite often hide an excess demand that appears during the implementation stage, because either the quantity turns out to be lower than the one taken into account while drawing the balance, or lower quality generates demand for higher than planned quantity.

Interestingly, central planners' behaviour tends in some respects to confirm the existence of uncertainty about plan implementation figures. Since they are not sure as to what extent reported figures are realistic, they allocate supplies for the early part of the year at a level *lower* than that of the previous year (some 65–95 per cent of last year's actual supplies). Obviously, once they become convinced that supplies really increased — even if they are still uncertain by how much — they subsequently allocate higher quantities of supplies (for the USSR, see *Planovoye Khozyaistvo*, no. 3, 1977). Their perception of the situation continues, however, to be deficient in any case.

Next, even if planned quantity and quality of supplies happen to balance demand *in the aggregate*, it does not mean that inputs of the required quantity, quality and type will be delivered at the right time in the right place. Microeconomic shortages may appear even under the conditions of excess supply (if high inventories in STEs are taken into account),[11] but — as we have already noted in passing — there are no forces in a STE that, in the absence of a proper price system and a hard budget constraint for enterprises, would shift the excessive supplies to where they are needed.

Thus, it is system-specific features, on top of the problems arising from the size of the economy, that make uncertainty a twin brother of central planning at both the planning and implementation stages. For the same reasons outlined earlier, this uncertainty is not only great, but also unevenly distributed, increasing with the level of bureaucratic hierarchy. The latter feature may also be explained in the light of our earlier considerations.

The direct (or in modified STEs, indirect) subordination of enterprises to higher levels of the hierarchy does not prevent them from holding more trump cards at any stage. At the stage of plan preparation, enterprises are usually able to beat central planners in the game

11

where the centre wants to increase the level of planned output by a maximum percentage and the allocated inputs by a minimum percentage, while enterprises try to achieve the opposite outcome.[12]

It ought to be added that, in spite of the pressure from above, middle levels of the hierarchy usually support the resource claims of 'their' enterprises. (Therefrom stem recurrent fulminations of communist leaders against ministers that strive to take most and give least. Names are named from time to time, Gorbachev's speeches being the latest example,[13] but ministers come and go, while the practice remains, since slack plans with ample resources are easier to implement and figures look better when reported.)

However, even if the game is played with higher figures due to pressure from above, it is uncertainty everywhere in the system that increases, while enterprises usually find some valid excuses in case plans are not fully implemented (or at least reported as such). For they may be reasonably sure that there will be many shortages during the plan execution period that allow them to put the blame on somebody else, obtain reduction of plan targets and gain most of the plan-implementation-related rewards. In the Soviet Union, for example, 57 per cent of enterprises in 1980 obtained reductions in the output plan targets during the implementation period, some 33 per cent as late as in December (*Planovoye Khozyaistvo*, no. 11, 1981).

The knowledge of the game described above is not new in the literature. It dates back to the early works of Berliner (1952, 1956, 1957) on Soviet enterprises. Important here, however, is its impact upon the distribution of uncertainty. In the system in which everyone up to the highest but one level of the hierarchy is interested in producing performance figures which are better than they actually are,[14] the only undistorted figures may be those at the enterprise level or, to be more exact, those remaining *within* the enterprise (because figures reported upwards are quite often doctored to its advantage). Herein lies the relative strength of the enterprise. As far as its information needs are concerned, it is simply on a less shaky ground.

That relative strength continues throughout the whole stage of plan execution. The enterprise continues to rely on less distorted data than those available to its superiors in evaluating its prospects of plan implementation. Its managers know the true level of employment (not always truly reported upwards[15] for fear of being ordered to 'compress' it[16]), they know more or less the productive capacity (affected, however, by machinery breakdowns and variable input

Table 1.2: The structure of inventories in industry[a] in selected Soviet-type and market economies

Country	Year	Share in total stocks in industry (%)			
		Raw materials, purchased intermediate products, fuels, etc.	Unfinished production, produced intermediate products	Spare parts for equipment	Finished products, goods for resale
1	2	3	4	5	6
Czechoslovakia	1981	64.5	21.3	—[b]	10.4
Hungary	1976	—	—	—	11.9
Poland	1970	63.0	21.9	—[b]	15.1
	1980	63.5	24.5	—[b]	12.0
	1983	62.9	23.2	—[b]	13.9
Soviet Union	1970	59.3	22.3	3.9	14.6
	1980	57.7	23.5	4.4	14.3
GDR	1963	—	—	—	15.4
Austria	1976	—	—	—	32.1
Canada	1970	—	—	—	31.3
Japan	1975	—	—	—	53.2
Sweden	1977	—	—	—	38.2

Notes: a. Excluding intertemporal accounts.
b. Included in column 3.
Sources: For Czechoslovakia, Poland and Soviet Union — national statistical yearbooks and own calculations; for the rest, see Kornai (1982).

quality), and the inventories (but not the variable quality of stocked inputs). Uncertainty is greatest with respect to the inflow of inputs from other enterprises. On the other hand, there is almost no uncertainty with respect to outputs. They are sure to find demand on the seller's market for almost anything they care to produce.[17] Goods are shipped to purchasers almost as fast as they are produced. The comparative data for STEs and MEs on respective shares of inputs and outputs in inventories of manufacturing enterprises bear witness to this. In STEs, the share of the latter is 2–3 times lower (see Table 1.2).

The situation is different at higher levels of the hierarchy. The further one moves up the hierarchy, the more aggregated the figures are and the more distortions they contain. The figures look better, because some enterprises exceeded their monthly or quarterly plan targets while others fell short of theirs. These figures are misleading, however, because they contain an unknown share of non-existent or lower quality products and these will affect production elsewhere (see

13

above). Thus, aggregate economic growth figures may not deviate very much from planned ones due to the above-mentioned netting out procedure and a contribution of upwardly distorted reporting. However, other aggregated plan indicators, not affected by all these distortions, as well as more disaggregated indicators, will deviate markedly from the plan. Recent remarkably candid publication on the scale of these deviations in Poland, covering 182 disaggregated indicators for the period of 1960–76, prove the point. According to Maciejewski and Zajchowski (1982), only in 19.3% of cases were there no deviations at all from the plan, or deviations were less than 1%. In 39.1% of cases deviations were larger than 5% and in 19% of cases they were even greater than 10%. Thus, the number of cases of the exact plan implementation was equal to the number of those where it exceeded or fell short by more than 10% (with both over- and underproduction having disequilibrating effects in the basically closed economy. The details are shown in Table 1.3.

Significantly, the same publication stresses a high degree of uncertainty with respect to actual outcomes continuing almost until the last moment. Even September predictions of end-year production figures — made, therefore, only three full months before the end of the YP — missed the mark by more than 1% in almost two-thirds of cases, and in 20.9% of cases deviations were higher than 5% (details given in Table 1.3.). There are no data of comparable breadth and length of coverage for any other STE, but the doubters thinking that Poland may be a special case should be reminded that until the mid-1970s, and especially under Gomulka in the 1960s (two-thirds of the period under analysis), Poland was a fairly typical STE.

A Soviet survey made by the Central Statistical Office on the plan implementation in engineering industries in the 1976–78 period with respect to quantities of the 149 most important product groups found that only in 89, 94 and 86 product groups were plans fully implemented or exceeded (59.7%, 63.1% and 57.7% respectively). With respect to the remaining product groups implementation fell short of the plan targets (*Planovoye Khozyaistvo*, no. 8, 1979). The survey is fragmentary in comparison with the Maciejewski–Zajchowski study but its results display similar features. If we assume that the amount of upward deviations is similar to that of downward deviations (40.3%, 36.9% and 42.3%), we arrive at the 18–22% of cases of the exact plan implementation of output targets. That percentage does not differ from the 19.3 percentage figure obtained by the said Polish authors.

Table 1.3: The pattern of deviations of actual from planned and predicted[a] production figures in Poland for 198 indicators, 1961–76

The range of deviations in percentages	The deviations from the plan	The deviations from the predictions
	The percentage of cases within a given range	
1	2	3
0–1	19.3	36.6
1–2	14.2	19.7
2–3	11.5	11.3
3–4	8.4	6.9
4–5	7.5	4.6
5–6	5.7	3.6
6–7	4.9	3.4
7–8	3.5	1.7
8–9	3.0	2.4
9–10	3.0	1.7
10 and more	19.0	8.1

Note: a. Predictions conducted every year in September.
Source: Maciejewski and Zajchowski (1982).

Thus, uncertainty, pervasive under central planning, is, like shortage and excess demand, endogenous to the system. Those who maintain that the growth maximisation strategy, a policy-specific rather than a system-specific feature, is at the root of each of these phenomena would see all these phenomena as persisting under 'slack', 'modest' or 'reasonable' plans, as well as under more familiar 'taut', 'ambitious' and 'optimistic' ones. The centre (central planners and their political masters) may leave its imprint on economic performance as a result of whims and wishes but that would be *over and above problems generated endogenously by the system itself* — for example, shortage, excess demand and uncertainty persisted in Poland both under the cautious Gomulka and the reckless Gierek.

We ought to remember, however, that it is not only the centre which may leave its imprint upon the performance of an STE. Uniquely in communist countries there exists a strange type of linkage between political and economic hierarchies, and in consequence, multiple pressures on management persistently appear at various levels of the latter. Party organisations not only use their clout to assure a larger share of the investment pie for 'their' enterprises (located on their territory or otherwise under their control), but also intervene with respect to changes in plan targets, additional supplies, etc. Each time, political interventions set in motion the whole procedure of commands and reports throughout the bureaucratic hierarchy, clogging information channels and increasing uncertainty even further. The resultant *ad hoc* priorities superimposed upon earlier ones aggravate the supply situation. Thus, not only the Politbureau (a commanding segment of the centre), but also other Party bodies and individual apparatchiks adversely affect the performance of the economy under central planning, without bearing any responsibility for the results.[18]

1.3. INVESTMENT CYCLES: A DYNAMIC VIEW ON EXCESS DEMAND

So far we have outlined a picture of STEs as economies where shortage and excess demand continually persist for system-specific reasons. These phenomena are accompanied by yet another one, i.e. a high degree of uncertainty, as the system, with great effort but without commensurate effect, tries to substitute for the elementary allocational capability of the market. However, this picture, although true enough, is a static one. It is a well known fact that STEs are characterised by rapid accelerations and decelerations first of all of the investment component of their GNP equivalent (net material product — NMP).[19] It will be argued below that these fluctuations have had a powerful and, over time, an increasing impact upon the pattern of shortage and excess demand under central planning.

However, many different interpretations were advanced to explain cyclical fluctuations of investments in STEs (see, *inter alia*, overviews in Bajt (1971), Tamas Bauer (1978), Dahlstedt (1980), Winiecki (1982)). Thus I will begin with the refutation of certain most commonly held views, restate[20] my own view on investment fluctuations in general and within the FYP horizon in particular, and only then move on to describe the ideal type, i.e. 'model' investment cycle, and deviations from that model.

Analysts of the investment fluctuations usually agree that excess demand for investments stems from perceived shortage and resultant necessity to increase production. It is this demand, augmented by all formal and informal incentives inducing enterprises (and their superiors in the bureaucratic hierarchy) to strive for more investments, that is at the root of recurrent over-expansions followed, in due course, by cut-backs in expenditures. However, regardless of whether these authors evaluate excess demand positively in normative terms as a 'right to grow' (e.g. Pajestka, 1975) or negatively as a 'growth psychosis' (e.g. Romuald Bauer *et al.*, 1972), they all miss the most important point. If output growth is so highly regarded within each multi-level bureaucratic hierarchy in an STE, why should output grow only through putting on stream new capacities at the same level of technological sophistication? There exists an obvious (and less costly) alternative of output growth through innovation: technological change and/or reorganisation of production factors already at hand.[21] Obviously, it is not output growth *per se* but such growth through investments in new capacities that is sought by enterprises.

Yet another explanation of excess demand for investments is that it is a costless method from the enterprise viewpoint, since most investments were financed from the state budget (e.g. Khachaturov, 1975). However, cost (i.e. financial) considerations cannot be taken too seriously in an economy in which enterprises enjoy soft budget constraint. In any case various modifications of central planning in the 1960s and 1970s changed the financial structure of investments, increasing the role of self-financing and banking credit, while investments have continued to be the preferred method of expansion. Sources of excess demand for investments must then lie elsewhere. It is, again, as in the case of general excess demand, the structure of incentives to which we turn as the main source of this particular excess demand.

The present author stressed earlier (Winiecki, 1982)[22] the risk-averting behaviour under central planning in this respect. Enterprise managers evaluate their growth possibilities within the framework of the present and future plan targets first of all from the viewpoint of *minimising the risk* of non-implementation of output plan targets in the short term, be they formulated in volume or value terms. The lesser the risk, the lower the possibility of losing premiums and bonuses tied to the execution of the plan (as well as losing the high regard of their superiors). From where they stand the risk of expansion through investments, preferably new investments, is by far the lowest.

Firstly, every innovation, technical or managerial,[23] is introduced into the already existing productive facilities; and personnel operating these facilities are interested in implementing plan targets, first and foremost for the present planning period. The incentive system influences them strongly in this direction. Even if innovation would result in increased output, the risk associated with

17

introducing it — a risk of too long a period of technology absorbtion or resource reorganisation and resultant disturbances to production schedules — would cause managers generally to avoid such methods of expansion. In addition, as it has often happened in practice, increased productivity, if successful, would result in having the plan targets raised in the next planning period (the well-known 'ratchet' principle), so an extra effort could even be counterproductive, for it would be more difficult to implement the next year's plan and to get related premiums and bonuses.

In contrast, expansion of production capacity through new investments is achieved at no great effort, and what is more important, at no risk at all. A new plant or an expansion of the existing one is being implemented *outside* the already-existing capacity and without affecting production schedules there. There is no risk stemming from new investment with respect to plan execution. Even if production from new capacity is included in the plan and fails to materialise due to delays in completing a given project, the responsibility rests with a construction enterprise and material rewards for implementing or exceeding plan targets from existing capacity are still obtained.

Secondly, analysis of excess investment demand in terms of risk-averting behaviour also enables us to understand the commonly displayed preference for new investments rather than less costly modernising projects. The explanation is sometimes offered in psychological terms, viewing this preference as a carry-over from the early industrialisation era when new plants were status symbols of a rapidly industrialising country. Psychology, of course, may play a role, but preferences for new investments have a perfect economic explanation. Modernising investments, just like non-investment-based innovations, affect the existing productive capacity and bring with them a similar type of risk to which we have been pointing above. Seen from that angle, they are certainly less attractive for enterprises relative to new investments.

This explanation, incidentally, explains very well why various reforms in the 1960s and 1970s that tried to limit *absolute* attractiveness of investments were doomed to fail (and they did so): for it is the reduction of *relative* attractiveness of investments *vis-à-vis* innovations, coupled with other far-reaching changes in the system, that may decrease demand for investments of risk-averting managers of enterprises. This, however, would require reforms to change the fundamental features of central planning. It should be noted in passing that even the farthest reaching reforms of the period, i.e. the

Hungarian reforms of 1968, did not significantly reduce (if at all) excess demand for investments (see for example, Drecin, 1971; Drecin and Tar, 1978). In fact even modifications in Hungary and elsewhere, introduced in the 1980s, did not change the pattern of excess demand for investments. Although investment growth rates fell significantly in STEs, and in some of them investments declined in absolute terms, actual figures almost uniformly exceeded plan targets (see both sets of figures in *Economic Survey of Europe*, 1982/3–1985/6).

After explaining excess demand for investments in STEs, we turn to the issue of how this demand affects the aggregate behaviour of the national economy, i.e. how investments expand and contract in a cyclical manner. To this end we put the risk-averting behaviour of enterprises within the framework of planning with its typical FYP time horizon. We begin with the procedure of the preparation of the investment part of a FYP. Enterprises presenting their investment demands to the higher levels of the hierarchy are trying to present the proposals in the best possible light in order to obtain the desired funds. With that aim in view, they often underestimate the costs of proposed investment projects and/or overestimate the results. It is the time-honoured method of 'hooking into the plan' stemming from the conviction that cost overruns will be validated through increased funding under pressure of the argument that giving up the completion of unfinished investment projects will entail losses for the national economy.[24] This is, by the way, just another manifestation of Kornai's soft budget constraint principle.

Investment proposals of enterprises become aggregated as they move up the institutional hierarchy. Even if there are some preliminary limits drawn by central planners for ministries and by the latter for unions of enterprises, they are by and large disregarded, as each institution, given the incentive system, is vying to expand production. Thus, after aggregating the demand for investments at the central level, it usually turns out that the demand by far exceeds the funds (and capacities) earmarked for investment for the next planning period. In consequence, cuts are ordered down the line.

However, there is no possibility at the central planners' level for evaluating proposals on a project-by-project basis (it exists with respect to a few major projects and even here in general terms only). Cuts are usually of financial character, ministries are ordered to cut planned investment expenditures by a specified amount or percentage, and the procedure is repeated at each level. As a result, a few projects are dropped, while each remaining project is allocated somewhat less than requested. *Cuts from above are thus increasing the extent of distortions built in from below*, for real costs of planned investments have often already been underestimated.

Thorough assessments as to the size of the underestimates are rarely made, but in Hungary a 20–50 per cent range of cost overruns per project is being mentioned (Brody, 1983), while in Czechoslovakia a more precise figure of 25.4 per cent of cost over-runs on industrial investment projects in the late 1970s was put forward (Srejn and Novotny, 1980). The same figure for the late 1960s for the Soviet Union was 37 per cent (Plyshevsky, 1972). Projects not only cost more but also last longer. Gestation periods are often 50–100 per cent or more longer than planned (e.g. Brody (1983) for Hungary, and Khachaturov (1975) for the Soviet Union). Thus, the cost increase per project is spread over more years, while yearly expenditure overruns as compared with plans include not only cost overruns per project but also costs of the inclusion of new, originally unplanned, projects.

In consequence, the FYP typically starts with significant built-in distortions in its investment component. These distortions exercise, over time, an increased pressure on aggregate equilibrium (or, rather, lower-scale disequilibrium).[25] Shortages multiply and excess demand begins to grow. The producer goods sector of manufacturing and the construction sector are trying to meet invest-ment demand but it is here that underestimated costs and/or over-estimated results exert their strongest influence. On the one hand, new factories whose output had already been included in the planned output figures do not reach the expected capacity or do not even begin producing, while on the other, expenditures have already been made and wages, premiums and bonuses paid out.[26]

Aggregate disequilibrium usually reaches its peak in the middle of the medium-term plan, i.e., beginning with the early 1960s in the middle of the FYP. Those who would stress the lack of theoretical foundations upon which this assertion is based (e.g. gestation periods of investment projects may be shorter or longer than five years), should realise that a five-year horizon constitutes a corset put upon the real economic processes and exerts a strong influence upon the behaviour of economic agents. That influence is also strong in the case of those who put that corset upon the economy in the first place, i.e. upon central planners.

With their sights affected by the planning horizons, they see the investment cost increases and wage fund increases exceeding targets by substantial margins, while on the other hand, new capacities are not coming on stream to relieve shortages of both producer and consumer goods. Additionally, input shifts (see first section) aggravate the situation on the consumer goods market. Thus, with half of the planning period already over and increases in new capacities increasingly falling behind, they decide to intervene. At mid-point they resign themselves to the fact that all planned investment projects will not be completed by the end of the FYP. Thus, they decide to concentrate on those deemed to be most important and (optionally) on decreasing the disequilibrium on the consumer goods market. The second goal (if pursued) would also affect the selection of projects to be given priority at this point. All this makes the third year of a FYP a likely candidate for a policy change, usually with a year's lag effects of that change being felt throughout the rest of the FYP.[27]

Investment and production plans are then extensively revised and it is worth stressing that only now, when the scale of cost overruns and delays begins to be recognised, that cuts in investment plans are more project- than funds-oriented. Many projects are 'mothballed', with further construction postponed until the next FYP, and some others discontinued altogether. It is at this point that the economy begins to bear the burden of the so-called 'costs without results', for mothballed or discontinued projects appear only on the one side of the ledger.

The remainder of the FYP is usually a period when no substantial investment projects are started, while those started earlier are being completed. If the cuts are large and the share of the projects in the consumer goods' sector completed in that period is sufficiently large, excess demand for producer goods is decreased while the inflationary overhang on the consumer goods market follows suit. It sometimes happens, however, that the inflationary overhang is so large that it becomes impossible to close it through increased supply alone. A decrease in excess demand on the consumer goods market becomes necessary at the same time even to a lower scale of disequilibrium. It is then that price increases are declared.[28] Thus, at the end of that period, equilibrium, or low-scale disequilibrium, is restored and an STE enters the next cycle.

1.4. INVESTMENT CYCLES: EVIDENCE, CHARACTER AND IMPLICATIONS

The outline presented in the preceding section represents a standard, 'model' explanation of the investment cycle under central planning as an endogenously generated phenomenon. In fact, particular cycles may deviate from the model with respect to their timing. For the most part, however, they are in concordance with the pattern described above. Table 1.4. shows that average yearly investment growth rates for the FYP second and third years combined were higher than those for the fourth and fifth years of the same FYPs in over 60 per cent of cases (i.e. FYPs) in the 1961–80 period for all STEs considered here.

In reality, the concordance ratio is even higher (and much higher at that) if we exclude those cases in which factors exogenous to the cycle influenced investment growth rates. To begin with, we should exclude from the sample the 1961–5 FYP for the Soviet Union. In that country, a Seven-Year Plan (SYP) was inaugurated in 1959, but it was later abandoned. There were then a few more changes, with the 1964–5 period forming a separate plan.[29] Only *ex post* the 1956–60 and 1961–5 periods are presented in Soviet statistics as FYPs. In consequence, investments increased rather quickly over the 1959–61 period, while plan changes brought about a slowdown in the rate of growth (and also investments reaccelerated again during the 1964–5 plan).

Besides these changes in the planning horizon and related earlier starts of the acceleration phase, also excluded should be those cases in which important modifications of central planning institutions and instruments took place, especially those that were not introduced with the beginning of a new FYP. As it happened, all systemic modifications in smaller STEs were introduced in the middle of the respective medium-term plans.

Partial decentralisations that gave enterprises an increased room for manoeuvre (without imposing the accompanying hard budget constraint) invariably brought about an acceleration of the investment growth rate. The introduction in the GDR of the 'New Economic System of Planning and Management' from 1963 onwards more than doubled the growth rate of investments in the next two years. The same happened in Hungary with its more extensive 1968 modifications. The investment growth rate also doubled in the next two years, but this jump took place from the already high rate (an increase, on the average, from 10.5 to 25 per cent in each

Table 1.4: Average annual investment growth rates together for the second and third, and for the fourth and fifth years in subsequent five-year planning periods, 1961–80 (%)

	Average growth rate	1961–5	1966–70	1971–5	1976–80
Bulgaria	2–3	11.0	17.0	8.5	5.0
	4–5	9.5	6.0	12.0	3.0
Czechoslovakia	2–3	− 7.0	7.5	9.5	3.5
	4–5	9.0	7.0	6.5	2.0
GDR	2–3	3.5	10.0	6.5	3.5
	4–5	9.0	11.5	4.5	1.5
Hungary	2–3	11.5	10.5	1.0	8.0
	4–5	2.0	25.0	7.5	− 2.5
Poland	2–3	7.0	10.0	24.0	3.5
	4–5	6.5	11.0	18.5	− 8.5
Romania	2–3	10.5	14.5	9.0	14.0
	4–5	9.0	9.5	14.0	3.5
USSR	2–3	5.0	8.0	6.0	5.0
	4–5	9.0	16.5	8.0	1.5

Source: CMEA yearbooks, various years; national statistical yearbooks, various years.

two-year period). The restraining of the investment boom of this magnitude took more time. Investments still increased by 11 per cent in 1971, i.e. in the first year of the next FYP, and slowed down in the 1972–3 period. In this case the exogenous disturbance distorted the investment pattern in two consecutive FYPs.

Czechoslovakia's 1966-70 FYP should have been excluded on the same grounds, since the 1968 reforms there were also introduced in the middle of the FYP and investments immediately accelerated. However, the Soviet invasion brought about an abandonment of reforms in 1969 and the investment freeze slowed down the investment growth rate in 1970 to 1 per cent only (as compared with 13 per cent in the preceding year).

Furthermore, Poland, although it definitely did *not* introduce any reforms in 1968, introduced a strategy change aimed at increased specialisation of the national economy. Although doomed to failure for system-specific reasons (see Part Two of this study), this strategy change resulted, as might have been expected, in an increase in the investment rate in the 1969–70 period over the previous two years' already high rate (10 per cent on average). The strategy was abandoned with the fall of Gomulka and in consequence it did not affect the next FYP's investment pattern. Thus, if we exclude only four cases (and five FYPs, given the two FYPs affected in

23

the Hungarian case), leaving policy changes in Poland in the sample, the concordance ratio increases to over 73 per cent of all cases. However, we should extend the exclusion process to entail most or all of the 1971–5 FYP.

It is a well-known central planners' dream to execute *just once* a FYP without the necessity of putting the brakes on the investment programme and to complete in this way (or so the dream goes) all of the projects bringing in new productive capacities. The extra resources necessary for both the continued investment expansion and the reduction of the inevitable excess demand on the consumer goods market arising from the realisation of such a dream came, more or less by accident, in the early to mid-1970s, when the combination of *detente* and surplus liquidity (caused by the first oil price explosion) allowed all STEs to borrow capital in the West. At least five countries (Bulgaria, Hungary, Romania, Poland and the Soviet Union) borrowed relatively large sums in the 1971–5 FYP, allowing investments to continue growing at a high rate in 1974–5, i.e. the last two years of the FYP. The dream did not materialise but the investment cycle was exogenously disturbed by the strategy change. Thus, if we exclude these (with Hungary already excluded on other grounds), the concordance ratio will amount to over 84 per cent (16 out of the reduced sample of 19 cases).

Without exogenous disturbances (to which we may include, besides the change in time horizon, systemic modifications and major strategy changes), the not too numerous deviations from the model might have resulted from policy mistakes of three kinds: firstly, investment cuts undertaken too late with the effect of the policy change spilling over to the next FYP; secondly, investment cuts too modest to reduce excess demand on markets for producer and consumer goods and the period of restraint has to continue beyond the last years of a given FYP; and thirdly, investment cuts may increase rather than decrease excess demand if central planners and their political masters decide to press on with the large priority projects in the producer goods and infrastructure sectors at the cost of cuts in the consumer goods sector and nonproductive sector projects. This choice ensures the increase in disequilibrium and later, deeper cuts and longer periods of restraint extending to the first few years of the next FYP.

On the basis of the (superficial) similarity of investment fluctuations in STEs and MEs, some authors seem ready to equate the problems both systems have in coping with in this respect (e.g. Brody, 1983). Nothing is, however, further from the truth.

Business cycles in MEs may be regarded as continuous tests of efficiency and the 'creative destruction' process, to use Schumpeter's famous phrase. They ensure that firms, which for various reasons failed the test, pay for that in lost markets, sunk costs due to abandoned investment projects, and ultimately lower profits, while those who failed the test by a wide margin disappear from the scene. Thus, the process continuously weeds out inefficiency from the market place. Nothing even remotely similar is simulated under central planning, where profitability of projects — nay that of investing enterprises — is not even considered when investment cuts are to be instituted.

The decisions on investment cuts, just like on investments in general, are undertaken by central planners on the basis of the ill-defined, usually too numerous, priorities and rudimentary requirements of what passes as a balance in STEs (i.e. lower-scale disequilibrium), with stronger requirements of balance in the external sphere. The lack of scarcity prices and uncertainty generated by some system-specific features, outlined in section 1.2 above, scarcely allows more than that. In fact, it achieves *less* than that, because the centre, under strong pressure from various interest groups and armed with incomplete and distorted information, is rarely able to choose solely on the basis of its own, however vague, criteria.[30] It may not be surprising, then, that after renewed unsuccessful attempts at abandoning a part of unfinished investment projects, the deputy minister for economic reforms in Poland, exasperated, said that the best thing for the Polish economy would be if somebody would . . . 'bomb those projects out of existence'.[31] Obviously, had the central planners not shared the same heavy industry-oriented priorities as the strongest interest groups, their choices might have been more restrictive and wiser.

Altogether, if the market mechanism ensures the survival of the fittest, i.e. the most efficient, the mechanism of central planning ensures the survival of the strongest, i.e. those receiving the strongest backing of economic and/or political hierarchies. Without scarcity prices, almost everything can be 'proved' by the 'economic efficiency calculus', so in a bureaucratic sense, every investment project is defensible (see, for example, Libura, 1979). The wasteful character of the latter system should be seen by everyone. The wasteful character of the investment process under central planning is well evidenced by the fact that the changes in the GNP equivalent (NMP) in STEs are more strongly correlated with investment *efforts* than with investment *effects*. NMP growth rates move to a much higher degree in tandem with investment growth rates *without lag* than with a lag of a year of two. Thus, it is first of all the very process of investing that contributes to economic growth, while just when one could expect the effects of earlier investment activity to be felt more strongly (through coming on stream of new productive capacities), the correlation becomes weaker or even non-existent. Table 1.5 shows correlation coefficients between these two variables, without and with a lag, for 1961–77 and 1961–83 respectively.

An interesting feature of all this is that the process is not only wasteful but also *increasingly wasteful*. The addition of the last couple of years resulted in both markedly higher correlation coefficients, as well as in increasing the level of significance, in correlations of economic growth with investment efforts. *As the complexity of STEs increases, efforts seem to yield diminishing returns.* With respect to investments it means not only worsening outlays/returns ratios, but also lengthening completion periods, with all the resultant effects on equilibrium on both producer and consumer goods markets, on the level of modernity or the technology used in these projects, longer cost recoupment periods, etc. That the lengthy completion periods complained about in almost all Eastern publications dealing with investment (e.g. Stojkov (1983) for Bulgaria; Srejn and Novotny (1980) and Peknik (1983) for Czechoslovakia; Kornai (1982) and Soos (1983) for Hungary; Khachaturov (1975, 1979) for the Soviet Union, etc.), are lengthening further may also be evidenced by statistics showing the ratio of expenditures on unfinished investments to yearly investment expenditures for selected STEs. The ratios in Table 1.6, although not comparable cross-nationally due to different accounting practices,[32] show for all countries the increase of the ratios since the beginning or middle 1970s.

Given all the foregoing, the burden of central planning weighing upon the economy becomes heavier over time. Costly projects with obsolete technology need modernisation almost from the start. Thus, a new planning period is again considered as another period of ('obviously' necessary) rapid growth of investments. The long run, in which consumption would increase substantially due to an earlier lengthy period of high investment, never comes.[33] Investments become not so much deferred consumption, but *deferred further investments*.

Table 1.5: Product-moment correlation coefficients (r) for two variables: investment and net material product annual growth, concurrent, or with investments lagging by one and two years, 1961–77 and 1961–83 (both variables in percentages)

	1961–77			1961–83		
	Concurrent	With investments lagging one year	With investments lagging two years	Concurrent	With investments lagging one year	With investments lagging two years
Bulgaria	0.46[a]	0.12	−0.12	0.52[a]	0.09	0.12
Czechoslovakia	0.53[a]	0.55[a]	0.31	0.77[c]	0.66[c]	0.39
GDR	0.41	0.37	−0.46	0.49[a]	0.37	0.37
Hungary	0.31	−0.15	−0.07	0.64[c]	0.23	0.23
Poland	0.43[a]	0.52[a]	0.09	0.90[c]	0.78[c]	0.54[b]
Romania	−0.14	−0.27	−0.33	0.59[b]	0.45[a]	0.06
USSR	0.46[a]	−0.02	−0.23	0.56[b]	0.19	0.07

Notes: a. Correlation coefficient significant at the 0.05 level in two-tailed test.
      b. Correlation coefficient significant at the 0.01 level in two-tailed test.
      c. Correlation coefficient significant at the 0.001 level in two-tailed test.

Sources: see Table 1.4.

Table 1.6: Unfinished investments[a]: annual investments[b] ratio in selected STEs as an indicator of investment overexpansion, 1960–83[c]

| | Unfinished investments:annual investments ratio | | | |
	Bulgaria	Czechoslovakia	Hungary	Soviet Union
1960	0.64	–	0.59	0.69
1961	–	–	0.67	0.76
1962	–	–	0.74	0.76
1963	–	–	0.64	0.72
1964	–	–	0.65	0.68
1965	0.72	–	0.67	0.69
1966	–	–	0.70	0.71
1967	–	–	0.69	0.72
1968	–	–	0.79	0.77
1969	–	1.16	0.76	0.80
1970	0.87	1.20	0.78	0.73
1971	1.07	0.88	0.79	0.74
1972	1.13	1.00	0.83	0.78
1973	1.22	0.96	0.79	0.77
1974	1.05	1.03	0.83	0.77
1975	1.01	1.01	0.73	0.75
1976	1.13	0.87	0.76	0.80
1977	1.03	1.05	0.79	0.85
1978	1.06	1.06	0.84	0.85
1979	1.13	1.37	0.88	0.91
1980	1.03	1.31	0.94	0.87
1981	1.03	1.28	0.98	0.86
1982	1.01	1.39	1.03	0.84
1983	–	1.26	0.95	0.80

Notes: a. In actual prices of machinery and costs to the builder.
b. In current prices.
c. The indicator is not completely comparable on a cross-country basis due to different accounting practices with respect to the uninstalled machinery.
Sources: National statistical yearbooks; own calculations.

1.5. BEYOND QUANTITY: AN IMPOSSIBLE DREAM?

Before leaving the issues of quantity under central planning and turning to those of quality and innovation, one theoretical issue is worth pursuing, especially as it has also an important bearing on quality. It concerns effects of frustrated consumption expectations upon production. Obviously, households form consumption expectations[34] and if these expectations are frustrated by a significant increase in excess demand (and resultant shortages, long searches, etc.), they react by reducing both the quantity and quality of labour supplied. The lag with which such reactions set in is

Figure 1.2: Impact of frustrated consumption expectations and uncertainty resulting from the central planners' incomplete knowledge of the position of the real production possibility frontier

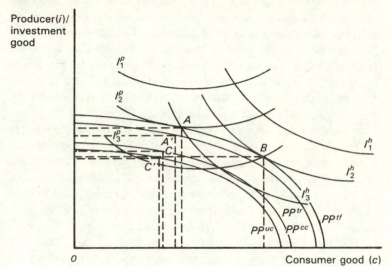

I_1^p I_2^p I_3^p — central planners' indifference curves

I_1^h I_2^h I_3^h — consumer indifference curves

PP^{tf} — technically feasible production possibility frontier according to central planners' perception

PP^{tr} — technically feasible production possibility frontier in reality

PP^{cc} — consumption constrained production possibility frontier had the inward shift taken place from PP^{tf} frontier

PP^{uc} — consumption constrained production possibility frontier in reality, with the inward shift taking place from the PP^{tr} frontier

difficult to estimate (and may be different in different STEs), but it may be assumed to assert itself within a time-span shorter than FYP. The reduction of labour supply then affects the level of production. The situation here is comparable with expected and unexpected money growth in the monetarist model of an ME. An unexpected increase in the level of shortage may cause no labour supply reaction. Over time, however, as the situation does not improve or even worsens, the households expect the new level of shortage to continue and reduce their labour supply.[35]

Diagrammatically, the impact of labour supply reduction resulting from the divergence between planners' preferences and household preferences may be represented as in Figure 1.2. Assume there are

29

two types of homogeneous goods: a consumer good (c) and producer (investment) good (i). The production possibility frontier PP^{tf} defines all combinations of (c) and (i) which are technically feasible, according to central planners' perceptions. Both central planners and households have expressed their preferences, depicted by the sets of indifference curves I^p and I^h respectively. The latter prefer a (c)–(i) combination at the point B, maximising their total utility with a relatively larger amount of consumer good (c) and a lesser amount of (i) than the central planners' preferred point A. Since B lies on a lower central planners' indifference curve I^p than A, a plan target reflecting central planners' preferences will be put forth. However, the withdrawal of labour supply (mainly through 'on the job' leisure) will make the attainment of any point on PP^{tf} impossible. The actual consumption–constrained PP frontier will be nearer to the point of origin as shown by the point C on PP^{cc} in Figure 1.2. The distance between A and C measured on both (c) and (i) axes reflects production consequences of labour supply reaction of households to the difference between actual and expected consumption.[36]

This is not the end of the story, however. The usual assumption is that production decisions concern combinations of products on a technically feasible PP frontier (PP^{tf} in Figure 1.2). However, as was stressed in section 1.3, this may not be true in an STE. Not only is the quantity of material inputs not fully known to central planners (see section 1.1), but they also base their decisions on a perceived PP frontier which does not exist if — in a growing economy — new capacities do not come on stream, or they do, but do not reach expected production volume on schedule. Then, the real PP frontier will be nearer to the point of origin (PP^{tr} in Figure 1.2) and an inward shift due to the labour supply reaction will take place from the real PP frontier, not from that perceived by central planners (PP^{tf}). A combined effect of both uncertainty constraint and consumption constraint will decrease production volume of both (c) and (i), making the attainment of any point, even on PP^{cc}, impossible. As production settles at point C' on the uncertainty and consumption constrained PP frontier (PP^{uc} in Figure 1.2), the distance between A and C' measured on both axes reflects production consequences of both constraints taken together.

The issue considered above also has quality implications, as indicated. The reduction of labour supply also entails lower quality, because working household members frustrated by the increasing level of shortage not only decrease time spent working (spend more time in a canteen, slip out of factories to queue for goods in short supply, take more sick leave, etc.), but also work less diligently, disregarding product quality requirements. This behaviour is tolerated by management due to the existing excess demand for labour and the stress on executing plan targets regardless of costs. Thus, we have a twofold negative impact on workers' attitudes towards quality, coming both from production and consumption experience under central planning. With respect to the former, their attitude is derivative. Workers perceive very well the extremely limited concern of managers with respect to quality of output that is turned out in a rush to fulfil plan figures (see section 1.1). With respect to the latter, their attitude is primary. This time it is managers who accept the temporary lack of interest of workers in maintaining even those already low quality standards that have been enforced so far. However, these attitudes towards quality obviously reinforce one another.

Low quality is thus an inseparable concomitant of production in STEs. The anecdotal evidence on the low quality of goods that can be found in the state-controlled press in these countries is over-abundant and, interestingly, seems to increase over time. Thus, for example, the tirades of the late Yuri Andropov, the then Secretary General of the Soviet Communist Party (CPSU), against the hopelessly low quality of many Soviet goods[37] drew the attention of Western journalists at the time. The low quality affects even the latest achievements, i.e. goods produced on licence bought from Western firms. Bulgarian party leader Todor Zhivkov used the term 'Bulgarisation' to describe the process of rapid deterioration of quality of these goods that accompanies the departure of Western specialists, as well as substitution of Bulgarian materials, parts and components for the initially imported ones.[38] This phenomenon is, let us add, well known in other STEs.[39]

The increasing frequency of these signals and of their critique is not surprising in view of the growing complexity of economic activity and increased sophistication of products that are outcomes of that activity. With higher input requirements and the increasing number of parts and components per product, the complexity increases, while the ability to cope with it on the part of STEs, with their slowly reacting multi-level hierarchies, simultaneously decreases. Besides, over time, the difficulties, and also those affecting quality, are aggravated by the long-term impact of central planning itself (this is developed in Part Two of this study).

It is worth stressing that the above considerations should not be construed as meaning that STEs are completely unable to produce goods of standard or even high quality. The Soviet weaponry, as well as some East European manufactures exported to the West, prove the opposite. What I am arguing is that *STEs are unable, for system-specific reasons, to produce standard, i.e.* world *standard, quality goods at standard cost.* They can reach and do reach lower–medium world quality standards with respect to some goods for military use or for the world market, but they do it at extra cost due to the use of (often imported) higher quality inputs or to the discarding of many defective standard ones. Moreover, further cost is borne by use of the additional quantity of labour inputs needed for more careful assembly, finishing, quality control, and packaging.

Even then it may happen that these products are not accepted on the world market because, in spite of the upgrading, they did not come within the quality range acceptable there. (This is returned to in Part Three). However, the fact that these upgraded goods, although of lower quality than required by the world market, are at the same time of very much higher quality than usual on the domestic market (or any other East European market for that matter . . .) did not pass unrecognised in Eastern Europe. For consumers and producers alike, the news that particular products were rejected by Western importers is a symbol of *superior* quality and these products are sought after in the first place.

One of the favoured myths of central planners and their political masters (and also of many orthodox Marxist economists in Eastern Europe) has been that it is excess demand that is at the heart of the quality problems. With excess supply, the situation would change for the better, and so they pressured for even greater quantity increases.[40] They are, however, severely mistaken. In cases (infrequent and temporary) of excess supply with respect to some consumer goods, the market was flooded with excessive quantities of goods characterised by the same low quality as under the conditions of excess demand.

The reasons for this absence of positive quality changes should have been obvious from the start. Without scarcity prices that would *inter alia*, differentiate between products of different quality, without the hard budget constraint that under the threat of bankruptcy would force enterprises to cease production for which there is no demand, and last (but definitely not least!), without domestic and foreign competition that, together with the hard budget constraint, would put pressure upon enterprises to raise the product quality, nothing is going to change for the better. Nor are bureaucratic measures and propaganda campaigns so loved by the communist apparatchiks of any help. Neither new laws on product quality nor declarations of party plenary meetings on the necessity of giving more attention to quality issues will change established practices in STEs in the absence of market discipline. Their increasing frequency is just another signal of increasing problems of STEs in this respect.[41]

So far I have highlighted the inability of STEs to produce normally (i.e. without extra effort) goods of acceptable quality but the concept of quality has been used in a narrower sense. It has been the quality of materials and that of labour input (craftsmanship) that have been considered to be beyond reach under central planning. However, the term quality, especially when contrasted with quantity, is used in a larger sense, comprising technological sophistication (or level of modernity) of products and processes. It follows that we have to consider here the issue of innovation as a factor contributing towards quality.

I have already stressed that the structure of incentives strongly discourages technical change (see section 1.3, above). Next, reasons for low average levels of technological sophistication will be explained as effects of the extreme import substitution and resultant underspecialisation that force an STE to produce with what is often outdated technology, since there are not enough resources to spread new technology over too many products. This outcome of the interaction between strategy and structure is discussed in the second part of the book. Finally, various obstacles to innovation, regardless of whether it is domestic or imported, are dealt with in Part Three, with regard to the impact of licences upon the foreign trade balance of STEs.

All these considerations imply that the issue of innovation is even more intractable than that of quality in the narrower sense. The same factors of incentive structure, soft budget constraint and lack of competition result in the lack of interest in innovation. New products and processes are most easily acceptable if they are turned out in new plants built for that very purpose.[42] As such they pass under the heading of investment rather than under that of innovation. Underpaid engineers and technicians[43] show scant interest in applying their knowledge to anything other than routine activities; and even if they do, they hit the barrier of disincentives at the enterprise level.

Thus, except when pressed from above to upgrade the technology, enterprises promote technical change in the already-existing facilities, which remains in concordance with their basic risk averting behaviour (see sections 1.1 and 1.3, above). It means

33

that technical change should not be too large-scale. Small changes in products or process minimise the risk of a failure or a delay, or any other rewards-threatening disturbance. A special, and highly profitable, kind of such changes is a small-scale technical change that passes as a large one, i.e. an introduction of a new product whose large increase in price in comparison with an old one is not compensated by the commensurate improvements in use value (on pseudo-innovations, see, for example, Csikos-Nagy, 1975, and Grossman, 1977).[44]

Under the circumstances technical change is slow in STEs and whatever new products and processes are introduced, they are in the main marginal improvements over the existing ones. What is introduced as new in an enterprise or even in a given STE is rarely new on the world market.[45] Altogether, *the closing of the quality differential, whether in the narrower or the larger sense, proves to be beyond the reach of STEs*. The distance does not even seem to decrease, in spite of the decade of relatively heavy technological borrowing.

NOTES

1. There are of course exceptions in this respect, too. In the East it is official apparatus and a shrinking number (especially in Hungary and Poland) of economists; in the West it is a minority of the latter, of which Portes (1974, 1977, 1979, 1981, undated) has been the most prolific in his refutations of the existence of system-specific sources of excess demand. For a critique of Portes by this author, see Winiecki (1985a).

2. Wakar (1959), Romuald Bauer *et al.* (1972), Beksiak and Libura (1974), Libura (1979), Beksiak (1982). Bauer's Christian name is included here to differentiate him from a Hungarian economist, Tamas Bauer.

3. Not surprisingly, statistical journals in Eastern Europe devote a considerable amount of space to proper statistical reporting, techniques of checking up the truthfulness of the reports, etc.

4. For a detailed analysis of the hidden inflation issue, see Chapter 2.

5. *Domestic* users, because, contrary to foreign (Western) users, they cannot count upon obtaining regular quality coal from other suppliers.

6. See, for example, almost ritual complaints on the behaviour of the Soviet steel-making enterprises in this respect (*Planovoye Khozyaistvo*, no. 5, 1974, no. 5, 1976, no. 8, 1979, no. 1, 1980, etc.).

7. This issue is examined in the third part of the book.

8. This is why netting out excess supplies here and excess demands there, as is done by disequilibrium empiricists trying to apply that theory to STEs, completely misses the point: for there are no forces in the system that would equilibrate the economy by reallocating excess supplies to reduce excess demand. For a critique of these approaches, see Kornai (1982),

Kemme and Winiecki (1984) and Winiecki (1985a).

9. It is worth mentioning that linkages between the two sectors occur not only through earnings but also through spending. Enterprises and bureaucratic institutions buy consumer goods (radios and TV sets, carpets, etc.), increasing the inflationary gap. On the other hand, consumers obtain otherwise unavailable goods that have slipped away from factories and construction sites, thus decreasing the inflationary gap.

10. This figure is from Wiles (1977). The approximate figures for some other STEs are as follows: 8–10 million for Poland (Lipowski, 1981), 5 million for Czechoslovakia (privately supplied figure), 2 million for Hungary (Wiles, 1977).

11. A point already made long ago by Grossman (1963).

12. This point has been very well made by Soos (1985), whose article this author received after having written this chapter.

13. See, *inter alia*, his speech of 11 June 1985, *Pravda*, 12 June 1985.

14. The economic history of Eastern Europe knows cases of self-deception at the top. Nonetheless, more frequent are cases where the centre prefers to know about actual facts, although at the same time it tries to deceive others (its own society, or the world at large).

15. See, for example, the Soviet report on discrepancies between higher average annual employment levels and lower end-of-the-year levels, the latter being important for reporting on plan implementation (*Planovoye Khozyaistvo*, no. 5, 1976).

16. One of the code words for redundancies.

17. If in some cases they do not, there will be almost no financial consequences, given the soft budget constraint prevailing in every STE.

18. It is worth noting that we stress here the problems arising out of *bona fide* interventions: we do not deal with the *parasitic* ones aimed at private enrichment of party apparatchiks (on this point see Winiecki, 1984c, 1986d). However, the latter are also of some importance, as well as being time-consuming, for managers, because kickbacks reinforce the willingness of apparatchiks to intervene in favour of a given enterprise. Besides, refusing kickbacks could incur the wrath of those who may have influence upon a given manager's position on the *nomenklatura*.

19. Net material product according to the Soviet methodology is equal to gross national product less fixed assets' depreciation and the so-called non-productive services.

20. The following discussion is based on my earlier publication on the topic (Winiecki, 1982).

21. The latter are what in economic theory has been called 'learning-by-doing' (Arrow, 1962) or the 'Horndal effect' (Lundberg, 1961).

22. For somewhat similar explanations, see also Tamas Bauer (1978) and Libura (1979).

23. The latter ought to be more properly called *entrepreneurial*.

24. This particular behaviour has been repeatedly pointed at in East European literature: see, for example, more recently Khachaturov (1975) for the Soviet Union, Tamas Bauer (1978) for Hungary and Czechoslovakia, and Krawczyk (1981) for Poland.

25. Tamas Bauer (1978), outlining his four-phase cycle, used two independent variables: number of investment projects started and total value

of investments in each period. The data for the former are not available, however, either in time series for longer periods or cross-nationally. Besides, as far as the scale of disequilibrium is concerned, the former independent variable is of lesser importance anyway, although it adds to it through excessive inventories of materials needed elsewhere, stocked at many investment sites. (Here again, by the way, netting out of inputs does not make sense!)

26. Given the regulations on the funding of construction enterprises, there is little association between the level of payments made to them by investors and the degree of investment project completion (for the USSR, see, for example, *Planovoye Khozyaistvo*, no. 1, 1976 and no. 3, 1980).

27. Incidentally, there is no contradiction between the investment cycle theory outlined here and some interpretations ascribing investment fluctuations to policy changes (Soos, 1983), for the latter are undertaken in response to recurrent endogenously generated investment expansions.

28. Or instituted without the declaration in this respect (see the next chapter on hidden inflation instituted from above).

29. On these changes, see Dahlstedt (1980) and the sources quoted therein.

30. This is a complaint heard from the centre everywhere under central planning (for the Soviet Union, see, for example, Khachaturov, 1975).

31. *Zycie Gospodarcze* of 21 October 1984. Incidentally, it also constitutes evidence that the Polish economy remains an unreformed one, since such typical features as excess demand for investments persists in the face of the 20 per cent fall of output.

32. For example, the value of uninstalled machinery is counted in Hungary as the increase in stocks, while in Czechoslovakia it appears to be included in the figures for unfinished investments. According to Dyker (1982), the same seems to be the case for the Soviet Union (what raises many doubts with the present author). Other cross-national differences arise with respect to the use of current or constant prices for current investment expenditures. On problems with the comparability of various investment and fixed assets series in STEs, see ibid.

33. In similar vein, see Libura (1979) and, more obliquely, Srejn and Novotny (1979).

34. Libura (1979) stresses that households (in the longer run, obviously — J.W.) react not only to frustrated private consumption expectations, but also to frustrated public consumption ones.

35. It follows from the foregoing that households may continue their labour supply reaction some time after the subsequent decrease in the level of shortage, i.e. until their expectations adapt again.

36. The foregoing considerations show, incidentally, a mistaken view of Kalecki (1969) that central planners have a choice between different mixes of investment and consumer goods that lie on the same *PP* frontier and the only limiting factor is the intensity of objections of central planners themselves to reducing consumption in the short run. As we have seen, the choice is between different points on *different PP* frontiers, since the reduction of consumption brings about a labour supply reaction that pushes the *PP* frontier inward. (As an aside only, we may note that Kalecki in his time believed that investments under central planning mean deferred

consumption, not deferred further investments.)

37. The short collection of his speeches is very long on critiques of that sort.

38. The term used. See *Rabotnichesko Delo*, 31 May 1983.

39. See, for example, Monkiewicz (1983) for Poland, and Dezsenyi-Gueuliette (1983) for Hungary.

40. For early critiques in STEs of the above view, see Beksiak and Libura (1974).

41. For those who see the relative quality differences between East German and Czechoslovak products on the one hand and, say, Bulgarian and Soviet ones on the other, and believe it is the case of the 'different stages of socialist development' rather than the effect of socialism itself, the present author points out that East German and Czechoslovak goods are also of lower quality in comparison with those produced in the West and that the difference *did not exist before World War II*, and, consequently, that the existing differences in quality are the consequence of different stages of *capitalist* development. It means that the labour force in countries which industrialised before communist rule cannot imagine, given its industrial tradition, that it is possible to worsen its performance by much more than it already has done under the circumstances, while the labour force in other STEs, without that tradition, can worsen its performance by much more (and from lower levels at that).

42. For example, according to the answers of managers of Czechoslovak enterprises to a poll conducted by the Planning Commission and Ministry of Labour and Social Welfare, a large majority of them stressed that they would not of their own initiative undertake to produce more technologically sophisticated products if that would entail abandoning any currently produced ones (Levcik and Skolka, 1984).

43. They are not only underpaid but their salaries relative to workers' wages tend to decline over time (for example, in Poland and the Soviet Union) or are already at or below the level of the latter (for example, in Bulgaria and the GDR).

44. See the following chapter on inflation.

45. A good evidence is the Czechoslovak economy where the share of new products in the gross value of industrial production in the late 1970s was equal to 6.7 per cent with respect to products that were new at the level of the Czechoslovak economy, but only 0.3 per cent with respect to products that were new at the level of world economy (Klvacova, 1982).

2

Prices

2.1. INFLATION SOURCES

In Chapter 1 quantity distortions under central planning — actual versus reported, actual versus assumed by planners, etc. — were pointed to, together with the much neglected issues of the extremely high degree of uncertainty affecting the behaviour of central planners and enterprises, as well as the quantitative outcomes of their actions. Below, the price outcomes of their actions are considered, including system-specific linkages between prices and quantities. Indeed, STEs are unique economies that may (and do) suffer from all three forms of inflation: open, hidden and repressed, simultaneously (see, *inter alia*, Jansen (1982), Winiecki (1982, 1985a and 1986e), Pindak (1983) and Wiles (1983)). The situation in which excess demand becomes open inflation — a typical one for MEs — is completely foreign to an STE.

Open inflation, understood here as a rise in the general price level measured by some price index, is nowadays an admissible idea in STEs[1] and one (increasingly) put into practice. However, even if the consumer price index (CPI) is published in STEs, it definitely is *not* an *ex post* measure of *ex ante* excess demand. It reveals only a part of price changes on the consumer goods market that central planners were able to register and of that part again a part which they (or rather, their political masters) are willing to concede in public. Under the dual impact of the inability to register and unwillingness to concede price increases, changes in the CPI have been small or negligible in comparison with the real scale of price changes there. The remainder have been hidden from the public and in part from central planners themselves. However, even if we devote most space here to outlining and evaluating all forms of inflation and linkages between them, it should not be forgotten that system-specific features do not fail to affect *sources* as well. Thus, it is inflation sources that need scrutiny before we turn to inflation forms, as well as manifestations and estimates thereof.

We have learned already how excess demand, an orthodox source of inflation, became *a very unorthodox one* in a shortage-ridden, uncertainty-permeated STE (see Chapter 1). Excess demand appears there first on the producer goods market and then quickly spills over to the consumer goods market via higher than planned payments from the total wage fund and lower than planned output of consumer goods. In fact, if the output of producer goods exceeds the plan target and the wage fund in respective industries does likewise, even the full implementation of the plan target for output of consumer goods will not prevent the spillover of excess demand. These spillovers, although a permanent feature under central planning, are subject to changes in intensity under the impact of investment cycles (see Chapter 1, section 3).

The contrast between orthodox excess demand inflation (meaning inflation known in MEs) and an unorthodox one extends also to the process by which excess demand transforms itself into inflation (of one form or another). This process is best described by contrasting the basic tenets upon which rests the thesis of near-impossibility of inflation under central planning, advertised for years (although decreasingly so!) in Eastern Europe and beyond. It seems to be all the more necessary, since these tenets (together with distorted official statistics) tend to confuse some disequilibrium theorists and empiricists dealing with STEs.[2]

There are essentially three such tenets. The first is related to wages. As central planners control wages, both the total wage fund and the specific wage rates, the earnings of labour cannot exceed the planned value of consumer goods supplies. Thus, excess demand may appear only as a result of planners' miscalculations. (The fact that these miscalculations have been occurring repeatedly year after year, according to the same pattern, and for decades at that, does not seem to matter for the believers.) Next, even if central planners make an error, and as a result of that error, excess demand appears on the producer goods market, the vertical control through the multi-level hierarchy ensures that it does not spill into the consumer goods market. (The fact that demand on the consumer goods market increases immediately due to overtime rates paid both to speed up the manufacture of needed producer goods and to put into

39

commission investment projects is also ignored.) Finally, central planners control prices and that control is supposed to be the final barrier against inflation. If by an error excess demand appears on the consumer goods market, price controls prevent the inflationary gap from translating into price increases. (The idea that *it cannot stay there indefinitely*, resulting only in greater shortages and longer queues alone, does not seem to bother central planners at all.)

An extensive literature, both Eastern and Western, showed these tenets to be contrary to STEs' realities (for an earlier critique, see, for example, Beksiak (1966), Kucharski (1969), Goldmann and Kouba (1969), Klacek and Klaus (1970), Kornai (1971, 1972), as well as Holzman (1956, 1960), Nove (1969)). Our considerations in Chapter 1 also disproved the first two tenets. Planned wage funds are exceeded most of the time.

No consistent series are available on annual planned wage growth for all seven STEs for the 1960s–1980s period. They are published together with other annual plan figures alternatively as nominal wage fund growth rates, nominal wage growth rates per worker, real wage growth rates per worker, or not at all. Thus, comparative study across STEs and over the longer period cannot be done even if references in the East European press often refer to failures in this respect. For more systematic evaluation we have to rely on the study of Poland where, *inter alia*, the data on wage fund plans were analysed for the 1960–76 period (Maciejewski and Zajchowski, (1982).

According to these authors, who had access to plan reports, actual payments from the wage fund did not miss planned figures or missed them by less than 1% only in 14.6% of cases, missed them by less than 3% in less than half of cases (46.2%), and in more than half of cases (53.8%) missed them by 3% or more.[3] More aggregated data in that study show the section of the plan listing 30 employment- and wage-related indicators[4] that deviate from plan figures in subsequent FYPs by 4.52% in 1961–5, by 3.17% in 1966–70 and by 5.94% in 1971–5. It should also be remembered that indicators on employment by their very nature tended to deviate by less than those on wages and distorted the aggregate indicator in the downward direction. Deviations on wage related indicators were undoubtedly *higher*.

The fact that output of consumer goods was falling below planned figures (or below the growth rate required to maintain equilibrium on the consumer goods market) may be inferred indirectly from the actual growth rate figures for producer and consumer goods-

Table 2.1: Growth rates of producer (A) and consumer (B) goods in East European centrally planned economies, in subsequent five-year planning periods, 1960–80 (%)

		1960–5	1965–70	1970–5	1975–80
Bulgaria	A	90	75	62	41
	B	57	59	44	23
Czechoslovakia	A	33	39	40	29
	B	22	37	37	21
GDR	A	37	41	39	29
	B	27	25	33	23
Hungary	A	47	33	37	17
	B	49	37	39	21
Poland	A	60	56	66	24
	B	38	37	64	26
Romania	A	108	85	90	63
	B	66	59	69	50
USSR	A	57	52	46	25
	B	37	49	37	20

Sources: *CMEA yearbooks*, various years; own calculations.

producing sectors for consecutive FYPs over the 1961–80 period. In many STEs, particular FYPs were officially proclaimed to be 'consumer goods oriented' within that period. However, in no East European country, with the significant exception of Hungary, did growth rate of the consumer goods exceed, even for one FYP, that of producer goods (see Table 2.1.).[5] As Hungary is widely regarded as a country in which the consumer goods market seems to be nearest to equilibrium of all STEs, the marked difference between its industrial production pattern and that of other STEs is significant.

The third and last tenet — i.e. that central planners control prices and thus prevent inflation — is no nearer to the reality of central planning than the other two. What central planners can prevent (to an ever smaller degree, as recent CPI figures point out; see Table 2.2) is only changes in the consumer price index, while other inflationary phenomena, specific for STEs only, make themselves felt all the time (albeit with a differing intensity). However, other sources of inflation under central planning should also be considered here. They, too, each in their own unorthodox way, add to the inflationary environment under central planning.

Thus, on the surface, wage-push inflation resulting from trade union pressure has been unknown in STEs, except during the brief Solidarity period in Poland. Furthermore, on the surface, profit-

Table 2.2: Annual changes in the consumer price index (CPI) in STEs, 1965–83

	Bul.	Cze.	Hun.	GDR	Pol.	Rom.	USSR
			yearly changes in CPI				
1965	−0.5	−0.4	0.4	−0.4	0.9	0.4	−1.0
1966	−0.3	0	1.4	0	1.2	0	−0.7
1967	0.2	1.2	0.2	−0.3	1.5	−0.4	0
1968	4.1	1.0	−0.4	0.2	1.6	0.5	0.1
1969	−0.2	3.9	1.4	−0.2	1.4	0.8	0.2
1970	−0.4	1.2	1.3	−0.3	1.1	0.4	0.1
1971	0	−0.4	1.7	0.1	−0.1	1.0	−0.1
1972	−0.1	−0.3	3.1	−0.7	0	0	−0.2
1973	0.2	0.2	3.5	−0.6	2.8	1.0	0
1974	0.5	0.6	2.1	−0.4	7.1	1.1	−0.1
1975	0.4	0.7	4.4	0	3.0	0.2	0
1976	0.2	0.9	5.3	0	4.4	0.5	0
1977	0.4	1.5	4.0	−0.1	4.9	0.6	0.3
1978	1.5	1.7	4.9	−0.1	8.1	2.0	0.7
1979	4.6	3.6	9.7	0.3	7.0	1.8	1.1
1980	14.0	2.4	9.2	0.4	9.4	1.5	1.2
1981	0.5	0.8	4.6	0.2	21.2	2.2	1.3
1982	0.3	6.0	6.9	0	100.8	16.9	3.3
1983	2.0	1.0	7.3	0	22.1	5.2	0

Sources: *Yearbook of international statistics, 1984* (in Polish).

push inflation, the other traditional source of cost inflation, has frequently been occurring in those STEs where profits have been performance indicators for enterprises. Such a view would be highly superficial, however.

It has been said before that system-specific distortions also affect inflation sources and *what appears as a profit-push is in reality a wage-push in disguise*: for profits are first and foremost indicators of performance, a means to an end for both managers and workers. The actual aim is a bonus tied to the execution of a given profit indicator. Therefore, it is not only a guise in which wage inflation appears under central planning that is of importance here: even more important is that, contrary to the situation in MEs, *management is not a constraint on wage-push inflation*. Managers' primary task is to execute plans. In the general climate of shortage, including labour shortage (see Chapter 1, section 1.1), they try to get the highest possible wages for their workers to keep them satisfied as an insurance against labour outflow. If a profit indicator is going to bring both managers and workers some tangible benefits, then various manipulations by the former take place with the tacit acceptance of the latter. *Managers and workers*, so to say, *play on the same team against the centre*: in terms of the market system they are workers' shop stewards, not owners' representatives (this point is made by Kornai, 1980).

A non-traditional source of cost inflation is so-called productivity inflation, and it has affected MEs since the mid-1950s. According to various strands of this theory (see, in particular, Streeten (1962), Baumol (1967), authors of the EFO model,[6] Skolka (1977) and Winiecki (1978), productivity growth rates in those manufacturing industries leading with respect to productivity increases determine wage growth rate there and elsewhere. This wage growth rate is set near the level of productivity growth rate in these industries and later becomes a 'norm' or a reference rate for wage claims elsewhere in industry and in services. A near uniform wage growth rate and different productivity growth rates bring about cost increases in industries and services with average and below average (or zero)[7] productivity increases. As different productivity increases are the rule rather than the exception, this inflationary pattern tends to perpetuate itself.

Even this non-traditional source of cost inflation can be found under central planning, although as usual reshaped to fit into the specific institutional and policy framework therein. The need to stimulate industrial production leads in STEs to the introduction of incentive systems which tie wages growth to the growth of productivity. However, differences in productivity growth rates lead over time to the increase in wage differentials between industries. As this may lead to the outflow of workers from the disadvantaged industries, across-the-board wage increases are granted from time to time to those employed in industries and services with low or zero productivity increases. Thus, it is not pressure from below but decisions from above which generate cost increases *of the same type*.

A Polish author calculated that during the 1961–5 FYP, wage growth in industry, transport and communications, and trade (the so-called productive sphere in STE parlance) amounted to 20.7 per cent while in other services (the so-called non-productive sphere), it amounted to 19.5 per cent. His calculations showed that the similar balance was held in the following 1966–72 period, in which these two figures were 38.2 and 36.4 per cent respectively. In his view the wage growth rate is determined by the leading industries, for it is in those sectors that payments for productivity increases take place even under the most stringent wage controls; and it is towards this growth rate that the wages growth rate of other workers tends to gravitate (Kucharski, 1983).

Other sources of inflation also present in STEs are once-for-all phenomena, but again, system-specific features make them different in comparison with their traditional versions found in MEs. Thus, for example, the oldest source, i.e. crop failure, either affects the CPI or not, depending on the coverage of a representative basket of goods: that is, if there is a price increase of fruits, vegetables and meat sold on the free (or *kolkhoz*) market and if goods sold on that market are included in the basket, then the CPI in an STE is affected much like in an ME. If it is not, however, then it is hidden inflation that increases the cost of living, while the CPI remains unchanged (see the next section).

In another context, STEs also suffer from imported inflation but the link between the cost increase and CPI increase is indirect only due to the levy-subsidy arrangement that separates domestic from foreign prices through surcharges levied on those foreign goods whose domestic prices are higher and subsidies accorded to those whose domestic prices are lower. Although distorted relative prices are a permanent feature of STEs, sufficiently large increases in world prices generated — usually with a lag of a varied length — increases in domestic prices. The two oil shocks are the best example in this respect.[8]

This brief overview of inflationary sources indicates that although excess demand inflation has been the main source of inflation under central planning (whether open, hidden or repressed), basic sources of cost inflation have also been present there, as well as more orthodox once-for-all sources. The difference has been in the processes set in motion by these sources, since the system-specific features make the participants behave differently from participants in MEs. *The outcomes are the same in substance*, i.e. the appearance of inflationary phenomena, *but these phenomena sometimes appear in different guise, often pass through different channels, and are partly hidden from view due to the variety of forms of these outcomes.*

2.2. INFLATION PROPER: OPEN AND HIDDEN

To begin with the traditional form of inflation, i.e. open inflation measured by the CPI, this phenomenon has not been unknown under central planning. Even if we leave aside the period of hyper-centralisation in the 'war communism' period in Soviet Russia that resulted (appropriately) in hyperinflation and the near collapse of economic activity, the first 20 years of central planning in the Soviet Union (1928–47) were a period of continuous high open inflation. Moreover, excluding the first post-war years, high open inflation accompanied in the early 1950s the imposition of the Soviet-type central planning and the forced industrialisation pattern upon smaller East European economies.

It is from the mid-1950s at the earliest that the claims about the eradication of inflation 'under socialism' began to emanate from STEs. Indeed, the CPI registered some price decreases, and the official index displayed remarkable stability for a period ranging from country to country from a couple to a dozen years. However, since the mid-1960s, CPI increases, although still small, began to be registered more frequently (in Hungary and Poland, almost annually), while since the late 1970s, open inflation became a fact of life, occurring everywhere on a yearly basis (see Table 2.2). The only exception to this picture has been the GDR, the last stalwart of the anti-inflationary orthodoxy. It will be seen below, however, that the GDR's data on quantities and prices are the most distorted ones of all STEs.

As to the sources of these distortions, we turn first to a Hungarian economist, Csikos-Nagy, a long time chairman of the Hungarian price commission. In a recent article (Csikos-Nagy and Racz, 1983), comparing the price record of Hungary with that of other STEs, he stressed the differences in CPI construction between the former since 1968 and the latter. Very circumspectly, as usual when 'brotherly' countries are criticised, he underlined that in other STEs, the sample of representative goods does not include: (a) goods sold on the free (*kolkhoz*) market, (b) goods produced by small local market-oriented enterprises and, in some STEs, even (c) services (thus, the *coverage* is narrower). Moreover, prices of representative goods are considered unchanged as long as these goods are produced and sold on the consumer goods market, regardless of their decreasing weights and increasing weights of higher priced substitutes (thus the *accuracy* is lower).

A major part of inflation in STEs other than in Hungary and, more recently, Poland,[9] has therefore remained hidden by the centre *by design*. The design regularly distorts the CPI in the downward direction. Besides these design distortions, the CPI under central planning has been affected by irregular distortions *by fiat*. As disequilibrium generated by the system-specific features accumulated, price increases became necessary. However, their true magnitude has sometimes been concealed from the public. Thus, for

45

example, a general rise in food prices in Bulgaria in 1968 ranging from 30 to 100 per cent on most products was officially registered as a 4–5 per cent increase in the CPI. Given the high share of food in total consumer expenditures (over half at the time), this CPI increase was grossly understated. Or, more recently, in Czechoslovakia the CPI increase for the 1982–3 period was officially put at 7 per cent. At the same time, however, prices of beef increased by 60%, veal by 42%, pork by 35%, ham and sausages by 20%, fish by 30–55%, etc.; prices of consumer durables like colour TV sets increased by 40%, automatic washing machines by 24%, electric kitchens by 23%, etc.; prices of gasoline by 23%, and so on.

However, *hidden inflation is not confined to inflation hidden from the public by the centre, but also includes* — figuratively speaking — *that hidden by the public from the centre.* Many Eastern and Western authors (see, in particular, Csikos-Nagy (1975), Grossman (1977), Katselineboigen (1977), Sokołowski (1978), Lokshin (1981), Nove (1982), Pindak (1983), and Wiles (1983), as well as the present author (Winiecki, 1982, 1985c, 1986e), show various ways in which enterprises doctor their reports on plan execution that not only distort quantity statistics upwards, but also price statistics downwards. Three such methods do both at the same time:[10]

(1) The crudest are changes in the product mix, i.e. those changes that increase the weight of higher priced substitutes in the output of an enterprise. The advantages for an enterprise are obvious: higher value that allows it to execute plan figures more easily or exceed it by some percentage and gain related rewards for managers and workers alike. These changes, called 'leaching' (see, for example, Pindak (1983) and Wiles (1983)) are not known to central planners if product mix is changed at the enterprise level, so the comments by Csikos-Nagy and Racz, cited above, do not concern *that* part of leaching.[11]

(2) Next are adverse changes in the quality of the product, due to the shoddy craftsmanship or substandard material inputs (or both). If quality decreases with unchanged prices, price level increases, even if controlled prices of these products do not.

(3) Finally, pseudo-innovations, i.e. products whose prices increased disproportionately in comparison with the improvements in product characteristics, also push the price level in an upward direction. This process is often accompanied by the disappearance of less expensive substitutes (leaching).

These three methods of doctoring enterprise statistics have, as indicated above, a dual impact: they distort price statistics downwards, because they increase the price level without increasing prices of particular products controlled by central planners, but they also distort quantity statistics upwards, because price increases are registered in the aggregate statistics as quantity increases. The net result is not only a lower real economic growth rate but also higher uncertainty under central planning. With respect to our prime concern here, i.e. inflation, *the above methods of hiding inflation from above and from below do not exhaust all possibilities, for they are accompanied by activities containing elements of both.*

Thus, as disequilibrium increases, central planners may, one way or another, encourage enterprises to increase prices by lowering quality or producing higher priced pseudo-innovations. To give but some examples, let us quote, firstly, two 1972 letters to meat industry enterprises in Poland from their superior, ordering them to reduce meat content in sausages, amounting to a 12.8 per cent price increase (see Laski, 1979). Next, it was an open secret in Poland that an unpublished circular letter of a prime minister was sent to all Polish enterprises in 1976 setting the *minimum* price increase for new products, in comparison with old substitutes, at 30 per cent. This was a roundabout way of mopping up excess demand when officially declared price increases were called off after the wildcat strikes had erupted in many places in Poland. The centre was, then willing to accept the misleading figures about quantities of consumer goods supplied if at the same time equilibrium on the consumer goods market was to be restored.

Our considerations here were limited to the CPI and the consumer goods market but all three methods listed above are also applied with respect to wholesale prices and the producer goods market (on the latter, see Pindak, 1983). Our concentration on the former market stems from the fact that contrary to enterprises, households do not enjoy soft budget constraint and, consequently, are more affected by hidden inflation. In comparison with Figure 1.1, Figure 2.1 shows the difference by the properly, i.e. negatively sloping (non-vertical) demand line. The demand line is steeply sloping to stress the scale of price increases necessary to equilibrate the market due to the existence of the sizeable inflationary overhang (the supply line is vertical, as in Figure 1.1, since plans set fixed quantities of goods, independent of price, as well as of demand).

All in all we have in STEs inflation hidden from above, inflation hidden from below and, so to say, inflation half-hidden from both

Figure 2.1: Budget constrained demand of consumers (demand line *D*) faces supply quantities fixed by plan and therefore price and demand are independent (supply line *S* drawn vertically). Excess demand at the given price level (P_o) may be, contrary to the situation on the producer goods market, eliminated through price increases. Due to the existing inflationary gap, equilibrium price is high and price increases would have to be substantial (demand line *D* sloping steeply upwards)

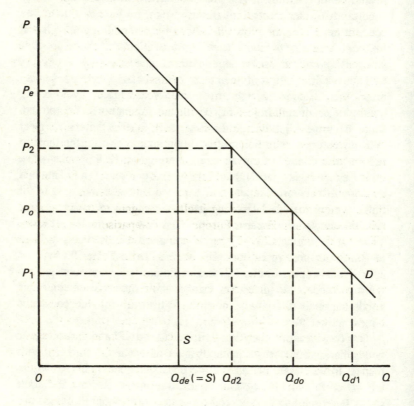

sides, all of them distorting quantity and price statistics. Given the picture painted above, only the gullible can seriously treat STE statistics with respect to either quantity or price. However, in economic research the price part of STE statistics is more often viewed with suspicion than the quantity part, even if in many cases of hidden inflation, what ought to be added to the inflation rate ought to be subtracted at the same time from the economic growth rate. For it is all those purely fictitious additions to production figures, quality-decreasing uses of substandard inputs, and value-added boosting pseudo-innovations that distort economic growth rates in the upward direction.

It is interesting that the only study known to this author showing systematic distortions of that sort both over long periods and across all STEs originated from outside the profession of area specialists. A UN Economic Commission for Europe comparative study of GNP *per capita* of MEs and STEs (*Economic Bulletin for Europe*, 1980) used a different estimation method than traditional GNP/NMP accounting. Using the physical-indicators methodology (called PIG in the said study, with G standing for 'global'), the said study showed the characteristic dual pattern of deviations of physical indicators-based[12] growth rates from official GNP/NMP *per capita*-based growth rates. Firstly, the scale of deviations in MEs was markedly smaller than in STEs (with the exception of Japan) and, secondly, physical indicators-based growth rates deviated in MEs in both directions, while in STEs deviations of volume-orientated growth rates were not only larger but in one direction only — that is, in all countries lower than officially reported ones. Only Hungary displayed deviations that, although one-sided, remained within the range typical for MEs, proving itself once again to have the most reliable statistics in Eastern Europe. The comparisons for all seven STEs for the whole 1951–73 period considered in the study, as well as for the respective sub-periods, are shown in Table 2.3.

It follows from Table 2.3 that more realistic economic growth rates in STEs, calculated on the basis of the PIG methodology employed in the UN study, constituted between 90 (Hungary) and 55 per cent (GDR) of the officially reported ones (the change from *per capita* to overall growth rates would not affect the percentages). However, even these ratios may be biased upwards. In the present author's opinion, the methodology of that study is not able to capture all economic growth-reducing manifestations of hidden inflation. Downward quality changes due to shoddy craftsmanship and the use of substandard material inputs would pass undetected, and forced purchases of these goods (due to their rapid deterioration) are counted as volume growth of output and consumption. Furthermore, growth rates of other goods and services than those on the list of physical indicators are assumed to be lower by the same percentage which need not necessarily be the case.[13]

That we are on the right track may be seen from a larger, painstakingly detailed study prepared for the US Congress on Soviet economic growth (US Congress, 1982). Using an eclectic methodology, i.e. time series on consumption or output in volume terms and official

Table 2.3: The difference between physical indicators-based GNP *per capita* growth rates, as estimated in the UN study, and official NMP *per capita* growth rates according to national statistics of STEs

	Bul.	Cze.	GDR	Hun.	Pol.	Rom.	USSR
1950–5							
V	7.2	3.7	5.2	5.3	4.1	5.7	5.1
O	8.1	6.9	13.7	4.6	6.6	12.6	9.1
diff.	− 0.9	− 3.2	− 8.5	0.7	− 2.5	− 6.9	− 4.0
1956–60							
V	7.9	4.5	4.7	4.0	3.9	4.9	5.2
O	8.7	6.2	8.0	5.7	4.8	5.6	7.7
diff.	− 0.8	− 1.7	− 3.3	− 1.7	− 0.9	− 0.7	− 2.5
1961–5							
V	7.4	4.0	3.5	5.1	4.8	7.5	5.4
O	5.9	1.1	3.7	3.7	4.7	8.3	5.1
diff.	1.5	2.9	− 0.2	1.4	0.1	− 0.8	0.3
1966–70							
V	6.1	3.7	3.2	5.0	4.7	5.8	4.4
O	8.0	6.5	5.1	6.5	5.1	6.5	6.5
diff.	− 1.9	− 2.8	− 1.9	− 1.5	− 0.4	− 0.7	− 2.1
1971–3							
V	3.4	3.5	3.4	4.5	5.5	5.8	3.9
O	7.2	4.5	5.4	6.3	9.7	10.2	5.1
diff.	− 3.8	− 1.0	− 2.0	− 1.8	− 4.2	− 4.4	− 1.2
1950–73							
V	6.6	3.9	4.0	4.8	4.5	5.9	4.8
O	7.6	5.0	7.2	5.3	5.9	8.5	6.7
diff.	− 1.0	− 1.1	− 3.2	− 0.5	− 1.4	− 2.6	− 1.9
V/O	0.868	0.780	0.556	0.906	0.763	0.694	0.716

Key: V   — physical indicators-based estimates
     O   — official accounts
     diff. — difference in growth rates in percentage points
     V/O — ratio of volume based on officially reported NMP growth
              rates
Source: UN ECE, *Economic Bulletin for Europe*, 1980.

time series in value terms where more reliable data could not be obtained, as well as a much larger number of products and product groups, the authors calculated the GNP growth rate over the period 1951–80, which constituted some 63.5 per cent of the officially reported NMP growth rate for the period (4.7 and 7.4 per cent respectively).[14] Thus, the larger coverage resulted in the greater differential between a realistically calculated growth rate and an officially reported one (for the Soviet Union a change from 71.6 to 63.5 per cent). Significantly, the authors of the study maintain that if their calculated growth rates are biased, it is in the upward direction.

Two questions arise that are of importance for our considerations with respect to both quantities and prices. The first is whether the 'law of equal cheating' suggested by Nove (1977) is really valid. Nove maintained that, in spite of the doctoring of the statistics in STEs, growth rates can safely be used because the imaginative reporting probably does not change over time. A tentative answer to the question on the basis of Table 2.3 (and some other sources)[15] is that it is not. The differential between real (or at least more realistic) growth rates and officially reported ones varies — often sharply — over time. At the same time, these variations seem to depend very much on the political and economic environment.

The best example is that of the STE with the most distorted statistics, i.e. East Germany. Economic growth rates as measured in the study for the 1950–5 and 1961–5 periods constituted 38 and 94.6 per cent of officially reported ones respectively. The extremely high differential in the former period can be explained by the propaganda needs of the country's communist regime, which thought it necessary to prove — at least on paper if not in reality — a superior performance in comparison with the German 'Wirtschaftswunder'. As the Federal Republic's economic growth rates, both overall and *per capita,* were then very high, the very high overstatements of actual rates were needed to demonstrate the communist system's 'supremacy'.[16] On the other hand, the extremely low differential for 1961–5 may be related to the only experiment with some decentralised economic management in the GDR history that, *inter alia,* required improved statistics so that they would not mislead one's own side.

Although it goes beyond the available evidence, the present author regards the 1980s as another period of extremely high differentials between the real, very low NMP growth rates and the officially reported ones. Many available input–output ratios are wildly off their trend values and all the partial indices of repressed inflation on the consumer goods market also point strongly in that direction. The aim of these large overstatements is also political: to show that the GDR, the stalwart of central planning orthodoxy, is immune to the marked economic decline visible elsewhere in the Soviet sphere. Incidentally, the change from the need to prove supremacy over the Western counterpart to the need to prove merely the ability to avoid decline is in itself saying a great deal about the lowered levels of expectations in Eastern Europe . . .

The law of equal cheating does not find much stronger support in the case of other STEs. The differential between the more realistic and official NMP growth rates varies markedly over time, with the tendency for most countries to have higher differentials at the beginning and at the end of the period considered in the UN study (the US Congress, JEC (1982) study also seems to confirm that for the Soviet Union).[17] Exceptions to that tendency were Hungary throughout the period, Bulgaria at the beginning and Czechoslovakia at the end of the period. All in all, the golden period of honesty in STE reporting occurred long ago — that is, in the period 1961–5.

Again, we may hypothesise that with mounting problems, cheating becomes higher or more frequent (which amounts to the same thing). It is less imperative for enterprises to doctor the reports showing that the plan was exceeded by 3 per cent when it was in fact exceeded by 1 per cent only, than to show that the plan was implemented after all, when in fact production fell short of the plan by 4 per cent. The temptation to doctor the statistics at the centre to show better aggregate performance also seems to be stronger under such circumstances. Thus, we may expect STEs to have entered another period of highly overstated economic growth rates (even if the officially reported rates are in themselves much lower than the past ones).

The second question concerns the scale of hidden inflation under central planning, whether in terms of the CPI or the GNP/NMP deflator. Unfortunately, most of the manifestations of hidden inflation are difficult to measure or are not measurable at all. Large-scale studies like those referred to above may allow us to estimate the differentials between the real (or at least more realistic) and the official economic growth rates. Those differentials, if put in percentage terms, as in Table 2.3, may then be regarded as estimates of hidden inflation rates. Nonetheless, many manifestations of hidden inflation, e.g. those of pseudo-innovations and adverse quality changes, would pass undetected anyway.

Worse still, the problems with hidden inflation under central planning do not end with the inability to capture the effects of all growth-reducing hidden inflation phenomena. There are also inflationary phenomena that increase the price level without distorting quantities at the same time, and examples abound. As system-specific features in STEs stimulate enterprises to increase production in volume (weight) or value terms, production of spare parts is less profitable than that of multi-part sub-assemblies (on this point, see Sokołowski, 1978). Permanent shortages of the former force other enterprises or consumers to buy the latter, increasing the price level in consequence. It may not matter much for enterprises, given their soft budget contraint,[18] but it does matter for consumers.

With respect to consumers there also exists a well-known phenomenon of 'secondary distribution'. Illegal sales of goods in short supply, either under the counter or outside the regular distribution channels at prices higher than the official ones, add to hidden inflation (as well as redistribute savings). These activities are barely measurable.[19]

Taking all the above into consideration, hidden inflation in STEs is a phenomenon that, true to its name, remains partly hidden from the view of the researchers poring over the distorted statistics of countries, where permanent price controls, a seller's market and incentives to cheat on output figures combine to spread inflation over its open, hidden, and (as discussed in the next section) repressed forms.

If pressed for some quantitative guesstimates on the scale of inflation in STEs, I would point to the growth-reducing hidden inflation shown in Table 2.3 as a starting point. After some rough recalculations from *per capita* to overall economic growth rate,[20] that part of hidden inflation would range between 3.2% for the GDR and 1.1% for Bulgaria (with that paragon of statistical virtue among STEs, Hungary, having only half the rate of Bulgaria). Next, I would conjecture that all other (both growth-reducing and purely price-affecting) phenomena contribute only as much as the above (not an exorbitant conjecture). Assuming also that the latter hidden inflation growth rates may have been distributed differently,[21] we would arrive at some 3–5 per cent range of inflation rates for STEs in that period, except for Hungary where the rate would be lower. Adding to the open inflation rates in some countries, we would have inflation rates in STEs in the golden period of economic growth that were no lower than those in MEs in the same period.

Estimates by researchers point at the hidden inflation measured by the CPI in various STEs, ranging between 1–2% and 5% on a yearly basis for the Soviet Union (e.g. Howard (1976), Schroeder and Severin (1976) and Wiles (1983)) and Poland (Dunajewski, 1979) respectively, for periods ranging from 10 to 15 years up to the mid-1970s.

As STEs encountered growing difficulties, estimates of hidden inflation went up. Thus, for example, Wiles (1983) put Soviet hidden inflation in the 1975–9 period at 2.9 per cent, while the US Congress, JEC (1982) study estimated the growth-reducing part of hidden inflation to be 1.4 per cent per annum in the 1971–80 decade, as compared with 0.9 per cent per annum in the preceding one.[22] This is, it should be noted, indirect, even if limited, evidence for the validity of my conjecture that the non growth-reducing hidden inflation sources may contribute as much as growth-reducing ones (2.9 per cent for the overall hidden inflation rate for 1975–9 versus 1.2 per cent for the growth-reducing one for 1975–80).

To round off our considerations, we note that the existence of hidden inflation is sometimes acknowledged in STEs, usually when it suits the current interests of central planners and their political masters. Thus, for example, after introducing systemic modifications in 1968, a study appeared in Hungary (Javorka, 1973) showing that it was never a period of price stability, either up to 1957 or in the 1957–67 period, because prices increased yearly on average by 2 per cent in the former and by 1 per cent in the latter period. Clearly, as Pindak (1983) rightly stresses, this was a part of the campaign preparing Hungarians for the inevitability of open inflation under the modified system.

The Soviet invasion and the subsequent restoration of the *status quo ante* in Czechoslovakia prevented the appearance of similar studies relating to the pre-Dubcek era. Thus, the existence of hidden inflation was hinted at rather than statistically verified there (see the sources quoted in Pindak, 1983). However, as it suited central planners, wholesale prices for investment goods were recalculated for the 1954–66 and 1966–73 periods in preparation of the wholesale price reform. They showed the hidden price increase for machinery of 48 per cent and for construction works of 43 per cent (see again the sources quoted in ibid.). It would be difficult to believe that enterprises producing consumer goods would, in contrast, remain so virtuous as to refrain from doctoring their reports and, consequently, forgo the related possibilities of monetary rewards.

These lengthy considerations can be closed with an appropriately brief comment, and I have opted for the shortest possible one, i.e. for a joke I heard on the three degrees of truth in official publications in STEs: true items — that is, obituaries; probable ones — that is, weather forecasts; and the rest. The issues considered above may have contributed at least in some degree to its invention . . . .

2.3. SHORTAGE — REPRESSED INFLATION — STANDARDS OF LIVING

Turning in this last section to repressed inflation, it should be noted that the term is sometimes used in a vague fashion, covering both hidden inflation analysed in the preceding section and repressed inflation (see, for example, Culbertson and Amacher, 1978). However, the latter is, strictly speaking, not inflation proper, in the sense of contributing to the rise in the general price level, but a variety of phenomena that stem from the pervasive excess demand and the accompanying climate of shortage seriously affecting the welfare of the population. Repressed inflation is variously described (see, for example, Holzman (1960), Bornstein (1976) and Pindak (1983)),[23] but all these and many other authors tend to look at repressed inflation in STEs as something going beyond excess demand which cannot be transformed into inflation due to price controls.

Again, as with inflation proper, definitions of repressed inflation applied to MEs cannot be used with respect to STEs without extensive modifications. The by now standard definition of disequilibrium theorists that repressed inflation is 'a situation in which, at existing wages and prices, the aggregate demands . . . exceed the corresponding aggregate supplies . . . (so) purchases of goods and labour services are rationed' and, in consequence, excess demand amounts to the inflationary gap that disappears once constraints (i.e. fixed wages and prices) are removed (Barro and Grossman, 1974), is simply not applicable to STEs.

Firstly, there is no *aggregate* excess demand to be measured, because *a class of economic agents, i.e. enterprises, is characterised by the soft budget constraint and their demands (notional demands in terms of disequilibrium theory) know no limits*, since any cost overruns are expected to be compensated for by subsidies, tax reliefs, price increases, or a combination of all three (see Chapter 1, section 1.1). Thus, it may be irrelevant to measure something that knows no limits.

Nonetheless, indicators of repressed inflation on the producer goods market have been suggested and attempts to measure it have been made, but they are definitely not measures of excess demand in terms of the received theory (equilibrium and disequilibrium alike). Kornai's macro-index of shortage (1982) includes two partial indicators from the producer goods market, but neither of them measures excess demand that is a distance from 'here' to the

Walrasian equilibrium, because 'here' in relation to the equilibrium point is unknown. In actual fact, neither his partial indicators for the producer goods market nor the macro-index itself measures distance between the level of shortage and the Walrasian equilibrium, but only deviations from the trend. It may be said on the basis of these indicators that shortage is increasing or decreasing, but not how far from the equilibrium point the economy finds itself.

Pindak (1983) proposed the value of unfinished investments-to-value of the yearly investments ratio as an indicator, but it again only tells one whether disequilibrium is increasing with the rise of the ratio or decreasing as it declines. The distance from the equilibrium point remains unknown. All these indicators are useful with respect to the dynamics but not the size of disequilibrium.

Secondly, the inflationary gap does not disappear under central planning. Contrary to the experience of a wartime ME in which households expected constraints to be removed later, households in STEs do not form such expectations. For them, constraints are expected to last for ever; it is their intensity that is expected to vary (see Kemme and Winiecki (1984) and Winiecki (1985a)).

Thirdly, changes on households' behaviour under the conditions of repressed inflation in STEs make it imperative to go beyond the attempts to measure the inflationary gap (or the inflationary overhang regarded as stock measure if the gap is regarded as a flow measure),[24] and also to look for the impact of the changed behaviour upon the welfare of the population. Both these aspects of repressed inflation will be considered below.

Thus, repressed inflation under central planning is characterised by many different manifestations of greater or lesser importance. Without making the list complete, those most frequently found are the following:

(1) first and foremost, pervasive shortages plaguing the consumer goods market that vary in intensity over time and across nations, but are nevertheless present all the time;

(2) forced substitution by households which, under the impact of pervasive shortages, change not only quantity expectations (as under a temporary disequilibrium in the market system), but also a pattern of spending (preferences);

(3) rationing that may be open (for the population at large) and hidden (for the ruling elite and their organised supporters and party apparatchiks, the bureaucrats managing the economic system, the military and the police);[25]

(4) illegal 'secondary distribution' under the impact of pervasive shortages (selling under the counter for a bribe or selling on the black market at a higher price);

(5) two-tiered prices, official or at least officially accepted (selected state shops selling higher quality goods unavailable in regular shops at higher prices; the existence of the parallel free market where certain goods, mostly food, are sold at higher prices);

(6) lastly, but certainly not least, forced saving that is also present all the time, although it, too, varies in size over time and across nations.

It is evident from the above that the manifestations are all derivatives of the overall climate of shortage and continuous excess demand, the sources of which have been analysed in Chapter 1.

Persistent shortages, or at least changes thereof, can be measured in two ways. To begin with, queuing is an activity typical for persistent shortages. We could measure time spent queuing. Changes in time spent queuing per household or per person, obtained from household surveys, could be a valuable indicator on the changing intensity of shortage in a given STE. However, we could not measure the 'size' of shortage, since the time spent queuing under the conditions of the equilibrated market is unknown (it is certainly not zero!).

There would be some who could maintain, as did Pryor (1977), that queues do not indicate shortage of goods but that of shops, i.e. they are due to the underdeveloped retail trade sector. The retail trade and other services are indeed underdeveloped. The reasons for this underdevelopment are also systemic, as will be shown in Part Two of this study, but this is only a part of the problem. Another question in the household survey would dispel any doubts in this respect. The number of shops that have to be visited to do a week's shopping would reveal that time spent queuing does not consist of one block of time per week in one shop, as should have been the case with respect to food products, but of many visits to various shops in search of even those goods that are bought regularly on a weekly basis. The Pryor vision of STE shops crammed with goods and crowded with people is misleading in the case of the first half of his vision. Crowds are indeed flowing in and out; only goods are not there in demanded quantity and variety (to say nothing about their quality).[26] Thus, time spent queuing, corrected for the underdevelopment of retail trade, could still be a good measure of the dynamics of shortage on the consumer goods market.

However, queueing has another aspect, too, since it is a welfare-reducing activity. This is best explained by Wiles (1983):

> To queue is to work; to do extra housework. Standing and waiting takes time and are more unpleasant than most money-earning work or normal housework. [Now] if the volume of consumer goods increases by 10 per cent we are, say, 7 per cent better off (for the marginal utility of income diminishes). But if we originally did 42 hours a week plus 5 hours queueing, and now it is 42 + 9.7, that [means] 10 per cent more work, or, say, we are 15 per cent worse off (for the marginal disutility of labour increases). So the orthodox statistics tell us we are better off . . .; yet we feel worse off and not being professors of economics we cannot account for it.[27]

Now, for example, household surveys on Poland show that the average daily time spent queueing per household increased between 1966 and 1976 by 55.6 per cent (from 63 to 98 minutes).[28] Taking the above into account, such data should also be included into any calculations of changes in welfare of the Polish population in that period.

Shortages can be measured in other ways, too: for example, a Czechoslovak household survey estimated the percentage of consumer goods that displayed no supply difficulties with respect to a sample of food products and industrial goods. The data for the 1972–8 (first half) period are presented in Table 2.4. They show the existence of pervasive shortages on this relatively well-supplied market, as well as their dynamics. Shortage not only varies but also tends to increase over time, particularly sharply towards the end of the period, when only about one-third of food products and one-fifth of industrial goods did not display supply difficulties. No data have been published, unfortunately (but significantly) for the most recent period.

The indicator used in the Czechoslovak survey, whether weighted properly by the shares of respective products in the sample or not,[29] shows only the width (extent) of shortage, and not its depth (intensity). We do not know the value of goods that would have been brought in the absence of supply difficulties.[30] Thus, again, it can be useful in stressing the dynamics of shortage, but not the distance from the Walrasian equilibrium.

The distance from the equilibrium point (no shortage) may be

Table 2.4: The share of consumer goods that displayed no supply difficulties in Czechoslovakia on a half-yearly basis, 1972–8 (on the basis of household surveys with respect to a sample of goods)[a] (%)

		Food products	Industrial goods
1972	I	58.5	52.0
	II	61.6	50.5
1973	I	72.5	43.2
	II	68.9	41.1
1974	I	75.0	36.6
	II	65.2	27.8
1975	I	66.7	28.2
	II	58.7	34.6
1976	I	47.1	28.7
	II	27.1	27.5
1977	I	27.9	20.7
	II	27.9	20.1
1978	I	35.9	19.0

Note: a. For some information on the methodology and the data, see
       Dolejsi (1979)
Sources: Klaus (1979) (Quarterly data are shown in Dolejsi, 1979).

measured with respect to particular goods only. Some fragmentary data exist with respect to cars, the consumer durables most difficult to purchase in STEs. Kornai (1982) used the waiting time (unfilled orders divided by yearly sales) as one of the partial indicators of his macro-index of shortage. The waiting time fluctuated between 0.6 and 5.5 years within the 1965–79 period, with a tendency for the waiting time to increase sharply after 1975. The same indicator can be calculated for the earlier 1962–72 period for Czechoslovakia from the national statistical yearbook of that country. It also shows fluctuations over time between 2.8 and 4.6 years, with the longer waiting time at the beginning and at the end of the period in question. As with the indicator of shortage in Table 2.4, it ceased to be published when it showed the situation to have worsened.[31]

There are no time series for other STEs of comparable length, but fragmentary data also show sharply increasing waiting time for cars in the recent years: for example, in Bulgaria, this waiting time increased from 10 years in the late 1970s to 20 years in 1984,[32] and in the GDR to some 12 years in 1983 for the smallest 'Trabant' car, and somewhat less for another available make.[33] In Hungary the waiting time continues to fluctuate around the upper bound of the range (4–5 years).[34]

It is not only with respect to cars that shortages became more pervasive in STEs in recent years, although evidence is mostly casual: journalists' reports, visitors' accounts, etc.[35] The worst shortages have been reported from Romania, Poland and the Soviet Union (where on top of it there is a world of difference between large cities and those parts of the country not accessible to foreigners, including the countryside). However, journalists' reports also regarded the GDR's supply situation in the early 1980s as markedly worse than in the mid-1970s.[36] A worsened supply situation has been recently stressed by visitors in Bulgaria. In that country, thefts of agricultural produce on co-operative fields by city dwellers multiplied (when the situation was additionally aggravated by the severe drought) to such an extent that the attorney general's office issued a special warning threatening offenders with severe punishments.[37] Even in Hungary, the STE with the least disequilibrated consumer goods market, the supply situation with respect to industrial goods has worsened since the mid-1970s, and not only with respect to cars.

Thus, in spite of investment cuts that were supposed to decrease the growth of demand for consumer goods through lower wage fund increases, and in spite of open and hidden inflation that reduced excess demand through the higher general price level (see the preceding section), shortages have become more pervasive of late: and again, greater shortages mean more queuing and, in turn, decreased welfare.[38]

Pervasive shortages also mean the existence of forced substitution. As we already stressed, it is not only quantity expectations that change, but also the preferences of households. The subject has been dealt with exhaustively by Kornai (1980), so we do not repeat the argumentation here. We add only that the so-called 'vodka factor' is related not only to the alienation and hopelessness,[39] but also, on a more practical plane, to pervasive shortages that undermine the willingness to save in order to buy a desired apartment, or a car, or some other product. Alcohol is certainly the most conspicuous example of the spillover effects of pervasive shortages, but it is not the only one.

Rationing will be dealt with even more briefly here. The extent of rationing, properly weighted by the share of rationed goods in private consumption, can be used as an auxiliary indicator of shortage, since the absence of rationing does not signify the absence of shortages.

The next two manifestations of shortage, that will also be dealt with very briefly, have some features in common. Both the illegal 'secondary distribution' and two-tiered prices, although suggesting the repressing of inflation, in fact add to inflation proper. While the former contributes towards hidden inflation under any circumstances, the latter adds to open or hidden inflation, depending upon the quality of the CPI in a given STE (see the preceding section). Moreover, differentials between the black market or free market prices and official ones can be used as indicators of change in the intensity *(but again not the size)* of shortage. Thus, for example, the differentials between the free market and official prices in the Soviet Union and Poland were increasing in the 1970s, while those in Hungary were decreasing slightly. As this squared well with increasing disequilibria in the former and a near-equilibrated food market in the latter, the usefulness of this indicator cannot be denied (Pindak, 1983).

Finally, we arrive at the last of the manifestations listed above, and one steeped in controversy, especially of late. Forced savings generate a lot of interest, since — properly estimated — they could give an answer as to the size of excess demand in STEs: but can they be properly estimated under central planning?

For a decade or so, certain Western economists of Keynesian and — more generally — disequilibrium theory orientation tended to apply the procedures valid only under equilibrium conditions to estimate supply functions, demand functions, savings functions, etc., for STEs (see Pickersgill (1976, 1980), Portes and Winter (1977, 1978, 1980), and Asselain (1981)). With misapplied theory and misunderstood data (see Winiecki, 1985a), the results showed that equilibrium had been by and large maintained and little (if any) forced saving was in evidence.[40]

Many others however, including this author, are less optimistic as to the possibilities of proper estimates of forced savings (and *eo ipso* excess demand) under central planning. Firstly, savings ratios are not a very good indicator under the overall climate of shortage and permanent excess demand, since they are calculated from the variables based on the demand side, i.e. on the 'long' side of the market (in terms of disequilibrium theory). Secondly, the supply side, i.e. the 'short' side of the market, is even shorter than it is assumed by the protagonists of the above approach. Both quantity-reducing hidden inflation (see above, section 2.2) and the 'unsaleables' (goods of such a low quality that they cannot be sold even on the seller's market) reduce quantities supplied much below the officially reported level. Thirdly, the aggregation hides the pervasive mismatch between supply and demand structures, an

61

important disequilibrating factor in basically closed economies. All the above STE distortions tend to raise savings above the desired level, as households cannot satisfy their demand with respect to quantity (too low a supply of saleables) and variety (wrong supply structure). Other factors tend to affect savings the other way round. Thus, fourthly, the non-quantity-reducing component of hidden inflation (again, see section 2.2. above) reduces savings by making people increase their expenditures on the same volume of goods. Fifthly and finally, forced substitution also reduces savings.

As neither of these distortions from the normal pattern of savings can be measured with any reasonable accuracy, forced savings have to be represented by indicators that, just like other manifestations of shortage, show more of the dynamics than the absolute size of the phenomenon in question; and if somebody tries to assess forced savings it has to be done on the basis of the highly uncertain data, like, for example, household surveys. It is on the basis of such unpublished surveys that, for example, the Czechoslovak authorities assess forced savings to be equal to about one-third of the savings stock in the early 1980s (private information from a reliable Czech source).

Besides, not all indicators should be those based on traditional demand-related variables.[41] Both the present author (1982, 1985c, 1986e) and Jansen (1982) came up independently with the same type of indicator: namely, a ratio of savings stock to retail sales at current prices or, for countries that publish data on money stock, a ratio of savings and cash to retail sales. My own time series of the former indicator are shown in Table 2.5. Of course, neither indicator measures the size of inflationary overhang, for we do not know how large a part of the numerator consists of forced savings. Mechanical division between demand and time deposits, as is sometimes done, is not sufficient. Besides, under the conditions of a buying panic, *all* of the numerator may constitute an inflationary gap (for more on this point, see below).

The data for the 1960–83 period show quite a few interesting regularities. Firstly, there is a marked negative association between the said ratios and the existence of open inflation in STEs. Savings-to-sales ratios are the highest in those countries in which changes in the official CPI are the lowest and the least frequent. Thus, the said ratio in the GDR has always been the highest, with Bulgaria, Czechoslovakia and the Soviet Union following. The savings-to-sales ratio has been the lowest in Poland and Hungary — that is, precisely in those two countries that registered open inflation almost all the time.

Table 2.5: Savings[a]-to-sales ratios[b] for six CPEs, excluding Romania, 1960–83

Year	Bul.	Cze.	GDR	Hun.	Pol.	USSR
1960	0.35	0.21	0.39	0.08	0.08	0.12
1961	0.38	0.23	0.41	0.10	0.09	0.14
1962	0.40	0.25	0.44	0.12	0.11	0.15
1963	0.42	0.27	0.48	0.16	0.14	0.15
1964	0.46	0.29	0.54	0.20	0.16	0.16
1965	0.50	0.32	0.60	0.23	0.15	0.17
1966	0.55	0.34	0.65	0.24	0.20	0.20
1967	0.58	0.36	0.70	0.23	0.23	0.22
1968	0.60	0.34	0.74	0.26	0.24	0.24
1969	0.64	0.35	0.78	0.28	0.23	0.27
1970	0.71	0.39	0.82	0.30	0.26	0.30
1971	0.76	0.45	0.83	0.32	0.27	0.32
1972	0.83	0.49	0.84	0.33	0.30	0.35
1973	0.90	0.49	0.87	0.35	0.34	0.35
1974	0.92	0.55	0.88	0.35	0.36	0.40
1975	0.94	0.55	0.91	0.37	0.37	0.43
1976	0.94	0.58	0.92	0.40	0.36	0.47
1977	0.96	0.60	0.95	0.41	0.35	0.51
1978	0.94	0.59	0.98	0.44	0.35	0.54
1979	0.95	0.59	1.00	0.43	0.36	0.58
1980	0.86	0.61	0.99	0.42	0.36	0.58
1981	0.87	0.63	0.99	0.42	0.43	0.58
1982	0.89	0.66	1.03	0.43	0.31	0.59
1983	0.93	0.69	1.07	0.44	0.29	0.61

Notes: a. Total savings (savings stock).
      b. Retail sales of goods and services at current prices.
Sources: *CMEA yearbook*, various years; national statistical yearbooks, various years; own computations.

Next, it is assumed on the basis of the long dominant (but now receding) received theory that the share of income saved rises with the rise in income *per capita*. Since the latter is assumed to rise with the rise in GNP *per capita*, savings-to-sales ratio should, *ceteris paribus*, be positively correlated with GNP *per capita* in STEs. This is not, however the case: for example, Bulgaria, with its lowest GNP *per capita* among the STEs in question[42] displays a much higher relative savings' measure than all countries with higher income levels, except East Germany. Besides, differences in savings-to-sales ratios between the GDR, Bulgaria, Czechoslovakia and the Soviet Union on the one hand, and Hungary and Poland on the other, are so large (up to two-and-a-half to one) as to be inexplicable in terms of the differing propensity to save at different — but not *much* different — levels of income *per capita*. Obviously, sources of the different ranking of and large differences across STEs must be rooted elsewhere.

It is the trade-off between open inflation in Hungary and Poland and the higher inflationary overhang in the remaining STEs that explain much of the differences. The support for this thesis can be found also from the marked association between the greater levels of open inflation in all STEs except the GDR (see Table 2.2) and more slowly growing savings-to-sales ratios (see Table 2.5) in recent years. As STEs other than Hungary and Poland resorted to open inflation to reduce growing disequilibria, the ratios slowed down or declined temporarily.

Thus, we arrive at the conclusion that although all three forms of inflation — open, hidden, and repressed — affect STEs, at the same time there are obvious trade-offs between the three. In the preceding section we pointed to the substitution between open and hidden inflation: STEs that do not change (or do not change frequently) the official CPI register the highest hidden inflation growth rates. Here we established the trade-off of the same type between open inflation and repressed inflation: countries that do not register open inflation have markedly higher savings-to-sales ratios. As to the inflationary overhang-hidden inflation trade-off, the rise in the general price level generates continuous 'leakages' from the former to the latter. In other words, while paying more for the same quantity the nominator (savings) decreases, while the numerator (sales) increases. Higher hidden inflation means lower inflationary overhang and vice versa.

Another conclusion that can be drawn from the above, is that *there is no possibility of avoiding inflation once disequilibria are generated somewhere within the national economy.* In the case of STEs, they are generated within the producer goods sector (as shown in Chapter 1). *However, even if inflation itself is inevitable, the specific form that it takes is dependent upon the economic system.* In STEs, system- and policy-specific features assure that inflation appears in all three forms simultaneously.

Before we turn to the final conclusion concerning the dynamics of inflation, I would like to introduce some evidence linking the disequilibria in the producer and consumer goods sectors. Since investment-related activities tend to be the main disequilibrating phenomena, it is the fast rising wages in the producer goods sector that do not meet correspondingly rising supplies of consumer goods. This, in turn, results in all forms of inflation on the consumer goods market.

There ought to exist, then, an association between investment rates and savings, both rates and levels. I regressed two savings-related indicators: yearly changes in savings of households (a savings flow indicator) and yearly savings-to-sales ratios (the non-traditional savings stock indicator analysed above) upon yearly changes in investments for the period 1965–80. I decided to use yearly investment rate for the same year and the same investment rate lagging one year, because consumers affected by pervasive shortages carry more cash for longer periods. Thus, parts of their earnings in a given year may appear, after an unsuccessful search, on savings accounts next year. There is also a more compelling reason why two consecutive years ought to be taken into account. The hectic activity to execute plans, upon the execution of which depend various premiums and bonuses, results in large payments taking place at the very end of the year or at the beginning of the consecutive year. In consequence, they can appear as savings mostly in the latter year.

Regression results are presented in Table 2.6. Changes in investment rates explained between 25 and 50 per cent of changes in savings rates. Results were more varied for the alternative dependent variable, where the R^2 values for Poland, Hungary and Czechoslovakia were below the 0.25 level. It should be noted, however, that it is the above countries that most often used officially registered price increases to reduce the inflationary overhang, with the already noted effects upon the savings-to-sales ratio. Thus, I decided to add the third independent variable, i.e. annual changes in the consumer price index, to subsequent regressions. Regressions of annual savings-to-sales ratios on three independent variables resulted in much improved R^2 values for all three countries in question. Annual investment growth rates and CPI increases, i.e. open inflation rates, explained over 75 per cent of changes in the dependent variable for Hungary ($R^2 = 0.78$), almost two-thirds for Poland ($R^2 = 0.65$) and over one-third for Czechoslovakia ($R^2 = 0.35$).

Thus, a distinct link has been established empirically between the producer goods sector and the consumer goods sector, or — to put it differently — between the enterprise and household sectors. The strength of that link, i.e. the ability to explain at least one-quarter to half of the variance of each savings-related indicator by investment growth rates, ought to be regarded as satisfactory, given all the distorting systemic influences upon indices of prices and quantities.

Moreover, the markedly higher R^2 obtained by addition of open inflation as a third independent variable in the above regressions

65

Table 2.6: Impact of investments upon savings: results of regressions of annual savings growth rates and annual changes in savings-to-sales ratios on annual investment growth rates (i.e. on two independent variables: investment growth rates run concurrently and lagged one year), 1965–80

	Dependent variable: annual saving growth rates		Dependent variable: annual changes in savings-to-sales ratios	
	R^2	F statistics	R^2	F statistics
Bulgaria	0.33	2.93	0.34	3.29
Czechoslovakia	0.24	2.09	0.07	0.49
			$(0.35)^a$	$(2.13)^a$
GDR	0.53	7.27^c	0.44	5.04^b
Hungary	0.40	4.08^b	0.16	1.24
			$(0.78)^a$	$(14.20)^{a,d}$
Poland	0.52	7.07^c	0.18	1.47
			$(0.65)^a$	$(7.48)^{a,c}$
Soviet Union	0.36	3.62	0.27	2.46

Notes: a. Savings-to-sales ratios regressed on three dependent variables: the above two, and the official inflation growth rate.
b. Correlation coefficient significant at the 0.05 level.
c. Correlation coefficient significant at the 0.01 level.
d. Correlation coefficient significant at the 0.001 level.
Source: Winiecki (1985c).

empirically linked open and repressed inflation. Where there is open inflation, as there is particularly in Hungary and Poland, the savings-to-sales ratio which contains an (unknown) share of forced savings, a most telling manifestation of repressed inflation, is less strongly correlated with investment growth rates. It is precisely CPI increases that reduce both disequilibrium and forced savings, decreasing accordingly savings-to-sales ratio and weakening the link between investments growth rates and savings. This link again becomes stronger where annual CPI changes are added to explain the savings-to-sales ratio.

Finally, yet another conclusion — and one having an important bearing upon the future performance of STEs — can be drawn from analysing Table 2.6. Savings-to-sales ratios (as well as savings cum cash-to-sales ratios not shown there)[43] tend to increase over time. They grow more or less rapidly, stabilise for a year or two or even fall slightly, reflecting short-term effects of investment cycles and price policies, but in the longer term they have been increasing inexorably in all STEs.[44] It suggests that forced savings may be ever higher over time,[45] and it means, in turn, that whatever economic aims central planners and their political masters pursue in the future, they will pursue them in a more disequilibrated, i.e. less conducive, environment. There is, however, the major difference between STEs and MEs with respect to economic performance and economic policies in a disequilibrated environment. Distorted prices resulting in the simultaneous existence of all three forms of inflation — open, hidden and repressed — make disequilibria infinitely more difficult for central planners to deal with (and for households to bear).

NOTES

1. It was not always the case and even now its acceptability is in some countries limited to explanations pointing at central planners' mistakes (and/or external disturbances) as sources of inflation. The best example of changing communist orthodoxy is in this respect subsequent post-war editions of the Great Soviet Encyclopaedia. For a brief, useful survey of these changes, see Pindak (1983).

2. For a more detailed critique, see Winiecki (1985a).

3. This, *inter alia*, contradicts the study of Farrel (1975) who found the average amount by which the plans were exceeded in Poland over the 1957–70 period to be only 2.6 per cent.

4. An average (unweighted) of the set of indicators.

5. Over the period 1976–80, Poland was, for many reasons, an exception.

6. The so-called EFO or Scandinavian model was first presented to the non-Scandinavian audience in Edgren *et al.* (1969) and Aukrust (1970).

7. By definition in public administration, health and education.

8. Theoretically, uncompensated productivity increases offer a trade-off for price increases, but in a period of low growth, such productivity increases may be too small to offer a trade-off. Besides, other factors strengthen the willingness of the centre to increase prices and decrease living standards (to generate enough resources to pay the foreign debt).

9. Changes in the way CPI is constructed took place in Poland in two stages: in the mid-1970s and in 1981. At present the CPI in Poland does not differ much with respect to its construction method from that used in Hungary.

10. The following few pages are a revised version of Winiecki (1986c).

11. The situation is different if commands are issued by central planners to some enterprises to produce higher priced substitutes in spite of the unsatisfied demand for lower priced representative goods.

12. The methodology and the list of indicators are found in the said study.

13. More differentiated products lend themselves more easily to doctoring than, for example, steel, cement, cars, or sugar, all found on the list of physical indicators.

14. The calculations of an NMP equivalent showed slightly smaller differentials ranging from 78.5 to 61.9 per cent over the six five-yearly sub-periods, but ones only marginally different from those for difference between the calculated GNP and official NMP growth rates.

15. See, for example, the US Congress, JEC (1982) study on the Soviet Union, and the Askanas and Laski (1985) study on Poland (the latter shows differences in real consumption and consumer goods prices only).

16. I assume that during that period, almost all the doctoring of the data was done because reliable German workers and technicians succumbed more slowly to the doctoring of the reports, as something entirely foreign to their tradition.

17. The acceleration of hidden inflation in Poland in the 1970s, as measured by the prices of consumer goods, has also been found in Askanas and Laski (1985).

18. This is also one of the sources of extremely high input inventories in STE enterprises.

19. Although the Polish weekly *Zycie Gospodarcze* has been reporting recently on price divergences between the official and free or black markets, the volume of transactions is impossible to calculate.

20. Assuming for simplification the 1 per cent *per annum* population growth for all countries for the whole period (except the GDR where population has been regarded as constant).

21. For example, the noted reliability of German workers and bureaucrats may have compensated greater than average doctoring of official figures by the centre at the macro level with lower than average doctoring of plan reports at the micro level.

22. Although on a FYP basis, the latter estimated the 1976–80 yearly rate to be slightly lower than the 1971–5 one (1.2 versus 1.5 per cent respectively).

23. Kornai (1980) is somewhat vague on this point, in spite of dealing in an authoritative manner with most (if not all) phenomena of excess demand and shortage. This vagueness is also noted by Pindak (1983).

24. This distinction was not made in the earlier works of the author: see Winiecki (1982, 1985a and 1985c).

25. This issue has been dealt with at some length by the present author in Winiecki (1984a, 1984c, and 1986d).

26. See, for example, a comment by a representative of a large department store in the Soviet Union (actually, the largest one in Vilnius in the Lithuanian SSR) that 'crowds are large but not those of buyers. Purchases are made by every 30th person visiting the store' (*Chervonyi Shtandar,* 20 February 1986).

27. The only addition to the above would be that professors of economics who write about welfare of the population under central planning do not always take it into account either.

28. Quoted in Okólski (forthcoming).

29. The methodology was only partly revealed in Dolejsi (1979).

30. Soviet sources sometimes gave estimates in billions of roubles, or in percentages of satisfied demand (see, for example *Planovoye Khozyaistvo* (9–10, 1981) but these figures refer to differences between the demands of retail trade organisations and actually concluded contracts with producing

enterprises. These figures are, however, of highly uncertain nature. First of all, contracts do not equal shipments, since enterprises very often change the assortment of produced goods and supply other, more easily produced goods than those specified in the contracts. Usually it is goods already in short supply, i.e. less easily produced ones, that are turned out in smaller quantities. Thus, excess demand for them is actually larger than the Soviet figures show. On the other hand, retail trade organisations may overstate the size of excess demand because excess demands for various goods are obviously interlinked and — on the equilibrated market — actual purchases of some goods would reduce excess demand for other ones.

31. Interestingly, the situation in the early 1980s improved markedly for very specific reasons. Obsolete Czech 'Skoda' cars, whose subsequent models did not differ much from the basic mid-1950s model, registered a sharp fall in demand on West European markets (in spite of ludicrously low prices) and suddenly became more easily available domestically.

32. Quoted in *Przeglad Techniczny*, no. 6, 1985.

33. Quoted in *Polityka*, no. 38, 1984.

34. Quoted in *Przeglad Techniczny*, no. 40, 1984.

35. A lot of such evidence has been reported, e.g. in Drewnowski, 1982.

36. See, for example, *Financial Times*, 20 December 1983.

37. Quoted after *Polityka*, no. 12, 1985.

38. In Bulgaria and Romania, the welfare of the population also suffered from prolonged power cuts that reduced, sometimes drastically, heating and lighting hours in winter time.

39. In Poland, alcohol consumption fell sharply during the Solidarity period (by about one-third).

40. Interestingly, some East European economists reproduced the procedures to achieve the same (politically desirable) results. On both procedures and motives, see Pindak, 1983.

41. The following pages are based on my earlier article (Winiecki, 1985c).

42. Romania does not publish savings data.

43. Officially they can be calculated for Czechoslovakia, the GDR and Poland. Unofficial calculations for Hungary and the Soviet Union also exist.

44. Unpublished data for Romania for the period 1961–74 also show a similar trend.

45. It has already been demonstrated why it is impossible to explain differences in savings-to-sales ratios across STEs by varying propensities to save at different *per capita* income levels. The same applies to a large extent to changes in the savings-to-sales ratio over time. Savings may increase but raising levels of income *per capita* may account for a part (and probably a smaller one) of the increase in the numerator. Given the 2.5:1.5:1 ratios of the value of our indicator across countries with similar *per capita* income levels, the larger part of the increase in the savings-to-sales ratio stems from the different rates of forced savings: higher in countries with no or lower open inflation and lower in those with higher open inflation (with hidden inflation intermediating between the two and accounting for most of the distortions).

Part Two

The Distorted Structure of Soviet-type Economies

3

The Overgrown Industrial Sector

3.1. SOURCES OF THE OVERGROWTH OF THE INDUSTRIAL SECTOR

A casual look at statistics, whether national or international, on the structure of the national economy or, more precisely, on the production structure of the Soviet-type economies indicates something amiss with the industrial sectors of STEs. The share of industry in STEs has been increasing continually, while elsewhere, even in countries within the same GNP *per capita* range as that of STEs, the pattern has been different. It is a well-known characteristic of structural change in the world economy that industry's share in GDP increases over time, then at a certain level of economic development that share stabilises and later begins slowly to decline.

This stylised pattern of structural change is typical enough to be called uniform, although there are obviously variations around the trend shares of industry across countries for each level of GNP *per capita*. Determinants of such a uniform pattern of structural change are consumer demand (that ultimately determines investment demand), technical change (that, jointly with final demand, determines intermediate demand), and foreign demand. These unifying variables reflect an attained level of economic development that, in turn, is roughly reflected in the level of GNP *per capita*. If there are deviations from that pattern, they are due to the influence of diversifying variables such as the size of a national economy, its natural resources (climate, surface, minerals, etc.) or institutional factors (system- and/or policy-specific features that affect the production structure).[1]

Thus, if there are increasingly visible signs of the overgrowth of the industrial sector, they must stem from the impact of diversifying variables. However, strangely enough, this continuous overgrowth of the industrial sector, beyond any limits known elsewhere, largely continued unrecognised.[2] What is more, when recognised, it was disregarded and ascribed to differences in relative prices in comparison with market economies that statistically inflated the share of industry in GDP in STEs (*Economic Survey of Europe*, 1969). Not surprisingly, without the recognition of a problem, its sources remained unexplored until very recently (see Winiecki (1984d, 1986b) and Winiecki and Winiecki, 1987).[3]

It should not come as a surprise that sources of the overgrowth of the industrial sector under central planning are institutional, i.e. system- and policy-specific. Of the three above-mentioned diversifying variables, only institutional factors are common to all STEs. Industry's ever-increasing share in GDP observed in *all* STEs could not result from their similar size since these countries differ greatly in this respect. Nor could it result from their similar natural resource endowment. It is only the Soviet economic (and political) system that constitutes a common denominator for this economically diverse group.

Once institutional factors have been singled out as potential sources of deviations from the pattern of structural change under central planning, the next step is to set forth particular system- and policy-specific features affecting the production structures and indicate the expected deviations in STEs resultant therefrom.

To begin with, the overgrowth of the industrial sector may be expected from the inward-oriented economic development and concomitant *import substitution-oriented strategy* pursued under one or another name during the last 40 (and in the Soviet Union, during the last 60) years. Except for the Soviet Union, East European STEs are small countries, i.e. they belong to the textbook category of countries that are supposed to draw the largest benefits from the participation in the international division of labour. However, the application of the inward-oriented Soviet development model has forced upon these countries the extreme version of import substitution, causing them to forgo most of the advantages of international specialisation.

This semi-autarkic development results in the overexpansion of intermediate input-producing industries: iron and steel, chemicals, cement, paper, etc. The share of these industries expands beyond what is uniform for countries at their level of development and size, which satisfy to a much larger extent their demand for intermediates through international specialisation. The smaller the country, the greater the burden of what may be called *underspecialisation*:[4]

Poland, for example, produces 8–10 million intermediate and final products, Czechoslovakia five million, and Hungary three million.[5] As a result, all smaller STEs produce too large an assortment of goods in too small quantities per production run, using too many material inputs and production factors in the process. These goods not only cost too much, but they are more often than not technologically obsolete, since there are not enough resources to modernise production technology for too many goods (Winiecki (1984a) and Okólski and Winiecki (1984)).

These effects are fairly typical for all countries that choose an import substitution-oriented strategy. A line of research, which began with Little *et al.* (1970) and Balassa *et al.* (1971), established that less developed countries (LDCs) pursuing import substitution have many common structural characteristics: a higher share of industry in GDP reached at earlier stages of economic development, a higher share of intermediate goods-producing industries in industrial production, etc. These common characteristics were empirically distinguishable, in spite of the impact of other, both unifying and differentiating, variables.

Given the extreme variant of import substitution practised for much longer periods in STEs, the overgrowth in these economies may be expected to be greater than in LDCs and other market or mixed economies. Indications of such underspecialisation may be found in East European economic literature, especially in more recent complaints about parallel development of industries in CMEA countries and resultant suboptimal production runs (e.g. Karlik and Kormnov (1980), Belovic (1982), Mosoczy (1983)). However, it is pointed out that suboptimality, the other side of underspecialisation, is almost as prevalent in the Soviet Union as it is in smaller STEs (Karlik and Kormnov, 1980). Obviously, underspecialisation due to import substitution is not *the only* source of structural deviations. Indeed, the similarity with other countries pursuing import substitution cannot be stretched too far. STEs are burdened with distortions stemming not only from policy-specific, but first and foremost from system-specific features. These systemic distortions not only distort macroeconomic relationships (see above, Part One) but also exert lasting influence upon production structures.

The most serious of these features is underspecialisation at the micro level stemming from *the tendency of each enterprise in STEs to turn out as much as possible for the production of its final output within a given enterprise.* In the overall climate of shortage, low reliability of supplies[6] and uncertainty permeating STEs, enterprises

— to minimise the risk of non-execution of plan targets — tend to produce internally as large a share of intermediate inputs as possible. Even parts and components, as well as instruments, for the productive equipment installed there are in many cases produced within a given enterprise. Thus, enterprises pursue their own 'import substitution' strategy, trying to 'import' as little as possible from other enterprises. Furthermore, if what is traditionally called import substitution lowers the optimum production scale across the national economy, with resultant structural distortions, then that type of 'import substitution', or *do-it-yourself bias*, has no less grave distortionary consequences for production structures.

The small scale, often one-of-a-kind production of intermediate inputs, instruments, parts and components for the equipment, etc., uses up much more materials and labour inputs than in the case of specialised subcontractors, instruments suppliers and servicing by equipment producers. In consequence the already suboptimal production scale (due to extreme import substitution) becomes even lower, as an important part of the resources of the enterprise has to be devoted to these unspecialised activities.

In consequence, in STEs the size of an enterprise measured by the size of its labour force is not equal to that measured by its production volume. The more complex the product, the more parts and components are necessary; the more sophisticated, and 'maintenance-intensive' the equipment, the larger the discrepancy between the former and the latter. For these very reasons most affected are engineering industries, in which even in such a large country as the Soviet Union 70 per cent of engineering factories are estimated to produce at below optimal production scale (Karlik and Kormnov, 1980).[7] This percentage is certainly higher in smaller STEs. This is, incidentally, an explanation of the fact, invariably surprising for Western industrialists, that STE enterprises — comparable with Western ones as far as technology of final product is concerned — tend to employ more production factors, use more material inputs per unit of output and generally register higher costs.[8]

The do-it-yourself bias that makes sense at the micro level in a shortage-plagued economy due to the higher probability of plan execution by the enterprise is an economic nonsense from the efficiency viewpoint of the national economy. Nonetheless, it is sometimes raised to the level of a principle. In the GDR one of the plan indicators for large industrial groupings (combines) has been the ratio of intra-combine turnover to sales, and the combine is regarded as increasingly specialised if the numerator grows faster than the denominator(!). That may ensure supplies of intra-combine produced parts and components for the combine's own final output, but makes them even less available — and disruptive for production schedules — elsewhere. Shortages do not disappear; they are only redistributed (see Csaba, 1983a).

In the overall atmosphere of shortage, both types of import substitution, or underspecialisation, blend in some cases into one. Thus, for example, various Hungarian and East German enterprises are known to substitute intra-enterprise produced inputs for those supplied by enterprises from other CMEA countries (ibid.). In another example, the GDR combines established the so-called rationalisation divisions (*Rationalisierungsmittelbau* — RMB) that are supposed to produce new productive equipment and instruments for their own combines, to modernise the existing equipment, to perform repairs, etc. According to the East German source, modernisation of the existing equipment takes 20 per cent of their time, repairs account for another 20 per cent,[9] while the rest is devoted to substituting for unavailable imports (see Boot (1983) and the literature quoted therein). It is assumed that substituted imports are both from the East (uncertain supplies) and from the West (scarcity of convertible currencies).

Thus, system- and policy-specific features created what may be called a *twofold underspecialised economy* that is unable to follow the uniform pattern of structural change observable in the world economy. The deviations are only to be expected and, if import substitution strategy-oriented LDCs have displayed deviations from the pattern due to their underspecialisation of the first type, the scale of deviations (and adverse effects thereof) in the case of countries affected by *both* types of underspecialisation are expected to be much larger.

This is all the more so, moreover, as structural change in STEs as also affected by other system-specific features. The distorted structure of incentives adds to the greater demand for inputs in relation to outputs. As it was formulated earlier (see Chapter 1, section 1.1), material and other incentives for enterprises are under central planning positively correlated with the volume or value of output, but are not negatively correlated with the cost of inputs. The most important gross indicators (both volume, like tons, metres, etc., and value indicators, like gross production or sales) encourage waste of material inputs that have to be produced somewhere, inflating further the size of the industrial sector without increasing value added commensurately.

Moreover, these problems are not alleviated over time, as is the case under the market system, since there are no scarcity prices under central planning. In a shortage-plagued economy without scarcity prices, the very existence of scarcity is not a sufficient condition for the reallocation of resources to expand production of the scarce goods or, better, their less expensive substitutes. As scarcity signals appear everywhere, resources are reallocated to products and product groups that are preferred by central planners and their political masters and/or are successfully pressed upon them by various bureaucratic pressure groups at lower levels of the bureaucratic hierarchy: ministries, unions or enterprises, etc. (on the latter point, see Greskovits, 1985).[10] Thus, shortages continue unabated as before. Furthermore, innovation is slow because the structure of incentives strongly discourages enterprises from using less costly inputs or changing anything in the production routine (see above, Chapter 1, sections 1.1 and 1.3, and below, Chapter 6). Thus, not only the reallocation of resources from above, through investments, but also innovation-based change at the bottom of the multi-level hierarchy, i.e. in the enterprises, fails to relieve persistent shortages.

All told, four hypotheses can be advanced. Firstly, one would expect the industrial sector in STEs to be markedly overgrown in comparison with other economies at the same level of economic development. Secondly, these deviations from the uniform pattern would be in the same direction, given the similar impact of institutional factors in all STEs. Thirdly, this overgrowth would be distortionary in the sense that increases in outputs would not be commensurate with those of inputs, causing STEs to produce less with more (contrary to what economics is all about . . .). Fourthly, since both the size of the economy and the degree of sophistication of industrial production tend to increase, these distortionary deviations are expected to be greater over time and across the GNP *per capita* spectrum (i.e. at higher levels of economic development).

3.2. EVIDENCE OF THE OVERGROWTH OF THE INDUSTRIAL SECTOR

To test the above hypotheses on the most important characteristics of production structures under central planning, I began with applications of the methodology formulated and applied by Chenery *et al.*[11] I selected 38 market and mixed economy countries at different stages of economic development, i.e. from the early stages of industrialisation to mature industrial (or post-industrial, as some would have it) economies, for a sample.[12] Next, I applied multiple regression analysis, resorting to the by now well-known Chenery-type regression equations in using their simplest semi-logarithmic form, that is:

$$X = a + b_1 \ln Y + b_2 (\ln Y)^2 + c_1 \ln N + c_2 (\ln N)^2$$

where: X = the share of industry[13] in GDP;
$\quad\quad Y$ = GNP *per capita*; and
$\quad\quad N$ = population in millions of inhabitants.

These regressions were subsequently run for the sample of 38 countries for the years 1965 and 1979. The choice of time points was determined by the availability of the (reasonably) comparable data on GNP *per capita* for market and mixed economies on the one hand and STEs on the other. Such data for the latter had been estimated for the mid-1960s by the Secretariat of the UN Economic Commission for Europe (ECE), with the assistance of the physical indicators-based methodology estimating the NMP and then converting it into GNP (for the methodology and the estimates, see UN ECE, *Economic survey of Europe*, 1969). At the same time 1979 was the last year when the World Bank published the data on GNP *per capita* for all CPEs, applying the same methodology devised by the ECE Secretariat (*World Development Report*, 1981).

Furthermore, the choice of dependent variable i.e. the share of industry (mining, manufacturing, construction and utilities) rather than that of manufacturing industry, as in Chenery's estimates, was also determined by availability. A choice of the latter would have to eliminate a majority of STEs for which no data on manufacturing industry's share in GDP could be obtained. This change, however, does not distort the shares in the 38-country sample to any significant extent. Construction and utilities shares vary little across countries at the same level of development. Consequently, their addition does not change the expected relationship between dependent and independent variables. The only sub-sector that *does* vary is mining, but it varies most strongly at the lowest development levels and/or in the smallest countries. Since both least developed countries and countries below two million inhabitants were excluded from the sample, the possible distorting impact of the inclusion of the mining sub-sector has been minimal.

The first dependent variable, GNP *per capita*, was to represent the impact of unifying variables upon structural change (here, each sector's share in GDP). The second dependent variable, population, was to capture the differences arising from the size of the respective national economies. It was possible to assume, then, that the residual differences would stem from the impact of the remaining differentiating variables, i.e. natural resources and institutional factors. In addition, with the extreme cases of the impact of natural resources excluded (that is, the main oil-exporting countries excluded from the sample), a substantial if not actually dominant part of the residual would be due to institutional factors.

The results of the regressions showed strong-to-moderate explanatory power of the above independent variables in explaining variations of the industry's share in GDP, but were highly significant in each case (see Winiecki, 1984d, 1986b). Simultaneously, interesting changes took place over time. The ability to explain the variations in industry's share decreased between 1965 and 1979. At the same time, the ability of the above independent variables to explain changes in services' share increased in the same period. It is worth noting that simultaneously, the degree of linearity of the relationship between the share of industry and the independent variables — represented by GNP *per capita* — decreased in the 1965–79 period, while the degree of linearity of the relationship of services' share and the same variables increased in the same period.

The relationships established by the regressions were subsequently used to predict the shares of industry in GDP in seven East European STEs: Bulgaria, Czechoslovakia, Hungary, the German Democratic Republic, Poland, Romania and the Soviet Union for both 1965 and 1979 on the basis of their GNP *per capita* and population data. The actual and predicted shares are presented in Table 3.1.

Of the four hypotheses that were formulated at the end of the preceding section, the test referred to above tentatively confirmed three of them (the distortionary character of industrial growth requires different methodology — see below). Thus, the overgrowth of the industrial sector in STEs was strikingly high, as shown by comparison with actual and predicted shares of industry. All STEs showed an extremely high share of industry in GDP, not found in any other country in the sample,[14] including countries within the same GNP *per capita* range.[15]

Next, deviations from the uniform pattern were, as hypothesised, in the same direction. Not only was industry's share in GDP *on the average* overgrown under central planning, but it was also

Table 3.1: Actual and expected shares of agriculture, industry and services in the GDP of STEs, 1965 and 1979 (%)

| | 1965[b] | | | | | | 1979 | | | | | |
| | Agriculture | | Industry | | Services | | Agriculture | | Industry | | Services | |
	A	E[c]	A	E[c]	A	E[c]	A	E[c]	A	E[c]	A	E[c]
Romania	22[d]	15	54[d]	38	25[d]	46	14	11	50	40	36	48
Bulgaria	26	14	47	37	28	49	19	9	63	38	18	52
Czechoslovakia	9	10	58	40	32	49	8	7	71	39	18	52
GDR	11	9	53	41	35	49	10	6	69	40	21	53
Hungary	16	12	52	39	32	48	15	9	59	39	26	51
Poland	18	11	49	41	32	47	16	8	64	41	20	56
USSR	18	5	49	40	33	57	16	3	62	40	22	56
Total[a]	17	11	52	39	31	49	14	8	63	40	23	53
Total (excl. USSR)[a]	17	12	52	39	31	48	14	8	63	39	23	52

Notes: a. Unweighted.
b. 1967.
c. Predicted from Chenery-type regressions in the semi-logarithmic form

$$X = a + b_1 \ln Y + b_2 (\ln Y)^2 + c_1 \ln N + c_2 (\ln N)^2$$

where Y = GNP *per capita* and N = population in millions.
d. At constant 1963 prices.

Sources: *World tables*, World Bank, Washington, D.C., 1980. The Second Edition (1980); Chenery and Syrquin (1975); UN ECE, *Economic survey of Europe*, 1969; and *World development report*, 1981, 1982, and 1983.

overgrown in each STE under consideration.[16] Finally, the differential between the uniform pattern of structural change in the world economy and deviations from that pattern displayed by all STEs increased over time. From 1965 (in fact, from 1967) to 1979 it increased on the average by 10 percentage points (from 13 to 23 per cent). (All averages are unweighted.)

It is at this point that certain misconceptions as to the pattern of structural change under central planning should be dispelled. It has sometimes been maintained in Eastern Europe that the rapid increase in the share of industry in GDP resulted from the so-called 'steep ascent' strategy of (forced) industrialisation. The gist of the 'steep ascent' strategy is, in a nutshell, the sharp increase in the share of investments in GDP (effected through forced savings) and a rapid and broad-based expansion of the whole industry, with strong preferences for intermediate and investment goods producing industries. Only the establishment of a minimal industrial complex able to produce all types of goods (consumption, intermediate and investment), according to this autarky-coloured reasoning, may pull the economy out of its backwardness and supply it with the investment goods necessary for rapid industrialisation.

In other words, STEs behaved in their inward-orientated, import substitution-based strategy as if they were large countries. Industrialisation in large countries, less dependent on foreign trade, displays certain characteristic features. The share of industry in large countries increases faster, i.e. at the lower levels of GNP *per capita*, and within it intermediate goods-producing industries requiring economies of scale are established at an earlier stage. Also established earlier (although somewhat later than intermediate industries) are investment goods-producing industries (on these characteristics, see the works of Kuznets and Chenery referred to in section 3.1). In contrast, smaller countries increase the share of industry in GDP more slowly, because they establish economies of scale-based industries, usually as a part of their (inter-industry) specialisation patterns at higher levels of GNP *per capita*.

Since STEs behaved as if they were large countries (although only the Soviet Union *is* a large country), the 'steep ascent' strategy undoubtedly contributed to the fast increase in industry's share in these countries *at the early stages of forced industrialisation*. The evidence from the world economy tells us, however, that over time, i.e. at the later stages of economic development, the differences between large and small countries tend to disappear in this respect: the shares of industry become very similar. Diagrammatically different

Figure 3.1: Changes in the share of industry in GDP in small and large countries across the GNP *per capita* spectrum (trend lines after Chenery and Syrquin, 1975)

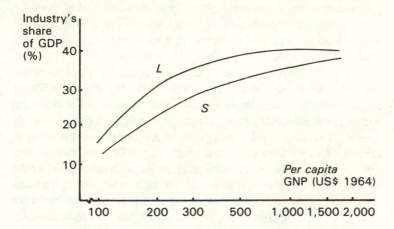

paths of large and small countries in the world economy are shown in Figure 3.1 (taken from Chenery and Syrquin, 1975).

Thus, in the case of STEs, the differences between the actual and predicted shares of industry, large in the 1950s, should have gradually disappeared throughout the 1960s and 1970s. However, the reality was opposite to the expectations formed on the basis of the 'steep ascent' strategy. The share of industry might have increased rapidly in the 1950s, but the evidence shows that it *continued to increase* in the 1960s and 1970s. Consequently, it is not the early industrialisation strategy, but first and foremost industrialisation under the influence of system-specific features of the Soviet system that results in increasing deviations from the uniform pattern of structural change in the world economy.

There are no doubts whatsoever that of the two differentiating variables left out of account in the regressions, i.e. institutional factors and resource endowment, it is the former that influences the pattern of deviations under central planning. The differences in the natural resources endowment of the Soviet Union on the one hand and, say, Bulgaria or Hungary on the other are so great that the similarity of deviations from the uniform pattern of structural change cannot be logically expected to stem from the impact of that variable. It is, then, institutional factors that are at the root of the problems under consideration.

There are two objections which it is possible to raise and which have to be answered before shifting attention to the evidence of the distortionary character of industrial growth. Firstly, it may be argued that neither the structural change nor development theories give an unequivocal answer to the question at what level of development industry's share ceases to grow. Accordingly, STEs in 1979 may still have been at the ascending part of the curve, reflecting changes in the share of industry across the GNP *per capita* spectrum. To dispel the doubts in this respect, the present author compared the change in industry's share between 1965 and 1979 for the Soviet-type economies in question with those of other countries within the same GNP *per capita* range (US$2,500–6,000 — 1979 prices). The latter group consisted of six countries: Yugoslavia, Greece, Israel, Ireland, Spain and Italy. Out of this group, industry's share declined a little in Greece and Israel, stayed at the same level in Spain and increased a little in Yugoslavia, Ireland and Italy. Altogether, fluctuations from -2 to 3 percentage points were registered, as compared with the increase from 5 to 16 percentage points in CPEs (averages, unweighted, were 1 and 10 percentage points for each group of countries respectively).[17]

Within this range of GNP *per capita* market and mixed economies pass through the final phase of industrialisation or, at an upper part of the range, reach the mature industrial economy stage. In consequence, industry's share on average ceases to grow. Any further transformations of industry take place within the slowly shrinking industry's share in GDP. The fact that STEs' share of industry continued to grow over the range in question and beyond (see the GDR case) indeed makes them different in this respect.

A further objection might be that the differences in industry's share in GDP between countries conforming to the uniform pattern of structural change and that of STEs simply does not exist. In fact, this objection was raised by claiming that the whole difference is the result of different relative prices in STEs, i.e. higher priced industrial goods and lower priced agricultural products and services (UN ECE, *Economic survey of Europe*, 1969). It is probably this knowledge of differences in relative prices that has been responsible for the surprising lack of interest in an issue of such significance for the performance of STEs.

To test the validity of this objection, the author performed yet another test, running regressions for the share of industry in employment as a dependent variable on the same independent variables for the same sample of 38 countries[18] for the same years, and using the same simplest Chenery-type equation form. The idea behind the test was that if the share of industry in GDP in STEs is higher due only to different relative prices in favour of industry, then the latter test would show the predicted shares of industry in employment not to be different from the actual ones.[19]

The results of the regressions showed strong and highly significant explanatory power of the independent variables in explaining variations in industry's share in employment. This is not surprising because the sectoral data for employment were free from price distortions, accompanying the sectoral data for GDP in the sample countries. The relationships established by the regressions were, again, used to predict the shares of industry in employment in CPEs for both 1965 and 1979 on the basis of GNP *per capita* and population. The actual and predicted shares are presented in Table 3.2. Comparing both, we find that all three hypotheses were reconfirmed.

Firstly, the overgrowth of the industrial sector in terms of employment was also substantial. The absolute differentials — in terms of percentage points — were smaller than in the case of the share in GDP. It meant that differences in relative prices *did* play a role, although the remaining differences were nonetheless large enough to set STEs apart from the rest.

Secondly, the deviations were increasingly uniform. If in 1965 there were still two STEs (Poland and Romania) where actual shares of industry were lower than predicted ones, then in 1979 all STEs showed deviations in the same direction — and much higher at that. Obviously, institutional factors exerted a powerfully (and increasingly) unifying influence upon structural change.

Thirdly, deviations from the uniform pattern became greater over time. On the average, for all seven STEs, deviations from the uniform shares of industry in employment in 1965 amounted to 4 percentage points. Between 1965 and 1979 the extent of deviations almost tripled to 11 points (all averages unweighted).

With all three hypotheses reconfirmed, we may regard the above evidence on the overgrowth of the industrial sector as conclusive. The difference between the uniform pattern of structural change in the world economy and that of STEs is illustrated diagrammatically in Figure 3.2. The curves reflecting changes in industry's share in GDP and employment in market and mixed economies are estimated from equations; while those for STEs are drawn on the basis of assumptions reflecting expectations of faster growth of industry's share at lower levels of economic development, i.e. during the forced industrialisation period, and slower growth of industry's share in the last few years preceding 1979. The latter assumption is

Table 3.2: Actual and expected shares of agriculture, industry and services in total employment of STEs, 1965 and 1979 (%)

	1965 Agriculture		1965 Industry		1965 Services		1979 Agriculture		1979 Industry		1979 Services	
	A	Eᵇ	A	Eᵇ	A	Eᵇ	A	Eᵇ	A	Eᵇ	A	Eᵇ
Romania	57	35	25	29	17	37	33	27	34	29	33	43
Bulgaria	46	34	32	29	22	37	38	22	38	31	24	46
Czechoslovakia	21	21	46	36	31	43	11	15	48	35	41	48
GDR	16	18	47	37	36	45	10	12	50	37	40	50
Hungary	31	30	38	31	31	38	16	21	52	32	32	47
Poland	44	27	30	32	26	41	31	20	39	33	30	46
USSR	32	24	35	33	33	41	15	20	54	31	41	54
Totalᵃ	35	27	36	32	28	40	22	20	44	33	34	48
Total (excl. USSR)ᵃ	36	27	36	32	27	40	23	19	43	34	33	47

Notes: a. Unweighted.
    b. See note c at Table 3.4.
Sources: See Table 3.4.

Figure 3.2: Changes in the share of industry in GDP and employment in market and Soviet-type economies across the GDP *per capita* spectrum (trend lines with respect to market economies; assumption-based lines with respect to Soviet-type economies)

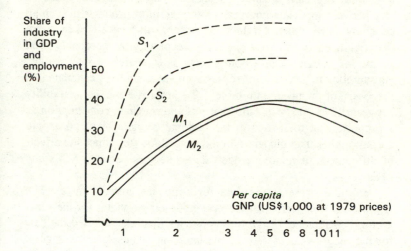

Key: M_1 and S_1 = share of industry in GDP of market (*M*) and Soviet-type (*S*) economies.

M_2 and S_2 = share of industry in employment.

based, in turn, upon expectations, that, with the labour reserves in agriculture largely exhausted (at least without fundamental changes in that sector) and with labour- and capital-hungry services, the possibilities of industry drawing upon the resources, especially labour, of the remaining sectors have been sharply reduced. This situation is expected to continue (see the next section), but in any case, the comparison of curves for STEs and MEs in Figure 3.2 shows a strikingly different — and lasting — pattern of structural change.

The distortionary character of industrial growth in the Soviet system, our fourth hypothesis, is a corollary of the above. It is obvious that, if a given economy or — as in this case — a group of economies with similar institutional (system- and policy-specific) features needs a greater share of industry in GDP to reach the same GNP *per capita* level, it or they must have suffered from an inefficient allocation of resources. It is all the more obvious since these countries cannot boast greater final output of industrial goods

87

commensurate with their overgrown industrial sector as a quid pro quo for reduced supply of services.

The inefficient allocation of resources in the twofold underspecialised and plainly wasteful economy of the Soviet type is, *inter alia*, expected to show through the disadvantageous relationship between inputs and outputs. Although most products in such an economy need more production factors, they need even more material inputs relative to a specialised economy. A reasonably good proxy for underspecialisation effects is a share of intermediate consumption in total uses of resources by an economy, calculated on the basis of input–output tables. To improve the comparability between STEs and MEs, the share of intermediate consumption as a proportion of total uses in the national economy was taken into account rather than the share in industry alone (to reduce the effects of differences in relative prices across sectors between STEs and MEs).

Table 3.3 presents the data for countries covered by the UN Economic Commission for Europe input–output tables for the years around 1965 and 1975. Not all countries that had supplied the data for the earlier year did so for the later one. Thus, the coverage of the 1975 data is less complete. Moreover, for both years there are only three STEs (Czechoslovakia, Hungary and Poland) in the group. Nonetheless, in spite of all the limitations in comparability and coverage, the data in Table 3.3 show a very distinct pattern, confirming our fourth hypothesis. To begin with, the share of intermediate consumption in the three STEs in question was very much higher than in comparable small industrialised MEs: 51.1 versus 38.8 per cent around 1975, and 49.6 versus 37.2 per cent around 1975 (unweighted averages). In fact, the share of intermediate consumption in the STEs was also much higher than in large MEs. It was even higher than in a very large country like the United States (but not higher, on the average, than in Japan).

Over time, the differences in intermediate consumption's share slightly increased in relative terms. The average (unweighted) share was higher in STEs than in small MEs by 31.7 per cent around 1965 and by 33.3 per cent around 1975. Interestingly, the relative differences in intermediate consumption's share were higher in comparative terms than differences between the actual and predicted share of industry in STEs (if the differences in employment's share, as undistorted data, are taken into account).

We may conclude that STEs, especially smaller ones (i.e. all except the Soviet Union), are strongly and increasingly affected by

Table 3.3: The share of intermediate demand in final uses of gross output of selected East European and Western countries according to input–output tables, 1965 and 1975 (%)

	Intermediate demand share	
	1965	1975
East European countries		
Czechoslovakia	50.8	51.6
Hungary	48.8	45.7
Poland	53.6	51.4
Small industrialised Western countries		
Austria	38.7	36.8
Belgium	40.2	—
Canada	36.7	—
Denmark	36.3	35.6
Finland	42.1	—
Netherlands	39.4	38.6
Norway	37.1	37.3
Sweden	40.1	37.7
Medium-sized industrialised Western countries[a]		
France	41.4	37.2
FRG	45.0	46.2
Italy	41.7	42.1
United Kingdom	40.8	43.1
Large industrialised Western countries[a]		
Japan	51.9	49.1
United States	45.2	—
Industrialising Western countries[a]		
Ireland	43.8	—
Portugal	37.1	37.0
Spain	46.0	45.0
Turkey	37.3	37.6

Sources: *Standardized input–output tables of ECE countries for years around 1965*, UN, New York, 1977; *Standardized input–output tables for years around 1975*, UN, New York, 1982.

the twofold underspecialisation and plain waste inherent in the system. It is these distortionary effects of system- and policy-specific features that find evidence in the inflated levels of intermediate consumption under central planning. All these distortions have far-reaching and varied adverse consequences for STEs' ability to implement structural change, to raise welfare of the population, and even to accelerate economic growth itself.

3.3. THE SELF-PERPETUATING CHARACTER AND CONSEQUENCES OF DISTORTIONARY INDUSTRIAL GROWTH

Before turning to the consequences of distortionary industrial growth in STEs, it is necessary to stress a characteristic feature that makes these (adverse) consequences more difficult to eradicate. Structural distortions are not only embedded in these economies, but tend to self-perpetuate themselves. The dynamics of this process are as follows. The overgrown manufacturing industries in STEs use, for the system- and policy-specific reasons explained above, much more material inputs per unit of output[20] than their counterparts in MEs. Excessive use, together with excessive inventories (another system-specific feature), create the overall climate of shortage. This in turn generates the pressure to expand extractive industries which are regarded by central planners and their political masters as a lagging sub-sector of industry. This is, however, a complete misreading of the reality. A comparison of extractive industries' shares in output and employment[21] in industry shows that the reverse is true. Extractive industries in STEs continually displayed a *very much* higher share in industrial output and employment than those industries in mature, developed MEs, and *much* higher than in middle developed MEs, i.e. countries that remain within the same GNP *per capita* range as STEs. The details for the 1963–80 period are shown in Table 3.4.

It should also be noted that over the period in question, the differences between STEs and other countries tended to *increase*, which points to the increasing distortions in this respect also. STEs tended to expand extractive industries in relative terms to a greater and greater extent, as shortages in the increasingly overgrown manufacturing industries have been giving the impression of lagging supplies of raw materials. Thus, the overgrowth of manufacturing industries forced the overgrowth of extractive industries.

All this fits neatly into the pattern of distortionary industrial growth and, looked at from that angle, extractive industries are not lagging but are in fact also overgrown. However, for decision-makers, shortages of raw materials are very real (Goldmann and Kouba, 1969) and, in consequence, they allocate a very large share of investments to extractive industries (as well as to basic processing industries, like steel-making, bulk chemicals, cement, etc.). Since international specialisation is a solution of last resort (see Part Three of this study), even more resources are devoted to extractive

Table 3.4: Extractive industries' share in industrial employment in some STEs and MEs, 1963–80

	Year		
	1963	1970	1980
STEs (unweighted average)	10.5	8.8	7.8
Bulgaria	10.5	10.6	8.0
Czechoslovakia	9.0	6.7	6.5
Hungary	11.1	8.7	7.8
Poland	13.1	11.2	10.2
Soviet Union	8.7	6.8	6.2
Developed MEs[d] (unweighted average)	3.9	2.6	2.6
			(2.2)[a]
Belgium	7.5	4.0	3.0
Finland	1.3	1.3	1.3
France	—	—	2.6
Germany, F.R.	6.7[b]	4.0	3.0
Italy	1.6	1.4	1.0
Norway	2.3	2.3	3.3
Sweden	1.9	1.5	1.5
United Kingdom	7.0	4.3	4.4
United States	2.9	2.3[e]	2.8[b]
Middle developed MEs (unweighted average)	6.0	5.0	4.2
Greece	4.6	4.6[c]	5.8
Ireland	5.0	4.8[c]	4.6[f]
Portugal	6.3	5.7	2.2
Spain	8.1	5.0	3.9[g]
STEs/DMEs ratio	2.69	3.38	3.00
STEs/DMEs ratio (excl. new oil producers)	—	—	3.54
STEs/MDMEs ratio	1.75	1.76	1.86

Notes: a. Excluding countries where now large-scale reserves of oil significantly increased employment (and production value) in extractive industries (Norway, United Kingdom). The exclusion of the United States due to the production from new oil fields in Alaska would increase the STEs/DMEs ratio to 3.71.
   b. Estimates.
   c. 1969.
   d. DMEs with zero or near zero extractive industries' share were excluded from the table.
   e. 1967.
   f. 1979.
   g. 1977.
Sources: UN yearbooks of industrial statistics, various years; own calculations.

industries, because less and less advantageous reserves have to be exploited.[22]

It is interesting to note that the impression of lagging resource supplies is so strong in STEs that even the best economists in Eastern Europe sometimes tend to be misled in this respect and characterise

91

these economies as 'resource-constrained' ones (see, for example, Kornai, 1979). Our considerations lead to a different conclusion. Theirs are not so much resource-constrained as waste-constrained economies, since they actually have at their disposal much larger amounts of material inputs per unit of output than other economies.

Having made this typological correction, let us return to the self-perpetuating character of structural distortions. Complaints about transportation bottlenecks are no less (or even more) frequent than those about the inadequate raw materials base. Again, however, this is in absolute terms an impression rather than the reality.

A recent study by a Hungarian specialist (Major, 1983) presents some evidence in this respect. According to this study there is a marked difference between transport intensity of developed and middle developed MEs on the one hand, and STEs on the other. Transport intensity in the latter measured by freight ton/kilometres per US$ is not only very much higher than in MEs, but does not display any tendency to decline at higher GNP *per capita* levels as it does in the former (see Figure 3.3).

In fact, the respective curves reflecting divergent patterns of transport intensity of market and Soviet-type economies across the GNP *per capita* spectrum in Figure 3.3 resemble those of industry's share of both in GDP and employment in Figure 3.2. The only difference is that the decline in transport intensity begins in MEs at the lower GNP *per capita* levels and is steeper than the decline in industry's share.

Significantly, as Major points out, the differences in both equipment (stock) and road and track networks between STEs and partially developed MEs within the same GNP *per capita* range are very small. Lagging supplies of transportation services contribute only a few percentage points to the overall imbalance between supply and demand: over 90 per cent of the imbalance stems from inflated demand; and demand is first and foremost inflated for the reasons explained above, i.e. the necessity to move all the raw materials and bulky basic intermediate manufactures produced by the overgrown industrial sector. Under central planning there exists, however, an additional contributing factor of inflated demand for transportation services — namely, the vertical control by a multi-level hierarchy. It prevents users to order material inputs from least-cost suppliers. Thus, there exist nearby suppliers who could ship bulky inputs at low transportation cost, but they are subordinated to different ministries and, accordingly, are ordered by their superiors to supply 'their' enterprises located in distant parts of a country,

Figure 3.3: Transport intensity in market and Soviet-type economies over time and across the GNP *per capita* spectrum (STEs except Romania and the Soviet Union; only West European market economies; trend lines from Major, 1983)

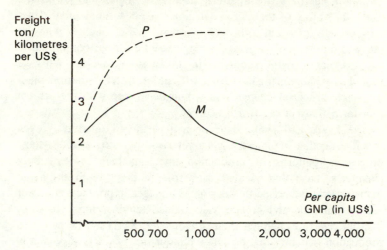

while needy nearby users have their own bulky inputs shipped from 'their' suppliers, i.e. ones subordinated to the same ministry, but again located away from their sites.[23] Such a pattern of supply not only increases demand for transportation services, but also raises production costs.[24]

This linked pattern of excess demands sets in motion economic growth that by its very nature distorts the structure of a national economy. Under the impact of the twofold underspecialisation and other contributing (and also system-specific) factors, the dynamics of growth in STEs are approximately as follows. An overgrown, wastefully resource-using manufacturing sub-sector creates excess demand for material inputs. This, in turn, generates demands for investments in the extractive sub-sector and in intermediate goods-producing industries of the manufacturing sub-sector itself. It ought to be noted that under inward-oriented development, it is only investments that are expected to alleviate shortages. Pressure for more investments in the above sub-sectors creates excess demand for machinery and equipment and for construction materials. This in turn increases demand for production of and, consequently, investments in, engineering industries. However, engineering industries also need material inputs (steel, energy) and this, again, increases demand for raw materials and intermediate goods.

93

Moreover, at each step, excess demand for transportation services is also generated. Such economic growth feeds upon itself in a self-perpetuating fashion.

Now if such a growth pattern displays a tendency to perpetuate itself, the ability of the STEs' decision-makers to implement structural change turns out to be very limited. The difficulties with the rate and direction of structural change will be further considered in the next chapter, with manufacturing taken as an example. What we should stress here is the *increased* difficulties for STEs in implementing such structural change that would be in step with the present transformations in the world economy.

The 1970s and 1980s have been a period of relative or even absolute decline of industries characterised by vertical multi-stage processing patterns of production (steel-making, cement, bulk chemicals, etc.) that yielded their role of the growth engine to industries characterised by horizontal linkages in production, lower use of materials and greater value added (engineering industries, instruments, fine chemicals, etc.). However, STEs self-perpetuate a production structure that prefers the industries of the past, which in turn only amplifies the scale of problems normally associated with structural change. Moreover, these countries are handicapped by other system-specific features, since the expansion of these new engines of growth is based upon innovation, flexibility, quality and reliability of after-sales servicing, i.e. features that are antithetical to central planning. Thus, a shift is to take place from industries more easily manageable under central planning to less easily manageable ones. Whether and to what extent it is at all possible is a matter of debate.

Furthermore, the service sector, understaffed and underinvested, cannot give industry the necessary support what becomes visible at higher levels of development. It is not only traditional infrastructure (transportation, communications, distribution), but even more sophisticated business services that — due to scarcity and inefficiency — adversely affect both growth *and* change in STEs. The underdevelopment of services, the concomitant of the overgrowth of industry, increasingly affects performance.

As economic growth of the above type distorts production structure, also by shifting resources away from consumer goods, the growth of the welfare of the population is very weakly related to the economic growth rate. Consumers suffer directly from the distorted structure, because the overgrown industry 'sucks' in a disproportionate share of resources, and because the lion's share of these is

94

allocated to production of investment and intermediate goods that are inputs to investment goods. They also suffer indirectly, because the underdevelopment of services reduces the quantity and quality not only of business, but also of personal services.

In his perceptive considerations, Kuznets (1971b) envisaged the prospective failure of STEs to attain the much higher level of aggregate economic performance already achieved by Western countries (although he did not concentrate on structural distortions as obstacles to that aim). He also implied that without substantial changes in the Soviet system, only modest increases in supply of consumer goods are to be expected. Our analysis of self-perpetuating distortionary industrial growth bears him out on both points. Performance failed to improve and supplies of consumer goods increased only at a modest rate. Structural distortions contributed in that way to what may be called *growth without much prosperity*, a very important characteristic of STEs. This type of growth is as tedious an endeavour as working the sweat mopping machine shown on a cartoon.

At the same time, Kuznets did not see any problem for the Soviet Union (and, presumably, other STEs) in pursuing 'more of the same' strategy. This has, however, been decreasingly possible in the last 10–15 years and seems to be even less possible within the similar time-span in the future. Economic growth that feeds upon itself, i.e. growth without increasing the welfare of the population, has been possible as long as industry has been able to draw the lion's share of resources at the expense of other sectors. However, there is no labour that can be drawn from agriculture any more (at least under the present collectivist reality); and the service sector in STEs is already drained of resources, including labour. The share of that sector in employment is already now on the average 14 percentage points lower than in other countries at STEs' GNP *per capita* range (see above, Table 3.2). In fact, services, underdeveloped as they are, had to increase their share in employment over the 1965–79 period just to keep going at the low level of performance. Even the increments in the labour force (also falling) will have to be shared in the future by industry and services.

Next, the availability of material inputs has increasingly become a problem even for the resource-rich Soviet Union (to say nothing of other STEs that are net raw materials and energy importers). The quantities required by the wasteful Soviet system to grow in a self-perpetuating fashion would require such immense investments that they are beyond the reach of the Soviet Union (again, to say nothing of smaller STEs). Thus, investments are the production factor whose lion's share can still be allocated to industry, especially heavy industry, but the falling economic growth rates in STEs cannot generate *absolute* volume of investments compatible with the input requirements of these waste-constrained economies. However, either labour, or — in consequence of the above — material inputs are simply not there for the continuation of the 'more of the same' strategy. In consequence, even another industry-oriented investment drive could not last long, since the much-neglected and often decaying infrastructure would become yet another drag on traditional economic growth feeding upon itself (these prospects are examined further in the concluding part of this study).

NOTES

1. On determinants of structural change see, first of all, Kuznets (1930, 1966, 1971) and Chenery (1960, 1977, 1982), as well as Chenery and Taylor (1968), and Chenery and Syrquin (1975). On institutional factors as a diversifying variable, see also Sakai (1956), Allen (1967), Ueno (1976–7) and others.

2. See, however, a perceptive comment by Solow in discussing Chenery's paper on transitional growth (Ohlin *et al.*, 1977).

3. It is upon the theoretical considerations and evidence in these earlier publications of the author that this chapter is based.

4. It is sometimes maintained that, measured by foreign trade-to-GDP ratio and allowing for the size of the economy and the development level, smaller STEs ceased to 'undertrade' (see, for example, Brzeski, 1979). However, given the system-specific features hampering export orientation in manufactures, STEs, even if they might not 'undertrade', certainly 'underspecialise'. Due to the permanent shortages and the resultant pressure for imports, these countries import more that they would like to and, consequently, are forced to export more as well. However, in the absence of a sufficient specialisation, STEs export increasingly scarce commodities, standardised semi-manufactures and low quality consumer goods sold at a heavy discount. The absence of 'undertrading' may thus go hand in hand with the presence of 'underspecialising' (Winiecki, 1985b).

5. The data for Poland are from Lipowski (1981), for Czechoslovakia from private sources and for Hungary from Wiles (1977).

6. The theoretical foundations of this feature of central planning have been outlined above in Chapter 1. As far as evidence is concerned, innumerable cases of supply failures can be found in the daily press in Eastern Europe, although aggregate estimates are rare. In one such rare case, a Soviet planning commission (Gosplan) official estimated that up to 40 per cent of allocating decisions of supply organisations are either cancelled or changed (*Planovoye Khozyaistvo*, no.1, 1970).

7. Estimates of this non-equivalence abound in the East European

literature: e.g. the Soviet Union Central Statistical Office checked 214 factories in 1969 and found that their employment was 21 per cent higher than planned. See *Planovoye Khozyaistvo*, no. 10, 1969.

8. These are known to have adversely affected cases of East–West industrial co-operation.

9. To give an idea of the order of magnitude of cost increases resultant from such unspecialised repairs, a Soviet example is illustrative: to manufacture a 1K62-type lathe in the early 1970s, 216 hours of work were needed, while major repair by its user needed, according to the prescribed norm, 540 hours (sic!), while in reality, it needed 800–900 hours (*Planovoye Khozyaistvo*, no. 2, 1972).

10. Contrary to often heard complaints in Eastern Europe that pressure groups distort investment structure (presumably ideally envisaged by the centre), the reality is different. Divergences between pressure groups and the centre mostly concern the *size* of investments (see Chapter 1, section 3), while those concerning *structure* of investments are very much smaller. Without scarcity prices that would signal where expansion is needed most and without realistic exchange rates that would draw international specialisation into consideration, the centre is going to prefer the same large-scale projects from heavy manufacturing and extractive industries that are the strongest pressure groups in STEs (after all, they became strongest due to the continuing support from the centre . . .).

11. See note 1 above.

12. The following countries with GNP *per capita* ranging from 380 to 11,930 (1979 US dollars) were included in the sample: Kenya, Ghana, Senegal, Egypt, Zambia, Thailand, the Philippines, Nicaragua, El Salvador, Nigeria, Peru, Colombia, Syria, Ivory Coast, Ecuador, Turkey, Malaysia, Republic of Korea, Mexico, Brazil, Portugal, Argentina, Yugoslavia, Venezuela, Greece, Spain, Italy, the United Kingdom, Finland, Austria, Japan, France, the Netherlands, the United States, Norway, Belgium, the Federal Republic of Germany, and Sweden. In selecting the sample that, for computational reasons, had to include less than 40 countries, main oil exporters and city-states were excluded in the first place, because they both register large deviations from the uniform pattern of structural change.

13. The author understands 'industry' to refer to mining, manufacturing, construction and utilities.

14. Only in 1965 was the share of industry in the Federal Republic of Germany near the average for all seven CPEs (53 versus 52 per cent). West Germany's share in 1979 was already more in line with the uniform pattern.

15. Although it is precisely at that range that the share of industry is the highest (see below).

16. Chenery (1982) has shown that China's share of industry in GDP was also strikingly high for the country's level of economic development.

17. Romania is an exception, but given the traditionally low reliability of Romanian data, it does not disprove our case in the least.

18. Thirty-seven countries in 1965 (except Nigeria).

19. The tenuous character of the second objection may be shown by noting that, given the increasing difference in the shares of industry in GDP between the uniform pattern and that of STEs, the above objection could

hold only under the additional assumption that the differences in relative prices had been increasing over time, an assumption contrary to the facts, at least for some STEs.

20. For example, with respect to energy or steel, STEs use 2–2.5 times more than MEs per US$ 1 of GDP (see Table 1.1. in Chapter 1).

21. Both output measures, i.e. gross value and value added, are distorted for reasons to be explained below in Chapter 4. For an early estimate of the extent of distortions, see comparisons of the official gross value and value-added data with estimates of inputs at standard cost as a rough substitute for value added for 1963 in United Nations (1977). The employment measure is free from price distortions but it may entail other types of distortions, i.e. radically different endowment in extractables, possibly reinforced by radically different extractive technologies due to the very different relative prices of capital. Neither of these distortions can be said to exist in the case of East European STEs, though, as witnessed by basic similarities of gross value and employment shares of the extractive industries in these countries.

22. For example, according to a Polish specialist, coal is produced in Poland at two to three times the production cost in other coal-exporting countries (Szpilewicz, 1985). It should also be kept in mind that Polish coal reserves are much better located (and thus less costly to extract) than, say, those of Czechoslovakia or Hungary.

23. This additional source of high transport intensity is reinforced by other systemic sources and consequences. The distorted structure of incentives may sometimes induce enterprises to consciously *raise* transportation costs to increase the value of gross output, an important indicator under central planning. In addition, a systemically generated overall climate of shortage and concomitant uncertainty makes it less risky for an enterprise to get material inputs from 'their' (i.e. captive) suppliers, regardless of transportation costs, than from lower-cost suppliers, subordinated to a different ministry.

24. For example, the average mileage for construction materials-producing enterprises in the Krasnoyarsk region were, in 1971, 886 km for sand, 883 for stone and 386 for gravel. As a result, the cost of a cubic metre of each ranged between 36 and 42 roubles, i.e. markedly more than a cubic metre of high-quality cement (*Planovoye Khozyaistvo*, no. 2, 1972).

4

Peculiarities of Intra-Industry Change

4.1. OUTLINING THE ISSUES

In the previous chapter I pointed to the distortionary industrial growth in STEs, generating deviations in the pattern of structural change from what may be called the uniform pattern. These deviations tend to grow over time, increasingly setting STEs apart from the rest of the world with respect to structural characteristics. In this chapter, *intra-sectoral* distortions in STEs are outlined and explained.[1] Industry, rather than any other sector, has been chosen for obvious reasons. Since distortions affecting the whole economy are generated within that sector, characteristics of intra-industry change are of greater importance than those elsewhere.

To formulate meaningful and verifiable hypotheses, we begin by contrasting the uniform pattern of change in the process of economic development within the manufacturing sub-sector (as well as variations in the process) with the pattern observed under Soviet-type industrialisation.[2]

Thus, the normal pattern of industrialisation and the resultant change in manufacturing structure would look like the following. At the low level of economic development, dominant (in terms of shares in manufacturing value added) would be industries doing primary processing of agricultural, forest and mineral commodities. It means food, leather and leather products, textiles, and to an extent also wood products and non-metallic mineral products.[3] Unsophisticated technology, low skills, and production unrelated to scale economies would all combine to add little value to that of processed commodities. At the middle levels of development, clothing, footwear, pulp and paper, petroleum and coal products, rubber, and metal products all become more important than at the lower level. Steel and (depending on natural resources) non-ferrous metals come later. Heavy manufacturing industries usually follow the light ones. At the same time early industries both expand horizontally and add more value, i.e. expand vertically (wood products to furniture, non-metallic mineral products to pottery and china and, later, to cement, and glass and glass products).

At the higher levels of development, chemical and engineering industries expand most rapidly. Within the latter, production of consumer durables precedes that of machinery and transport equipment. In terms of shares in manufacturing value added, engineering industries take the lead at that stage, surpassing food industries. If at all, chemicals surpass the share of food industries usually long after the industrialisation process is completed i.e. at the level of a mature industrial economy. Thus, further changes in the manufacturing structure are taking place under the conditions of a stabilised or, later, slowly decreasing share of manufacturing in GDP.

The pattern sketched above does not necessarily repeat itself in its entirety, but the sequence has been occurring so often as to be discernible through both empirical (see sources quoted above) and historical (see, for example, Maizels (1963) and Rostow (1960, 1978)) analysis. Whatever variations to that pattern have existed, they were mainly the results of the impact of size and resource endowment.

Large countries expanded scale economies-based industries earlier due to the existence of the sufficiently large domestic market which could absorb most of the output, even at lower levels of GNP *per capita*. That timing affects basic metals, chemicals and those engineering industries in which scale economies matter. On the other hand, the existence of ample natural resources results in delayed and less dynamic expansion of some labour-intensive light industries (whose products rarely become exportable), while the manufacturing structure evolves partly around the resources with which these countries are endowed.[4]

Now the Soviet-type industrialisation pattern had been strikingly different. The so-called 'steep ascent' industrialisation strategy envisaged the large-scale shift of resources (entailing not only the shift of incremental resources but the shift of the already-existing ones)[5] towards investment in industry. Special preference was given to investments in heavy industries producing intermediate and investment goods. They were regarded, according to the official dogma, as the necessary ingredients of the basic industrial complex that every socialist country (whether large or small) had to establish *on its own* to be able to industrialise successfully. Such a strategy resulted in a very rapid transformation of the industrial (especially the manufacturing) structure in STEs which already, by the end of the 1950s, resembled — in terms of shares of heavy industries — that of MEs with markedly higher levels of GNP *per capita*. This 'modern' outlook has had lasting consequences, since the rapid expansion of heavy industries has been achieved at a very high cost. The traditional development costs due to the (varying) lack of industrial competence[6] were compounded by those stemming from system-specific features. The extreme version of import substitution, bordering at the time on autarky, increased the costs of establishing plants at below optimum scale in smaller STEs. It also increased the degree of technological obsolescence, already present in a too extensive industrialisation and the accompanying inability to supply an up-to-date technology for a too numerous number of plants. Not only underspecialisation of the above type but also the do-it-yourself bias (on both, see the previous chapter) contributed to the situation by further decreasing the scale of production and increasing the demand for labour, investments and material inputs. Moreover, the incentive structure added considerably to excessively high resource use, especially that of material inputs. In consequence, the 'modern' manufacturing structure in STEs has been turning out low-quality, technologically obsolete products (a point conceded at times even by dogmatic Marxists: see, for example, Marciniak, 1970).

High costs that resulted, *inter alia*, in the swelling of industry's share in GDP (see Chapter 3) did not disappear at more advanced levels of economic development: on the contrary, they became even higher over time. A comparison with less developed countries (LDCs) seems relevant at this point. Various studies of LDCs' industrialisation stressed the wastage of materials, particularly high in newly established, more sophisticated industries.[7] This excessively high resource use was mainly the effect of the lack of industrial competence. However, LDCs, especially those which are export-oriented, have the incentives to learn, because to stay competitive, they have to reduce input costs continuously. These incentives have been weaker in import substitution-oriented LDCs, whose protected markets allowed a lot of slack without the concomitant lower profits.

In the case of STEs, not only the above incentives to learn are almost non-existent, since they have been institutionally separated from the world market, but the structure of incentives strongly

Figure 4.1: Decreases in the use of material inputs per unit of output correlated with rising industrial competence. The latter rises with the GNP *per capita*, as shown by the downward sloping continuous line (near horizontal continuous lines exemplify the range of the use of materials at a given level of GNP *per capita*). The normal pattern does not apply to STEs, in which system- and policy-specific factors exert greater countervailing influence than the rising industrial competence. In consequence, the rise in the latter is not accompanied by decreases in the use of material inputs in spite of the increasing GNP *per capita* (broken line).

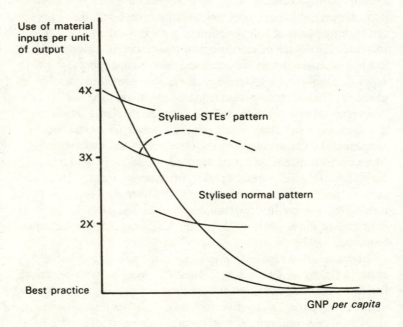

pushed producers in the opposite direction — that is, towards using *more* inputs per unit of output than necessary (see Chapter 1). The strength of the systemic sources of excessively high resource use becomes more clearly visible if we point out that even countries with relatively high industrial competence, i.e. Czechoslovakia and the GDR, conformed to the pattern and displayed as high a level of resource use as other, less developed STEs: two to three times higher than MEs in terms of resource use per US$ of GDP (see Table 1.1 in Chapter 1 with respect to energy and steel). The impact of systemic features has obviously been much stronger than the impact of increasing industrial competence, and excessively high resource use continues to plague STEs (the difference between the normal pattern and that of STEs and its impact upon resource intensity are shown in Figure 4.1). Since neither system-specific features nor the import substitution strategy has changed to any important extent, they have had a varied but generally adverse impact upon the size of the industrial sector and its internal structure. Since the former was analysed in the preceding chapter, we now turn to the latter.

The foregoing brief outline of the industrialisation process and its important characteristics allow us to draw the following hypotheses as to the expected intra-industry change over time and across the GNP *per capita* spectrum under central planning.

(1) The manufacturing structure in STEs would basically resemble that of MEs at higher levels of economic development, at least since the implementation of the 'steep ascent' strategy (i.e. since 1960, and for at least developed STEs — Bulgaria and Romania — since the mid-1960s at the latest). Such similarity would be expected from the rapid (even if only quantitative) expansion of heavy industries normally expanding at higher levels of economic development than that then achieved by STEs.

(2) The manufacturing structure of STEs would be more similar to large than to small MEs. Large MEs are able to establish scale economies-based industries at lower levels of economic development and, being generally less trade-dependent, have a less specialised manufacturing structure (see, in particular, the works of Chenery and Kuznets). Analogously, in STEs the 'steep ascent' strategy was substituted for the large scale and inward orientation for the lesser trade dependence, both with similar effects. In contrast, smaller MEs generally establish more specialised structure in response to their specific resource endowment, as well as to stimuli from the world market, and are expected to differ more from underspecialised smaller STEs.

(3) Regardless of resource endowment and size, the manufacturing structures of STEs would resemble each other more than those of large MEs. Since the impact of system- and policy- (here, extreme import substitution policy) specific features is expected to dominate, high structural similarity would be its logical outcome.

(4) The high structural similarity of STEs stipulated above would tend to increase over time. The dominant impact of system- and policy-specific features would continue to be felt throughout the development process of STEs, but the effect would be increasingly strong. The more sophisticated the technology, skills and other

requirements, the more costly is the expansion and, consequently, the more inflated is the share of a given industry.[8] With repeated attempts to expand more value-adding industries, deviations from the normal pattern of structural change would become larger across all STEs, increasingly setting them apart from the rest of the world and making them ever more similar to each other.

(5) Smaller, less resource-rich and more trade-dependent STEs bear heavier costs of underspecialisation than the Soviet Union. We would hypothesise, then, that at some point the smaller STEs, while increasingly similar to the Soviet Union with respect to structural characteristics, could become even more similar to each other, since they would be affected by structural distortions to a larger extent than the latter — a very large country.

(6) The manufacturing structure is expected to change relatively slowly in STEs once the early 'steep ascent' strategy was implemented. Two factors combine to result in such slowness: the resemblance to MEs at higher levels of development, and the need to expand *all* industries under the conditions of the import substitution strategy. Since all industries have to expand, their respective percentage shares in the manufacturing total change rather slowly, but most or all expand *outward*, i.e. increase their shares in GDP (at the expense of sectors other than industry).[9]

The above closes the list of hypotheses with respect to comparisons across the whole manufacturing structure. The following ones deal with expected distortions *on a case-by-case basis*, i.e. with particular industries or industry groups. Thus,

(7) It is expected that, typically for import substitution-oriented economies, smaller STEs are characterised by the aforementioned higher share of intermediate goods-producing industries.

(8) Since engineering industries are by far the most sophisticated ones, and the greater the sophistication, the more inflated is the share of a given industry in STEs, we expect the share of these industries to deviate particularly strongly from the uniform share at each level of GNP *per capita*.

(9) Finally, going beyond manufacturing, we hypothesise that although the manufacturing structure of STEs has appeared to be modern, the share of manufacturing in industry's total (whether in terms of value added or gross output value) is not. Excessively high resource use has resulted in forced expansion of extractive industries[10] and that in turn has been reducing the share of manufacturing at each level of GNP *per capita*.

Since different types of problems demand different analytical approaches, it seemed advisable to separate them one from another. In consequence, the next two sections present evidence with respect to structural change in manufacturing as a whole across countries and over time and, separately, with respect to particular industries or industry groups.

4.2 THE STEs' INDUSTRIAL STRUCTURE: FROM SIMILAR TO NEAR-IDENTICAL

An empirical investigation of structural change in manufacturing that would encompass both STEs and MEs encountered serious problems of data availability and comparability. Both imposed changes on the scope of the analysis and the analytical procedure. To begin with the latter problem, i.e. comparability, most of the data for MEs are available in value-added terms and it is usually value-added data that are the object of empirical investigations. However, the disregard of relative prices as reflections of relative scarcities under central planning, as well as more specific 'wedges' put between costs and prices in the form of turnover taxes levied upon the consumer goods and/or differentiated planned profit rates, higher for consumer goods and lower for intermediate products and investment goods,[11] caution against the usefulness of value added for the purpose of comparative analysis.

Although price distortions in STEs make any comparative analysis difficult, some comparisons give less distorted results than others. Certain analysts prefer gross output value to value added as an appropriate measure for comparative analysis (see, for example, United Nations (1977), Fink (1981) and Tuitz (1983)). Their argumentation is convincing. The main advantage of the former is that even if both may include the same distortions, they obviously make up a smaller part of gross than added value and, consequently, the scope for errors in calculating shares for comparative analysis is smaller.

Accepting the logic, a gross output value measure was used (wherever possible) in the analysis. A consequence of the choice of gross output value was, however, a decrease in the number of MEs that could be included in comparison with those that publish data on the said measure. Yet another limitation was that only three STEs — Czechoslovakia, Hungary, and Poland[12] — publish data according to the International Standard Industrial Classification (ISIC) (and at the desired level of aggravation).[13]

Finally, nine countries were included in the analysis: the three

105

above-mentioned STEs, and six MEs: Germany, the United States, Spain, Austria, Sweden, and the Netherlands. The structure of gross output value was calculated for 1963, 1970 and 1980 at the level of 15 manufacturing industries according to ISIC classification: food products (including beverages and tobacco), textiles, clothing, leather and footwear; wood and furniture, paper and paper products, printing and publishing, chemicals (excluding petroleum refineries and miscellaneous products of petroleum and coal), petroleum refineries (including miscellaneous products of petroleum and coal), non-metallic mineral products (including glass and glass products, and pottery, china and earthenware), primary metal and engineering industries (including metal products). Data were calculated from UN industrial statistical yearbooks. Earlier data than for 1963 were not available on a comparative basis, and those on STEs for the 1950s were even more prone to distortion than the later ones. Next, correlations of manufacturing structures were made for each year for each pair of countries in terms of percentage shares of each industry in the manufacturing total. Product-moment correlation coefficients are presented in Table 4.1.

Thus, our expectations with respect to the similarity of the manufacturing structure of STEs and MEs at the higher levels of economic development turned out to be true. The manufacturing structure in STEs has already been highly similar to that of MEs in 1963. The average correlation coefficient for all STE–ME pairs (except those of STEs with Spain, a country at a similar level of GNP *per capita*) was high, at 0.82 for that year. It increased to 0.83 in 1970 and declined to 0.74 in 1980. It may be said that the 'steep ascent' strategy strongly influenced the manufacturing structure in STEs that already displayed in 1963 the desired 'modern' outlook. The first hypothesis has therefore been confirmed.

It is interesting to note, however, that the degree of similarity has been somewhat higher at the beginning than at the end of the period under consideration (although it has still been high). It can be explained by the fact that the early modern structure entailed higher shares of highly resource-intensive industries like primary metals. It is this type of a structure that STEs have been able to achieve, given their system-specific features. However, radical changes in relative prices in the 1970–80 decade accelerated the shift of the manufacturing structure toward a significantly less resource-intensive one and the first effects of that shift have already been reflected in the 1980 structure of MEs. A distortionary industrial growth of STEs prevented the occurrence of the same shift in the latter group of

Table 4.1: Product-moment correlation coefficient matrices of manufacturing structure according to gross production shares for pairs of selected STEs and MEs at the 15 industry-level of aggregation (ISIC classification), 1963, 1970 and 1980

1963	Pol.	Cze.	Hun.	FRG	USA	Spa.	Aus.	Swe.
Pol.	—							
Cze.	0.87	—						
Hun.	0.94	0.85	—					
FRG[a]	0.87	0.86	0.84	—				
USA	0.87	0.79	0.84	0.93	—			
Spa.	0.92	0.69	0.87	0.71	0.72	—		
Aus.[b]	0.90	0.72	0.82	0.77	0.72	0.82	—	
Swe.	0.78	0.83	0.74	0.78	0.81	0.60	0.80	—

1970	Pol.	Cze.	Hun.	FRG	USA	Spa.	Aus.	Swe.	Net.
Pol.	—								
Cze.	0.89	—							
Hun.	0.92	0.89	—						
FRG	0.90	0.86	0.82	—					
USA	0.92	0.78	0.87	0.90	—				
Spa.	0.77	0.81	0.84	0.75	0.72	—			
Aus.	0.88	0.88	0.92	0.88	0.83	0.91	—		
Swe.	0.74	0.74	0.74	0.73	0.83	0.58	0.74	—	
Net.[c]	0.79	0.69	0.90	0.66	0.82	0.72	0.79	0.68	—

1980	Pol.	Cze.	Hun.	FRG	USA	Spa.	Aus.	Swe.	Net.
Pol.	—								
Cze.	0.89	—							
Hun.	0.89	0.81	—						
FRG	0.74	0.78	0.78	—					
USA[d]	0.78	0.82	0.80	0.95	—				
Spa.[e]	0.65	0.74	0.88	0.71	0.71	—			
Aus.[d]	0.83	0.78	0.89	0.76	0.73	0.82	—		
Swe.	0.53	0.68	0.61	0.73	0.83	0.54	0.59	—	
Net.[f]	0.68	0.54	0.84	0.65	0.74	0.63	0.74	0.53	—

Notes: a. 1965; b. 1964; c. 1969; d. 1979; e. 1977; f. 1978. Note that all coefficients are significant at least at the 0.05 level in a two-tailed test.
Sources: UN yearbook of industrial statistics, various years; UN, *Structure and change in European industry*, New York, 1977.

countries and the structural similarity between MEs and STEs decreased.

The second hypothesis has also been confirmed. STEs display visibly greater similarity of their manufacturing structure to larger than to smaller MEs. For each of the years under consideration, the average correlation coefficient for each pair of STE–larger ME countries was higher than for each pair of STE–smaller ME countries: 0.84 versus 0.81 for 1963, 0.86 versus 0.81 for 1970, and 0.79 versus 0.73 for 1980 respectively. Since all STEs considered here are in reality small countries, their under-specialisation (see above, section 4.1, and earlier, Chapter 3) resulted in the more diversified, less specialised manufacturing structure.

On the other hand smaller MEs, more sensitive to world market stimuli, have all the time been more specialised on an inter-industry basis (taken into account here) and, consequently, differed more from underspecialised STEs. Smaller MEs also reacted more rapidly to changes in relative prices in 1970s and the difference between them and STEs increased. Average correlation coefficients fell by a little more in the case of STE–smaller ME pairs than in the case of STE–larger ME pairs: from 0.81 to 0.73, and from 0.86 to 0.79 respectively.

The third hypothesis has been confirmed as far as was possible (since only three out of seven STEs were compared among themselves). Although STEs have displayed greater similarity to larger than to smaller MEs, they displayed even greater similarity to each other. Average correlation coefficients for each pair of the three STEs were the highest: 0.89, 0.90 and 0.86 for 1963, 1970 and 1980 respectively. Thus, system- and policy-specific features not only made STEs similar to ME countries at higher levels of economic development, but made them even more similar to each other. Institutional factors seemingly dominate all other factors, as far as the impact upon the manufacturing structure is concerned. Further confirmation was, however, necessary, covering all seven rather than the three STEs.

The similarity of the STEs' manufacturing structure stayed on more or less the same high level, according to Table 4.1, first increasing and then decreasing slightly. Thus, it failed to confirm the fourth hypothesis on increasing similarity, again to the extent possible given that only three STEs were compared. Further tests are clearly needed in this case as well.

No other hypothesis can be verified with the correlation co-efficients presented in Table 4.1. Thus, we move to the next stage of the analysis, i.e. comparisons among STEs alone. Since barely three of them could be included in STE–ME comparisons, and the Soviet Union, the sole large country, was not among the three, there was an obvious need to extend the coverage. The problem lay with the comparability of available data. It was decided to compare the structure of gross output value of industry according to a COMECON classification that does not differentiate between mining and manufacturing, and electricity, gas and water, since it was the only one presented in comparable format (in COMECON yearbooks).

Industry (excluding construction) is divided according to that classification into 15 industrial branches: electricity generation; fuels (extraction and processing); iron and steel (extraction and manufacture); non-ferrous metals (extraction and manufacture); engineering (including metal products); chemicals (including rubber, but excluding oil refining, which is included into fuels); non-metallic mineral products (excluding glass and glass products, and pottery, china and earthenware); wood and furniture; paper and paper products; glass and pottery; textiles; clothing; leather, leather products and footwear; printing; and food (including beverages and tobacco).

The results of correlation analysis applied to the above industrial structure, even if not directly comparable with those presented in Table 4.1, possess nonetheless some important advantages. If the intra-STE analysis shows evidence of high structural similarity, which is only to be expected, given the identical system- and policy-specific features, then conclusions drawn on the basis of comparisons of three smaller STEs would be applicable to *all* smaller STEs (or, in some cases, to all STEs, including the Soviet Union). Beside these indirect advantages, there are also some direct ones, since there is no other possibility of comparing smaller STEs with the Soviet Union.

Correlations of the industrial structure of seven STEs were made at the above level of aggregation for each pair for percentage shares in gross output value for the years 1960, 1970, and 1980 — that is, for the same years as the correlations for STE–ME comparisons (except that 1960 is substituted for 1963). The exception was correlations for each pair between six smaller STEs and the Soviet Union, since the data for both primary metal industries and printing for the latter were not available. In consequence, they were made for shares of twelve industries only. All product-moment correlation coefficients are presented in Table 4.2.

Table 4.2: Product-moment correlation coefficient matrices of industrial structures according to gross production shares for pairs of STEs at the 15 industry-level of aggregation (COMECON classification)[a], 1960, 1970 and 1980

1960	Bul.	Cze.	Hun.	GDR	Pol.	Rom.	USSR
Bul.	—						
Cze.	0.72	—					
Hun.	0.68	0.96	—				
GDR	0.80	0.96	0.95	—			
Pol.	0.90	0.89	0.88	0.91	—		
Rom.	0.75	0.97	0.96	0.96	0.88	—	
USSR[b]	0.91	0.90	0.90	0.93	0.94	0.93	—

1970	Bul.	Cze.	Hun.	GDR	Pol.	Rom.	USSR
Bul.	—						
Cze.	0.83	—					
Hun.	0.84	0.99	—				
GDR	0.88	0.97	0.99	—			
Pol.	0.91	0.98	0.98	0.98	—		
Rom.	0.90	0.97	0.97	0.97	0.98	—	
USSR[b]	0.97	0.93	0.93	0.94	0.98	0.96	—

1980	Bul.	Cze.	Hun.	GDR	Pol.	Rom.	USSR
Bul.	—						
Cze.	0.94	—					
Hun.	0.94	0.98	—				
GDR	0.96	0.99	0.99	—			
Pol.	0.96	0.99	0.99	0.99	—		
Rom.	0.94	0.98	0.95	0.98	0.99	—	
USSR[b]	0.99	0.96	0.94	0.97	0.97	0.95	—

Notes: a. Industry includes mining and utilities (electricity and steam generation).
 b. At the 12 industry level of aggregation (excluding iron and steel mining and metal making; non-ferrous metals mining and metal making; and printing).
Note that all coefficients are significant at least at the 0.05 level in a two-tailed test.
Sources: *CMEA yearbook*, various years.

The results are extremely supportive of the hypotheses presented in section 4.1. To begin with, our expectations with respect to high similarity of the three STEs analysed earlier with the remaining STEs turned out to be true. Average correlation coefficients for industrial structures of Czechoslovakia, Hungary and Poland with other STEs were very high: 0.88, 0.94 and 0.97 for 1960, 1970 and 1980 respectively. As a result, generalisations made on the basis of the above three STEs can be safely extended to cover all smaller or all STEs. Thus, all STEs resemble MEs at a higher level of economic development and all are more similar to large than to small MEs. However, this cannot be regarded as a deviation from the uniform pattern in the case of the Soviet Union, which not only pursued an import substitution-oriented policy of a large country, but *is* a large country as well.

The third hypothesis concerning the highest structural similarity among STEs themselves (higher than with large MEs and still higher than with small MEs) has been reconfirmed.[14] The degree of similarity has, in fact, been so high that we can almost talk about the *identical* industrial structure among STEs at the end of the period, since average correlation coefficients for each pair of six smaller STEs increased from 0.88 in 1960 to 0.94 in 1970, and 0.97 in 1980. At the same time average correlation coefficients for the Soviet Union with smaller STEs displayed the same pattern of very high and rising similarity (from 0.92 to 0.95 to 0.96 respectively).

The above results also confirm the fourth hypothesis regarding the increasing similarity of the STEs' industrial structure. As we have already pointed out, the industrial structure is not only increasingly similar, but tends to be identical in all STEs over time. Whatever differences still existed in 1980, they were the residuals of the much larger differences that the East European countries displayed before adopting the system of central planning.[15] It is possible, of course, that at a lower level of aggregation we could find only evidence of high and increasing similarity — not of the *identical* industrial structure — but the trend is unmistakable.

It is evident that system- and policy-specific features are at the root of that phenomenon which sharply sets apart STEs from other countries. Out of the three variables that diversify industrial or, more narrowly, manufacturing structure, neither natural resource endowment nor size seems to play any role in shaping the STEs' industrial structure. The most striking evidence is the very high and increasing similarity of the structure of the resource-rich Soviet Union and resource-poor Bulgaria (correlation coefficients of 0.91, 0.97 and 0.99 for 1960, 1970 and 1980 respectively), and between the very large former country and comparatively small Hungary (correlation coefficients of 0.90, 0.93 and 0.94 for the respective years).

It could conceivably be maintained that the increasing similarity (in fact, the tendency toward the identical structure) is an outcome of differentiated economic growth rates and resultant decreasing differences in the level of economic development among STEs. After all, the manufacturing structure changes with the economic development level, and smaller GNP *per capita* differences tend to narrow share differences in such countries. However, it is only large countries that would display very similar structural characteristics at the same development level. Small countries like the six STEs would be expected to specialise in response to their own resource endowment and the impact of the world market (see above, section 4.1). Spain, a country within the range of GNP *per capita* of STEs, is a good example. The average correlation coefficients of the manufacturing structure between that country and each STE under consideration (Czechoslovakia, Hungary and Poland) were not only lower than those of the latter three countries among themselves, but also falling over time (0.83 and 0.89, and 0.81 and 0.90, and 0.76 and 0.86, respectively, for 1963, 1970 and 1980).

Besides, STEs ought to display greater structural similarity to those MEs whose GNP *per capita* is nearer to their own. A look at Table 4.1 and the data on GNP *per capita*, for example in *World development report 1980*, shows that the similarity is greater with respect to countries whose GNP *per capita* is *farthest* from their own, i.e. the United States and the FRG: for it is the size factor, not the GNP *per capita* differences, that determines the degree of similarity with STEs.[16]

Careful analysis of the correlation coefficients in Table 4.2 reveals one almost indistinguishable deviation from the trend toward the identical industrial structure. Between 1970 and 1980, the similarity of the Hungarian industrial structure to that of Czechoslovakia, Poland and Romania declined by 0.01, 0.01 and 0.02 respectively in terms of changes in the value of the correlation coefficients (the degree of similarity was still abnormally high, however).

There are two explanations that can be offered with respect to the above observation. The first is that the 1968 reforms pushed Hungary (albeit very slowly!) along the road of greater specialisation of its industrial structure. The second possible explanation is that the removal of certain price distortions, especially since 1980, made the re-priced Hungarian industrial structure look slightly different from those of other STEs. In other words it is not quantity but price changes that altered somewhat the shares of various industries between 1970 and 1980. A combined impact of both, i.e.

of *some* specialisation and *some* re-pricing, cannot be excluded either.

The Hungarian case also explains why the comparative STE–ME analysis of manufacturing structure did not confirm the fourth hypothesis concerning increasing similarity over time. Hungary was one of the three STEs taken into account therein and it was the decrease of correlation coefficients for both pairs; Hungary–Czechoslovakia and Hungary–Poland between 1970 and 1980 (see Table 4.1), that resulted in the decrease of the average coefficient for the group (after the increase between 1960 and 1970).

Next, it does not seem possible to verify the fifth hypothesis. The near-identical industrial structure of *all* STEs reduces the possibility of differentiating the degree of similarity among smaller STEs, bearing heavier costs of underspecialisation and having more distorted structures as a result, from that between smaller STEs and the Soviet Union. With the average correlation coefficients at the 0.97 and 0.96 levels respectively in 1980[17] differences are all but indistinguishable. It is possible that the hypothesis can be verified at a lower level of aggregation of the industrial structure (with the data unavailable at present). However, it is just as much possible that the hypothesis is completely unverifiable, since the identical industrial structure does not mean that the hypothesis must be rejected. It may well mean that the much longer impact of distortionary industrial growth on the Soviet Union offsets, in its adverse effects, the stronger impact on smaller STEs exerted in a shorter time-span.

Finally, the sixth hypothesis on the slowness of change needed correlation analysis, not between pairs of countries but between pairs of data points for each country. The rate of change of the manufacturing or industrial structure is higher, the lower the correlation coefficient between two data points. Thus, shares in gross output value were firstly correlated for the nine countries from Table 4.1, and secondly, for seven STEs from Table 4.2 between the years 1963 (or 1960 for the latter) and 1970, and between 1970 and 1980. The correlation coefficients are shown in Tables 4.3 and 4.4 respectively.

Both sets of results confirm the sixth hypothesis. All three STEs compared with the MEs in Table 4.3 displayed high correlation coefficients, higher than those of small MEs in both periods under consideration and higher also than those of large MEs between 1970 and 1980.

The comparatively slower rate of structural change under central planning than in small MEs indicates that the latter are benefiting

Table 4.3: Product-moment correlation coefficients of manufacturing structures according to gross production shares of selected STEs; and MEs at the 15 industry level of aggregation (ISIC classification), 1963–70 and 1970–80

	1963–70	1970–80
Czechoslovakia	0.93	0.97
Hungary	0.97	0.93
Poland	0.93	0.95
FRG	0.94	0.93
United States	0.99	0.93
The Netherlands	—	0.86
Spain	0.91	0.95
Austria	0.81	0.93
Sweden	0.95	0.92

Note that all coefficients are significant at least at the 0.01 level in a two-tailed test.
Footnotes and Sources: see Table 4.1.

Table 4.4: Product-moment correlation coefficients of industrial structures according to gross production shares of STEs at the 15 industry level of aggregation (COMECON classification), 1960–70 and 1970–80

	1960–70	1970–80
Bulgaria	0.92	0.94
Czechoslovakia	0.97	0.99
Hungary	0.97	0.98
GDR	0.96	0.99
Poland	0.90	0.96
Romania	0.97	0.95
Soviet Union	0.97	0.98

Note that all coefficients are significant at least at the 0.01 level in a two-tailed test.
Footnotes and Sources: see Table 4.2.

from international specialisation, while inward-oriented STEs are not. Import substituting STEs expand production of all industries and, in consequence, structural change occurs mostly through differences in *increments* of inputs and outputs. This type of change is of necessity slow.[18] Results in both tables confirm both the relative (in comparison with MEs) and absolute (coefficients in the high nineties) slowness of structural change under central planning. Again, the relatively higher rate of structural change registered by Hungary in manufacturing (but, interestingly, not in industry total) between 1970 and 1980 indicates either or both sources mentioned above: real, i.e. quantity, change and/or price changes.

Beyond the hypothesis advanced in section 4.1, no less significant than the slowness of change is an indication that the change is *increasingly* slow under central planning. Thus, the average correlation coefficient for all three STEs in Table 4.3 is imperceptibly higher for 1963 to 1970 than for the period 1970 to 1980; but the difference is too small and the number of STEs too limited to regard this as evidence of anything substantive. Somewhat stronger evidence of increasing slowness is given in Table 4.4, in which six out of seven STEs displayed higher correlation coefficients i.e. a lower rate of change, for the later period (with average coefficients for seven STEs at 0.95 and 0.97 respectively).[19] Even stronger evidence is provided, however, by the already-mentioned slower structural change in STEs between 1970 and 1980 than in large MEs, since it means that large mature market economies with a diversified manufacturing structure also adapt better to changing patterns of demand and, particularly in the 1970s, to those of supply than smaller STEs.

4.3. CASE-BY-CASE DISTORTIONS IN THE INDUSTRIAL STRUCTURE

Comparisons across the whole industrial structure have obvious limitations where *specific* deviations from the uniform pattern of change have to be taken into consideration. With the individual industries or industry groups analysed below, there is a need to shift predominantly towards case-by-case statistical evidence. The tasks, however, also change, for since price distortions are more important in the latter type of analysis,[20] the comparability of STE data has to come under closer scrutiny. Thus, we must devote as much space to interpreting the data as to interpreting the results.

To begin with, a typical characteristic of import substitution-oriented economies, i.e. too large a share of intermediate goods-producing industries in the manufacturing total, is analysed below. With the rising numbers and sophistication of final manufactures at higher levels of economic development, the demand for semi-manufactures, parts and sub-assemblies increases very rapidly. In the inward-oriented economy, this demand has to be satisfied by domestic industries. Since they produce too many of them, with overly small production runs with what is often obsolete technology

Table 4.5: Shares of intermediate goods-producing industries[a] in manufacturing structures according to gross production shares in selected smaller STEs and MEs, 1963, 1970 and 1980

	1963	1970	1980
STEs (unweighted mean)	35.4	39.6	40.2
Czechoslovakia	35.7	42.1	41.9
Hungary	36.1	35.9	42.2
Poland	37.8	37.7	34.8
MEs (unweighted mean)	31.9	35.5	37.0
Austria	34.5	44.0	42.2
Denmark	26.0	27.7	28.4
The Netherlands	32.3	35.9	40.0
Sweden	33.1	34.2	37.3

Note: a. Iron and steel, non-ferrous metals, pulp and paper, petroleum refineries, miscellaneous products of petroleum and coal, chemicals, rubber, textiles (all intermediate industries according to the Chenery–Watanabe (1958) classification, except printing and publishing, given the different scope of this industry in the ISIC and COMECON classifications).

Sources: *UN yearbook of industrial statistics*, various years.

(see Chapter 3 section 3.1), as well as using too many factors and other inputs per unit of output, their share in the manufacturing total becomes overgrown in the process. Since STEs are extremely inward-oriented, they should — as formulated in the seventh hypothesis — display the same characteristics (but, let us add, to a larger extent).

Table 4.5 displays shares of the intermediate goods-producing industries in the gross output value of manufacturing totals of some small MEs and the three STEs with available statistics. The results confirm the seventh hypothesis regarding the larger share of intermediate goods-producing industries in the latter: the said share was on average markedly larger in STEs in each year under consideration (35.4 and 31.9 per cent, 39.6 and 35.5 per cent, and 40.2 and 37 per cent for 1963, 1970, and 1980 respectively).

At this point the problem of comparability comes to the fore, because these results, although confirming the hypothesis under consideration, grossly understate the real size of these industries. Price distortions under central planning underestimate the shares of intermediate goods-producing industries within the manufacturing total, while the overgrowth of the industrial sector in STEs makes the shares of these industries appear comparatively smaller in terms of manufacturing as compared with the shares in the national economy.

To begin with the former, price distortions in STEs have traditionally underestimated shares of heavy industries in the manufacturing or industrial total.[21] Lower material input prices, i.e. those of most intermediate products, were subsidised by the state through lower planned profit rates in those industries and through turnover taxes levied on consumer goods. The extent of that subsidisation varied but it was nonetheless significant.[22] The extent of these distortions is unknown, but an indirect method used in the painstakingly detailed study by the ECE Secretariat (United Nations, 1977) gives us an idea in this respect. The authors of the said study used the concept of *inputs at standard cost*, calculated by aggregating wages, capital depreciation and an imputed rated of return on fixed assets, uniform for each industrial branch at 8 per cent. Through this valuation they obtained something much more comparable with Western data on value added than the official value-added data of STEs. The constraint on comparability was, however, of a different kind: the data available for calculating inputs at standard costs were only according to the COMECON classification of industries (see above, the beginning of Section 4.2).

Nonetheless the present author decided to calculate respective shares of heavy and light industries in STEs according to inputs at standard cost, since all intermediate industries, except textiles, belong to the former industry group. The distortions in favour of heavy industries ought to be regarded as indirect evidence of the understated share of intermediate goods-producing industries. Table 4.6 shows the shares of heavy and light industries in STEs (except Romania) according to inputs at standard cost, official value added and gross output value at producer prices (used throughout most of this chapter). The differentials in percentage points between shares according to inputs at standard cost and those according to the two most often-used measures are also shown.

The shares in Table 4.6 are for 1963, i.e. the beginning of the period under consideration; and for that year, the realistically calculated shares of heavy industries exceeded officially presented ones by a very substantial margin: from 12 to 20.8 percentage points compared with official value-added data and from 5.4 to 19.7 percentage points according to official gross output value data.[23] Thus, in reality the share of intermediate goods-producing industries in industry's total *was much larger in all the STEs* under consideration, with the largest differentials (meaning distortions) in the Soviet Union, the GDR[24] and Bulgaria.

Table 4.6: The shares of heavy[a] and light[b] industries in the industrial structure of STEs[c] according to inputs at standard cost, value added and gross output value measures (with differentials between them in percentage points), 1963

1	Inputs at standard cost	Value added (official data)	Differentials (2) − (3)	Gross output value (official data)	Differentials (2) − (5)
	2	3	4	5	6
Bulgaria					
Heavy	54.3	37.4	16.9	38.4	15.9
Light	45.7	62.6	−16.9	61.6	−15.9
Czechoslovakia					
Heavy	68.8	55.1	13.7	63.4	5.4
Light	31.2	44.9	−13.7	36.6	−5.4
GDR					
Heavy	73.9	54.4	18.5	67.4	6.5
Light	26.1	44.6	−18.5	32.6	−6.5
Hungary					
Heavy	69.3	57.3	12.0	61.2	8.1
Light	30.7	42.7	−12.0	38.8	−8.1
Poland					
Heavy	70.7	58.3	12.4	58.4	12.3
Light	29.3	31.7	−12.4	31.6	−12.3
Soviet Union					
Heavy	70.4[d]	49.6	20.8	50.7	19.7
Light	29.6[d]	50.4	−20.8	49.3	−19.7

Notes: a. Electricity, fuels, ferrous and non-ferrous primary metals, engineering, chemicals, construction materials, pulp and paper.
b. Glass and pottery, wood and furniture, textiles, clothing, leather products and footwear, food.
c. Except Romania.
d. Shares of paper on the one hand and wood and wood processing on the other have been split into two according to the approximate ratio between these two industries in other STEs.
Source: United Nations (1977); own calculations.

It was not possible within the framework of this study to repeat the calculations made by the ECE Secretariat for 1970 and 1980 (and even if it were not, the data base would not be available for some countries and some indicators). However, there are strong presumptions that the real shares of intermediate and, more generally, heavy industries continued to be higher than the officially presented ones. Although various price reforms in STEs usually raised the prices of raw materials and intermediate inputs by more than those of final goods and, in consequence, narrowed in each case the differentials between real and official shares, these revisions were so infrequent that, in the meantime, old patterns of low profits and high subsidies re-established themselves. Throughout the region electricity and fuels tended to be underpriced even in the early 1980s, after the two oil shocks. The same may be said about primary metals (even if to a lesser extent than fuels).

An exception to this pattern of self-reproducing distortions is, again, Hungary, where, already in 1963, differentials between realistic and official shares were the smallest. Since then, price reforms in that country have contributed to the substantial reduction of price distortions. Indirect evidence in this respect can be found in Table 4.5. According to the data presented therein, the share of intermediate goods-producing industries in the manufacturing total increased sharply in Hungary between 1970 and 1980, from 35.9 to 42.2 per cent, while that of the other two STEs decreased. Such divergent developments could be explained by the rising resource intensity of the Hungarian economy and, conversely, the falling resource intensity of Polish and Czechoslovak ones. It is known, however, that Hungary generally displays the lowest resource intensity among the STEs (see, for example, Winiecki, 1984b) and made most of the progress in this respect in the more recent period. On the other hand, resource intensity did not change in Poland and Czechoslovakia, while price distortions tended to increase, especially in the former.

Thus, it is price rather than the real share developments that are at the root of such divergent share changes in Hungary, on the one hand, and in the two remaining STEs included in Table 4.5, on the other. In consequence, it may be said that the share of intermediate goods-producing industries and, more generally, heavy industries continue to be underestimated under central planning (with the possible exception of Hungary). Further, the second-order consequence is that the extent of deviation from the uniform pattern is significantly higher than that suggested by official data on industrial output (even those least distorted ones).

However, higher, upwardly revised, shares shown in Table 4.6 reveal only a part of the overgrowth of intermediate goods-producing and, more generally, heavy industries. As evidenced in the previous chapter, industry's share in GDP is itself grossly overgrown in comparison with MEs at the same (or, in fact, any other) level of economies development. Consequently, shares of both largely overlapping industry groups, i.e. intermediate and

119

heavy industries, would show even larger deviations from the normal pattern if they were calculated not as shares in the manufacturing or industrial total (whether in value added or in gross output value terms), but as shares in the GDP total. In conclusion, both revisions reconfirm — and much more strongly at that — the seventh hypothesis formulated earlier.

The eighth hypothesis concerns the oversized engineering industries under central planning, since it is not only intermediate goods-producing industries but also engineering industries that are expected to display a similar tendency. It is particularly strong in the latter because of many stages of processing and high numbers of parts and components necessary to make the final product and, subsequently, because of the correspondingly high costs of the do-it-yourself bias in engineering enterprises in STEs. Moreover, the production of new, more sophisticated products demands more and more fragmented — and therefore costly — internal efforts within these enterprises. In other words their production becomes increasingly suboptimal.

The test of the hypothesis of engineering industry overgrowth was more rigorous than the simple comparison of industry shares applied in the case of the intermediate goods-producing industries. It was made possible because of the less distorted STE data on engineering value added than those on value added in most other industries, including intermediate ones (that necessitated the use of gross output value as a measure). The dual nature of engineering output under central planning (investment goods with planned lower profit rates and consumer goods with planned higher profit rates plus turnover taxes) generates two-way deviations which to a large extent cancel each other out. This assessment is largely confirmed by the already-mentioned ECE study (United Nations, 1977), in which deviations between engineering shares according to inputs at standard cost and those according to value added differed little in 1963, except in the Soviet Union.

As a result, a larger sample of market and mixed economies could be selected to establish the normal pattern of change in the share of engineering industries at different levels of economic development and at different sizes of national economies via a simple Chenery-type regression equation of the following form:

$$x = a + b_1 \ln Y + b_2 (\ln Y)^2 + C_1 \ln N + C_2 (\ln N)^2$$

where: x = the dependent variable (in this case, the share of engineering industries in manufacturing value added in 1979);

Y = GNP *per capita* in US dollars (1979 prices); and

N = population in millions.

The *World development report* (1981) data for 1979 engineering[25] value added for 28 countries were used in the regression (which yielded a high and highly significant coefficient of determination) and the regression was later used to predict the expected shares of STE engineering industries in manufacturing value added. Next, expected shares were compared with actual ones. The results are shown in Table 4.7.

On average, small STEs showed significantly higher actual than predicted shares, thus confirming the hypothesis in question. Engineering industries' shares were larger than expected by some 8 per cent on the basis of STEs' GNP *per capita* and country size. The overgrowth was not found among smaller STEs in the case of Bulgaria (actual, 15 per cent and predicted, 18 per cent shares

Table 4.7: Shares of engineering industries (ISIC 382–4 industries) according to value added in STEs, 1979 (A — actual; E — expected from regression equation)

	Shares (%)	
	A	E
Bulgaria	15	18
Czechoslovakia	34	22
GDR	31	24
Hungary	29	19
Poland	31	22
Romania	31	18
Soviet Union	27	30
STEs (unweighted mean)	28	22
STEs, excluding the Soviet Union (unweighted mean)	28	20

Source: *World development report*, 1981.

respectively). This, however, could be the result of an error in the *World development report* data, in which engineering industries' share in value added in Bulgaria was shown to be about half that of other STEs. Neither gross output value data shown elsewhere (*CMEA yearbook*, 1981) nor other data (including those on inputs at standard cost that showed a 17.5 per cent share of engineering industries[26] already in 1963) support the data in question. Thus, in reality the average overgrowth of engineering industries in small STEs is *higher* than 8 percentage points.

The test did not show the overgrowth for the Soviet Union either (actual, 27 per cent and predicted, 30 per cent shares respectively). This outcome should be treated with caution, since the engineering value-added data for the Soviet Union were the only ones among STEs that deviated strongly from those on inputs at standard cost in the ECE study quoted above. If an almost 5 per cent underestimate continued to exist by 1979, it would yield a (moderate) overgrowth of 2 per cent. However, as other tests tend to show *increasing* distortions over time, we may hypothesise that the underestimate of value added in engineering industries has also increased in the Soviet Union since 1963.[28] Thus, the overgrowth could well be larger than 2 per cent. On the other hand, it would probably be smaller than in small STEs due to a much weaker influence of the import substitution-oriented strategy on a very large country.

The ninth and last hypothesis has, in fact, already been evidenced to an extent in the previous chapter. Table 3.4 in the previous chapter showed the abnormally high share of extractive industries in STEs (and, conversely, lower shares of manufacturing and utilities). It was — in terms of the share in industrial employment — already about 75 per cent higher in 1963 than in other countries at the same level of economic development. True to the general pattern of increasing distortions under central planning, the differential has been rising, albeit slowly, over time: from 75 per cent in 1963 to 86 per cent in 1980. Larger, but somewhat more erratic deviations have been observed with respect to the share of extractive industries in gross output value.[29]

It need not be added that the above deviations were even higher in comparison with mature MEs at higher levels of economic development.

Although the above evidence concerned only three STEs — Czechoslovakia, Hungary and Poland — the conclusions drawn from it can easily be extended to encompass all other STEs, given their near identical industrial structure. With their inward-oriented development, STEs in each case firstly turn to internal reserves in search of raw materials for their excessively input-using manufacturing industries. This orientation is reinforced by low export-earning capacity (see Part Three of this study). Forced expansion, regardless of cost, inflates the share of extractive industries, and conversely, deflates that in manufacturing.

A better indication of the too low share of STEs' manufacturing industries in industrial total[30] for their level of GNP *per capita* would be the one obtained by subtracting from it a share of not only extractive industries but also utilities. However, employment data on utilities are even less available than those on extractive industries, while gross output data are also misleading here due to underpriced electricity output under central planning. To be more exact, the outputs of all fuels and energy-related industries have been traditionally underpriced under central planing. Extremely high at the beginning of the period under consideration,[31] the degree of underpricing, although smaller, is still high in most STEs, except in Hungary, which went the furthest in reducing price distortions. In Hungary, however, the share of fuel and energy-related industries (coal mining, oil extraction and refining, electricity, steam and gas generation and distribution) in value added was 19.6 per cent in 1980, more than in all MEs whether at the same or higher level of economic development (except oil-rich Canada). At the same time the share in more energy-intensive Czechoslovakia and Poland was 13.3 and 11.4 per cent respectively, obviously due to downward distorted prices.[32] Using yet another measure, the share of energy and fuels in total costs of industrial production did not change in Bulgaria and Poland, while it increased very slightly in Czechoslovakia and the Soviet Union (according to official statistics).

Summing up, all the hypotheses that required the comparison of shares of industries or industry groups on a case-by-case basis have been confirmed in this section. It may be pointed out that it is heavy industries, whether as a whole or their partly overlapping subgroups (intermediate goods-producing industries, fuel and energy-related industries, engineering industries), that are substantially oversized. Consequently, heavy industries are responsible for the distortions in the intra-industry structure and its change over time under central planning. This conclusion has important bearings not only for the sources, but also for the effects of industrial growth at the intra-sectoral (as well as at the inter-sectoral) level.

4.4. CONSEQUENCES OF INTRA-INDUSTRY DISTORTIONS

It is the contradiction between the modern industrial structure of STEs in terms of its resemblance to that of MEs at higher economic development levels, and its substandard output (technologically obsolete, of low quality, and highly resource-intensive) that draws attention of both analysts and casual observers of the Soviet-type system. This is only an apparent contradiction, however. High (in actual fact *exceedingly* high) shares of technologically more sophisticated industries are inextricably linked with the above output characteristics.

It ought to be remembered that somewhat similar developments were registered in countries pursuing an import substitution-oriented strategy, whose more sophisticated industries, mainly intermediate and investment goods-producing ones, also increased their share in the industrial (or, more specifically, manufacturing) structure. The price they paid was in terms of technological obsolescence, since they could not afford all the modern technology needed to produce all the desired final goods, as well as the intermediate inputs required to produce them. Furthermore, they paid a price in terms of higher costs, since under import substitution they typically produced too many goods (both final and intermediate) from production runs that were too short, which in turn raised unit costs.

However, import substitution-oriented LDCs or MDCs (i.e. middle-developed MEs) have been enduring under the *single* disadvantage of import substitution, while STEs work under the double disadvantage of much more stringent import substitution and the very strong do-it-yourself bias, both reinforced by yet another system-specific feature, that of incentive structure. In consequence, the latter underspecialise to a substantially greater extent.

First, the do-it-yourself bias increases technological obsolescence. More intermediate inputs (and even parts and sub-assemblies for the installed equipment) produced at the user enterprise mean more products turned out in a technologically less sophisticated way, usually by underequipped labour. The above effect is reinforced by the lack of incentives to reduce costs through innovation, because it is the routine, i.e. the smooth execution of plan targets, which is at a premium at the enterprise level, while innovation is scrupulously avoided (see Chapter 1). Incidentally, that allows labour to take a lot of leisure on the job as well.

Secondly, central planning adds characteristic disadvantages of its own, unknown under traditional import substitution. Low-quality production does occur in LDCs, but it is mainly the outcome of low industrial competence, and its incidence declines with the rising level of economic development and the requisite competence. In STEs in which industrial competence is higher than in LDCs, quality is not commensurate with the level of industrial competence, because the incentive structure encourages enterprises to sacrifice quality in pursuit of quantity (see Chapter 1, section 1.4). Also system-specific in nature are various manipulations lowering product quality through the use of lower-than-required quality inputs in order to implement or exceed plan targets more easily (see Chapter 2).

Thirdly, enterprises producing too many goods, both final and intermediate, with production runs which are too short — an effect of both types of underspecialisation — produce at too high a cost in terms of labour and capital inputs[33] and material inputs per unit of output (see above, section 4.1). Excessively high material inputs are made even higher by the incentive structure that encourages pure waste of material inputs due to the dominant influence of gross (volume or value) indicators of performance set for enterprises by central planners.

All three output characteristics of STEs are linked with high shares of more technologically sophisticated industries, both intermediate and final goods-producing ones. All raise input usage and, indirectly, demand for inputs. The low quality of workmanship and materials directly increases demand for inputs through unsatisfied demand when purchased goods are discarded and new ones are being sought. The more technologically sophisticated industry is, the more it is forced to maximise inputs and, in consequence, the more inflated is its share in the manufacturing (and industrial total).

It is worth noting that our considerations in this chapter have been in terms of *intra-industry* but *inter-branch* structural change. Thus, intra-branch structural change, increasingly important at higher economic development levels, has not been considered. This omission looks, however, less important once the linkages of inter-branch structures of STEs with technological obsolescence, low quality and high material intensity of output are considered, because underspecialised STEs may shift output *structure* from one sub-branch or product group to another but — given the system-specific features — output *characteristics* would remain similar everywhere.

All in all, then, technological obsolescence, low quality and high material intensity are not an aberration but a concomitant to modern industrial structure achieved at too low a level of economic

development and — what is more — under the peculiar characteristics of central planning. This is a first and highly significant consequence of STEs' deviations from the normal pattern of intra-industry
change. Its significance stems from the fact that it indicates lasting
high costs of Soviet-type industrialisation. Moreover, since more
sophisticated industries display a stronger tendency to overgrown
shares, further structural change under central planning may lead
only to more overgrown shares — and higher costs.

More technologically sophisticated manufacturing industries in
STEs that both use excessively high quantities of material inputs per
unit of output and are larger than normal at a given economic
development level demand relatively higher supplies than do these
industries elsewhere. This higher demand is felt at each stage of
processing. As a result, shares of extractive industries and fuel and
energy-related ones are in fact also overgrown (although it does not
always show in the official statistics due to large price distortions).
Thus, high shares of these industries which resemble — for a change
— those of countries at the *lower* economic development levels than
the one already achieved by STEs are yet another consequence of
peculiar intra-industry change under central planning.

With extractive, energy, intermediate and engineering industries
having larger (more often than not, *much* larger) shares in the
industry total, it is light consumer industries at the expense of which
the expansion of heavy industries has been taking place. Relatively
shrunken consumer industries have been unable to maintain equilibrium at the consumer goods market; and since smaller STEs import
much less consumer goods than smaller MEs,[34] it is domestic
supplies that matter. Thus, not only did the linkage between structural
and output characteristics turn out to be a consequence of a peculiar
intra-industry change in STEs; so also did that between the structural
and disequilibrium characteristics of central planning.

A more general comment concerning both the analysed past and
the future should be made here. It was shown by Piotrowska (1982),
who repeated the Chenery (1960) analysis of patterns of intra-
manufacturing growth across the GNP *per capita* spectrum using
almost the same sample of countries, with the same methodology but
for 1975 data, that there is a different dynamics of producer (investment and intermediate) and consumer goods industries at different
levels of economic development. At low and middle levels of GNP
per capita (US$100–700 and US$700–3,000 (1975 prices) respectively), it is the intermediate and investment goods industries that
grow much faster than consumer goods industries, and their shares

126

in manufacturing value added increase rapidly (especially in the case of investment goods).

However, the pattern changes at higher levels of GNP *per capita* (US$ 3,000–7,000, 1975 prices). Consumer goods industries then grow as fast as investment goods ones, and faster than intermediate goods industries. As a result, between US$3,000 and 7,000 (1975 prices) GNP *per capita*, the share of consumer goods industries not only ceases to decline but even increases by 3 per cent.[35] The same happens to investment goods industries, while the share of the remaining group of industries falls by 6 per cent, i.e. by more than one-fifth (probably due to the lower material intensity of industrial growth at higher levels of economic development).

Now some STEs were in 1975 within the range of GNP *per capita* associated in the said study with higher levels of economic development (the GDR and Czechoslovakia), while most of the others (all except Romania and Bulgaria) approached the lower bound of the range.[36] However, in the five-year period preceding 1975, producer goods industries increased faster than consumer goods industries, thus maintaining the pattern of developing countries. In addition, by 1980, the Soviet Union, Hungary, Poland and Bulgaria entered the US$3,000–7,000 range. Again, however, in the five-year period preceding 1980, producer goods industries increased faster in the Soviet Union and Bulgaria, about as fast in Poland and more slowly only in Hungary. Moreover, producer goods industries continued to grow faster at still higher levels of GNP *per capita* in the GDR and Czechoslovakia (in fact, the differential between the two increased between 1976 and 1980 in favour of producer goods industries relative to 1971–75).[37]

The foregoing evidence supports the contention, formulated in the previous chapter, that the distortionary industrial growth of STEs is self-perpetuating, and without fundamental systemic changes these countries are locked into a pattern of growth that feeds upon itself and bears little relation to the welfare of the population. Moreover, the evidence carries with it a hint (or even more than a hint) of a *permanently developing country* status attached to STEs in the sense that their industrialisation process is never completed and they are not destined to become mature industrial economies under the Soviet system (in spite of the GNP *per capita* increases).

The question as to whether the status of the mature industrial economy is within reach for STEs may not be all that important, however. Even if it were possible, industrial maturity is a long way off, given the slowness of structural change under central planning

— and this slowness is becoming even more marked as time passes. In underspecialised economies that continue their inward orientation, there are no shrinking industries in absolute terms. They all grow at different rates (see Tuitz, 1983). Consequently, only the rate *differentials* influence structural change.

The evidence presented above in section 4.2 highlights the increasing slowness of structural change. This is not surprising, since the expansion of industries based on innovation, flexibility and quality is particularly difficult under the Soviet system and they demand exceedingly large quantities of inputs for that purpose. With smaller increments of inputs available, their shares in the industry total increase more slowly than before. At the same time it seems that the limits have already been reached, or are close to being reached, with respect to the *outward* expansion of all industries at the expense of other sectors. It seems all the more so, as most sophisticated industries need for their expansion an extensive supportive network of various (no less sophisticated) services. The linked patterns of intra-industry and inter-sectoral structural change under central planning tend to slow down the former to a snail's pace; and, as the latter seems to be slowing as well, we may talk about the approaching structural stagnation.

NOTES

1. This chapter is based to a large extent on a recent article by the author and his wife, Elisabeth Diane (Winiecki and Winiecki, 1987). Her permission to include it in this book is warmly acknowledged.

2. With respect to the former, determinants of structural change at the inter-sectoral level also have a dominant impact upon that at the intra-sectoral level (see in particular Chenery (1960, 1977), Chenery and Taylor (1968), Chenery and Syrquin (1975), and Kuznets (1966, 1971a)). Thus, at the latter level also, domestic consumer demand (and dependent investment and, partly, intermediate demand), technical change (and partly dependent intermediate demand), as well as foreign demand, are regarded as unifying variables. It is these variables that shape industrial and — at the sub-sectoral level — manufacturing structures according to the uniform pattern at each level of economic development.

On the other hand, the size of the national economy, the natural resource endowment and institutional, system- and policy-specific characteristics all have a diversifying impact upon the manufacturing structure. Specific diversifying variables create specific variations to the uniform pattern (see this chapter). The impact of the first two is more permanent, while that of system- and policy-specific characteristics may be more transitory (after all, policies, and even systems, do change from time to time, while the size or the natural resource endowment rarely does . . .).

3. See, however, Chenery and Taylor (1968), who classify, on an empirical basis, wood products and non-metallic mineral products industries to those expanding at the middle level of economic development. Non-metallic mineral products are found there primarily due to the level of aggregation problem. The fact of large shares of cement industries, glass products, and pottery and china expanding later versus that of basic building materials seems to be decisive in this respect. Aggregation problems do not seem to be so obviously at work with respect to wood products, however.

4. Another feature of the latter group of countries (which does not concern us here) is that their share of the manufacturing sub-sector in GDP is distinctly lower throughout most of the industrialisation process (see Chenery and Taylor, 1968).

5. Due to the net effects of falling real wages and consumption. In the extreme case, in the Soviet Union the level of food consumption *per capita* of 1913 was achieved after more than 40 years, i.e. in the late 1950s.

6. It ought to be remembered that Czechoslovakia and the German Democratic Republic were by 1950 already well advanced as far as the industrialisation process is concerned.

7. See, for example, World Bank studies on engineering industries in India (1974), Mexico (1977) or Korea (1978): respectively, Industrial Projects Department, *India, survey of the steel forging industry* (Washington, D.C., 1974; processed); Industrial Development of Finance Department, Latin America and Caribbean Region; *Mexico manufacturing sector: situation, prospects and policies, vol. II* (Washington, D.C., 1977; processed); and Industrial Development and Finance Department, *Korea: development of the machinery industries* (Washington, D.C., 1978; processed).

8. To give an idea of a range of these differentials, a comparison with the Soviet Union is made below. In the wood products industry, production costs were some 25–50 per cent higher (productivity some 30–35 per cent lower) at user enterprises non-specialised in wood production than at specialised enterprises of that industry (*Planovoye Khozyaistvo*, no. 10, 1973). At approximately the same time, in the instruments industry, these costs were between two and ten times higher (productivity between two and three times lower) than at specialised instruments-making enterprises (*Planovoye Khozyaistvo*, no. 11, 1974). Incidentally, these differences reflect only the impact of one type of underspecialisation, i.e. do-it-yourself bias. Thus, had we been interested in the absolute differences in resource use between STEs and MEs, we would have to take into account the fact that system-specific features make the production in STE specialised enterprises much more costly than that in respective ME enterprises (due to often outdated technology, lower quality equipment which raises costs of maintenance and repair, material incentives to use more inputs, etc.).

9. This is expected to take place in spite of high rates of production growth that have historically been associated with rapid change (see Paretti and Bloch (1956) for 1901–55 and *Economic survey of Europe* (United Nations, 1980) for the post-war period).

10. To give but one example, extraction of low-content iron ore in

Poland in the 1946–1980 period cost the economy US$1.4 billion (1983 prices more than the equivalent imports (in terms of Fe content) from the world market. Domestic costs exceeded world prices three or more times. See Szpilewicz (1984).

11. A point stressed in most if not all studies on Soviet-type planning, industrial policy, etc. See, for example, Davies (1979).

12. An additional problem was that 1963 and 1970 data for Poland were published which included highly distortionary turnover taxes while those for the preceding two STEs conformed in this particular respect to the ISIC requirements and were published net of turnover taxes.

13. The GDR publishes data for seven industries only.

14. Varga (1980) confirmed this rank ordering of similarities using the same type of analysis but for four countries only: Czechoslovakia, Poland, Austria and the FRG.

15. This observation was also made in the UN study dealing with industrial change in the 1950–70 period (United Nations, 1977).

16. Varga (1980) also pointed at the untenability of the GNP *per capita* differences as an explanation of the structural similarity of Poland, Czechoslovakia, Austria and FRG, but did not draw positive conclusions.

17. I also carried out a correlation analysis for six smaller STEs for twelve industrial branches, i.e. identical to that between six smaller STEs and the Soviet Union in Table 4.2 (results available from the author upon request).

18. These issues are discussed in Tuitz (1983).

19. The exception being Romania.

20. They are less important, especially in comparison with the industrial structure of STEs, whose types of distortions are obviously the same and they may differ by the degree of distortion alone.

21. For the early literature on the subject, see Little *et al.* (1970). The body of literature on this subject increased markedly later on.

22. To give but one example, wholesale prices of material inputs for manufacturing industries in the GDR covered only 45–75 per cent of their production costs until the 1964–6 wholesale price reform (*Die Wirtschaft*, no. 37, 1966).

23. Incidentally, somewhat smaller distortions of gross output value data confirm the choice of gross value as a relatively better indicator for comparative purposes.

24. With respect to value added in particular.

25. ISIC 382–4 industries, i.e. excluding metal products.

26. But this time including ISIC 381, i.e. metal products.

28. It is all the more probable, since the production of military hardware certainly weighs more heavily upon the output of heavy industries than in other STEs.

29. The respective differentials in comparison with other countries at the same level of GNP *per capita* for gross output value measure were 223 per cent for 1963 and 155 per cent for 1980.

30. In the industrial total, because the share in GDP has been much overgrown due to the inflated share of industry in GDP in all STEs.

31. The major part of the underestimated share of heavy industries in the industrial total under central planning resulted from the underpricing of

energy and fuels. According to the study it ranged from 6.8 per cent for the Soviet Union in 1963 to 11 per cent for Poland if shares according to the (distorted) value-added measure and more realistic measure of inputs at standard cost are compared (United Nations, 1977).

32. Even now, the coal price in Poland is three times lower than its value according to world market prices (see *Zycie Gospodarcze*, no. 2, 1986).

33. It is worth noting that the higher use of labour *and* capital per unit of output was found in the case of import substitution-oriented economies than in export-oriented ones at similar levels of GNP *per capita* (equated here with the levels of industrial competence). See, for example, the data for Mexico versus those for Singapore and Taiwan in Shen's (1984) estimates of x-inefficiency across countries at different levels of GNP *per capita*.

34. For example, the UN Economic Commission for Europe study, *Economic Bulletin for Europe* (1971), showed on the basis of input–output tables that smaller MEs imported almost twice as many final consumer goods and more than half as many intermediate inputs for domestically produced consumer goods in percentage terms relative to total final uses than the STEs under consideration (i.e. Bulgaria, Czechoslovakia, Hungary and Poland).

35. The same phenomenon was observed in a less methodologically rigorous way by Bobek (1975a, 1975b).

36. Data according to the methodology applied up to 1980 by the World Bank (see above, Chapter 3, section 3.2).

37. For detailed figures, see Chapter 2, Table 2.1).

Part Three

Soviet-type Economies and the World Market

5

Import Pressure
and Distorted Export Structure

5.1. UNDERSPECIALISATION, DISTORTED INCENTIVES AND PRESSURE FOR IMPORTS

In contrast with the problems of structural change under central planning, which received so little attention that the evidence of distortions generated by Soviet-type industrialisation had to be established from the very beginning, the problems of exchange with the world market have been analysed much more often. Since the surfacing of the indebtedness problem, they have become *the* focus of attention of both analysts and decision-makers in the East and West. Thus, the basic data are reasonably well known and, consequently, the present writer can concentrate to a greater extent on sources of permanent pressure for imports and underperformance in exports so characteristic for STEs.[1] He begins with the role of foreign trade under central planning. This role, declarations to the contrary notwithstanding, did not change much over time, with import substitution continuing to be, explicitly or implicitly, the guiding idea.

However, before I present the orthodox Soviet ideas on the role of foreign trade under central planning, one additional remark is necessary. This chapter is primarily concerned with trade with the Western MEs rather than with the total trade of STEs. This focusing on trade that at most reaches 30–40 per cent of the total has been made deliberately — and for two reasons. Firstly, all weaknesses of STEs are more clearly visible in exchange with the world market; and secondly, once deviations from the normal trading pattern in exchange with the West are explained, many aberrant trade features of intra-COMECON trade become understandable and can easily be explained within the same theoretical framework. These explanations are made at the end of the chapter.

The role of foreign trade in the early model of central planning — that is, one developed in the Soviet Union in the 1930s and replicated throughout Eastern Europe in the early 1950s — has been well described in the economic literature (see, for example, Brown (1968) and Holzman (1974)). Thus, these considerations are limited to the relevant aspects of the problem alone. In STE textbook terms, import and export plans are secondary to the national economic plan. Import plans reflect planned domestic demand for:

(1) unavailable raw materials and fuels;
(2) finished products not manufactured at home (mainly investment goods); and
(3) intermediate products unavailable domestically in demanded quantities.

Consequently, imports are mainly determined by compiling the so-called material balances at the central planner's level that give estimates of the differentials between planned domestic needs and planned domestic supplies. The same material balances also identify a considerable part of exportable surpluses, where planned domestic supplies exceed planned domestic needs. If imports cannot be reduced, it is the value of imports, necessary to achieve the planned economic growth rate, that determines the value of exports.

Import and export volumes and/or values are determined both for the medium term and annually. However, it is the latter which are obligatory for foreign trade enterprises. The reasons for the different importance attached in practice to each set of figures are system-specific. Given the state of permanent excess demand under central planning in general and investment cycles in particular (see Chapter 1), the further an STE finds itself from the first year of the medium-term plan, the more annually drawn plan figures differ from the original figures for a given year (i.e. annual figures in the medium-term plan).

These conditions strongly affect import and export plans, since excess demand for production factors and material inputs, generates, in turn, pressure for increased imports, mostly imports from MEs. Firstly, other STEs trade with each other on the basis of earlier trade agreements on mutual supplies, and secondly, face similar system-specific problems of permanent excess demand. Both severely limit their export flexibility at a short notice.[2] It should also be remembered that excess demand affects exports, for STE industry 'sucks in' exportable raw materials, fuels, and intermediate products.

Figure 5.1: Price elasticity of the demand for imports in import substitution-oriented STEs and export-oriented MEs

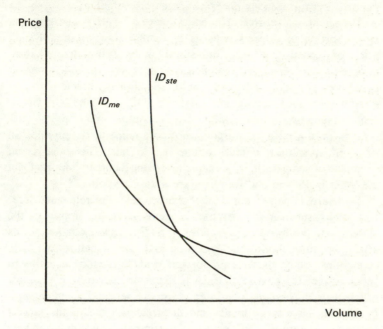

Excess import demand for investments goods, as well as for raw materials and intermediate products, not only puts pressure on the balance of payments, but also disrupts to a certain extent the flow of planned imports. Certain imports planned to alleviate shortages elsewhere or to improve production structure or (much more rarely) to increase the supply of consumer goods have to be postponed or abandoned altogether. Second-order adjustments by planning authorities have to be undertaken as a consequence.

Leaving until sections 5.2 and 5.3 of this chapter the difficulties concerning an increase in exports, it should be noted that a decrease in imports is also difficult in countries pursuing an import substitution-oriented strategy. These difficulties stem from these countries' specific import structure. Where almost all imports are necessary imports, reduction of import volume strongly affects output volume and, consequently, it is to be avoided if at all possible. This feature is reflected in Figure 5.1 by the shape of import demand curve ID_{ste}. The import demand curve of STEs is for the most part almost vertical. It means that after discontinuing a rather small part of

137

imports belonging to two categories (non-essential food products and industrial consumer goods), all remaining imports are necessary imports and further cuts decrease industrial output.

The situation is different in MEs where a large — and growing — proportion of imports consists of competitive imports. Rising prices of imported products result simply in the shift of demand from imports to lower-priced competitive products manufactured at home. Price elasticity of imports in MEs is high as reflected in a less steeply downward-sloping demand curve ID_{me} in Figure 5.1. Under central planning, however, there are no competitive imports, only *supplementary* ones. If imports do not supplement supplies in sufficient quantities, output volume has to fall. The most recent examples of steep declines in output after sharp cuts in imports from the West in Poland and Romania are a case in point.

There are, however, some other characteristics of relevance here. Just as pressure for imports mostly stems from the impact of the system- and policy-specific features of STEs, import characteristics affect, in turn, both the dynamics and the structure of these economies. Since there is no foreign trade efficiency calculus to speak of (see the next section), it is the strongest and not the most efficient producers who obtain *extra* import permits, when changes in the plan have to be made: and the *strongest* means the *largest* enterprises turning out priority investment and intermediate producer goods. Thus, changes in import structure reinforce changes in production structure in favour of producer goods over and above that built into national economic plans.

In Chapter 1, section 1.1, we stressed (following Kornai, 1979 and 1980) that enterprises turning out producer and consumer goods compete for the same inputs, and central planners' preferences for the former result in originally unplanned shifts of domestically produced inputs to the producer goods sector. What was stressed in the preceding paragraph highlighted the fact that the same process may be in existence with respect to imported inputs. Also since the more sophisticated the industry, the more distorted it is under central planning (see Part Two of this study), producer goods industries are by definition less efficient ones. Some comparative advantage-related consequences of the problem in question will be considered in section 5.3, below.

Next, unplanned changes in import structure affect export structure. With excess demand sucking in some exportable raw materials, fuels and intermediate products, foreign trade adjustments made by central planners instead entail increased exports of 'non-priority' consumer goods. We will discuss export structure in the following sections: at this juncture, we stress only the feedback effect upon the consumer goods market. Disequilibrium increases not only due to greater than planned demand for these goods, since higher wages were paid in the expanding producer goods sector, but also due to lower supply. Moreover, it should be kept in mind that the output of consumer goods is already lower due to input shifts stressed by Kornai (1979).

Permanent pressure for imports linked to macroeconomic and structural change-related distortions is not felt with the same strength over time, but changes both cyclically, i.e. over the length of the investment cycle, and trendwise, i.e. in the long run. The former feature relieves somewhat demand for imports due to shifts in the structure of imports over the cycle. With new investments approved for a new FYP, there is greater demand for investment goods in the first years of each FYP, while demand for raw materials and intermediate inputs tends to increase more evenly. At the expansionist phase, demand for imported inputs increases across the board, while at the restrictive one, either new capacities reveal new needs for imported inputs or some unfinished priority investment projects require more imports than estimated at the planning stage and various inputs have to be imported (mainly from MEs). At the same time, postponement or abandonment of unfinished projects and the freeze on new investment projects reduce imports of machinery and equipment. In consequence, more foreign exchange can be freed to import inputs without raising the overall import volume.

Besides, the later years of the FYP are altogether periods of greater restraint, and whatever deficits appeared in the expansionary phase of the investment cycle were usually made up in the restrictive one, not only through greater exports but also through lower imports from the West. As a result, fluctuations of both STEs' imports from and exports to industrialised MEs were distinctly larger than those of intra-Western trade. Cuts in imports of more than 10–20 per cent were not rare in both the stable 1960s and the turbulent 1970s; and nor were rare even larger import increases in the same period. As measured by the standard deviation (SD), these fluctuations were, for the 1960–80 period almost twice as high for both imports and exports (SD of 14.31 and 14.34) for Eastern imports from and exports to the West, respectively, than those of intra-Western trade (SD of 7.91).[3]

Incidentally, the supplementary character of many STE imports and cyclical shifts in import structure make it difficult to search for a pattern of revealed comparative advantage in Eastern trade with the West, as attempted, for example, by Weiss (1983) with respect to the FRG. Outside the machinery and equipment product group, which is largely a one way street, the trade pattern is often changing due to the fact that certain STE imports from the West in the earlier phase of the cycle appear as STE exports to the West towards the end of the FYP characterised at that stage by investment restraint (steel and steel products, certain bulk chemicals, cement, etc.).[4]

However, if intra-cycle shifts in import structure alleviate, somewhat, demand pressures for imports from the West, while general restraint holds down (also cyclically) the overall level of imports, the trend has been unmistakable. Over time, import pressures have been on the increase in all smaller import substitution-oriented STEs.[5] The paradox of import substitution generating increased pressures for imports has gained a wide and well-evidenced literature that started with Little *et al.* (1970), Balassa *et al.* (1971) and others. Import substitution,

> which was rationalised in many countries as a means of reducing dependence on the international economy, actually seems to increase it as import substitution activities are import-intensive and require imports of both intermediate and capital goods to sustain production and growth. (Krueger 1982)

The above effects upon developing countries summarised by Krueger have also been typical of smaller STEs, as outlined, for example by Köves (1978). Smaller economies are particularly strongly affected. They produce too many products and, in consequence, manufacture them in production runs that are too short, often use obsolete technologies because, producing too many products, they cannot afford to acquire (or develop on their own) more sophisticated technologies for all of them. It is already known, however, from our earlier considerations in the second part of the book that STEs are burdened not only with the aforementioned source of underspecialisation, but also with other, system-specific ones, stemming from the do-it-yourself bias of enterprises and the incentive structure encouraging the excessive use of resources. Thus, STEs' problems of high input intensity, technological obsolescence (and, additionally, low quality) are even more serious than those of import substitution-oriented LDCs. Moreover, given the higher level of development, with greater import pressure, STEs have of late been facing very severe adjustment problems. These problems are not only (or even not mainly) the heritage of the profligate 1970s when STEs discovered, some 20 years after LDCs, the lures and the costs of borrowed money-fueled expansion.

5.2. EXPORT UNDERPERFORMANCE OF STEs: OR HOW TO SPECIALISE WITHOUT KNOWING ONE'S OWN COMPARATIVE ADVANTAGES

If pressures for imports that increase with the level of economic development are typical for import substitution-oriented economies (although STEs also suffer from other distortions, generating similar pressures), then the weak ability to specialise in manufactured exports is a singular characteristic of STEs. Structural change in industry in STEs is not followed, with the usual lag, by changes in export structure with respect to their exports to the world market, i.e. to the market where normal competitive conditions prevail.[6] A look at Table 5.1, which presents shares of East European STEs[7] in Western MEs' imports of manufactures, suffices to indicate how disproportionately low is the share of each STE in question, and all of them taken together, compared with that of other countries at similar or even lower levels of economic development (i.e. countries of southern Europe and newly industrialising countries respectively).

We know, of course, from the earlier parts of this study, the real reasons of the underperformance. It is, then, the characteristics of the products which STEs turn out that make these products not very attractive on the world market. The contradiction between 'modern' industrial structure in terms of high shares of sophisticated industries and high cost, low quality and technologically obsolete products manufactured by this 'modern' industry is nowhere as clearly visible as in their world market-oriented exports.

Yet another problem is that manufactured exports which pass the test of the world market are not necessarily the least costly ones in terms of the domestic cost of a unit of foreign exchange earned. The problem of foreign trade efficiency, neglected from the start under central planning, remains unsolved to this day. To explain the difficulties (if not the outright impossibility) of STEs in achieving specialisation in manufactures, we return to both the role of foreign trade under the traditional model of central planning and to planning procedures in this area.

141

Table 5.1: Shares of seven STEs' exports in Western imports of manufactured goods, 1965–81

	1965	1970	1975	1977	1981
Bulgaria	0.10	0.09	0.07	0.08	0.06
Czechoslovakia	0.48	0.45	0.41	0.37	0.33
GDR	0.63	0.54	0.55	0.52	0.47
Hungary	0.20	0.20	0.24	0.26	0.23
Poland	0.31	0.29	0.41	0.45	0.31
Romania	0.07	0.18	0.28	0.28	0.26
Six smaller STEs	1.56	1.48	1.71	1.71	1.46
Soviet Union	0.82	0.56	0.60	0.70	0.51
All STEs	2.38	2.04	2.31	2.41	1.97
Memorandum items: Four 'middle' developed southern European countries[a]	0.84	1.10	1.85	1.90	2.10
Newly industrialising countries	2.74	2.99	4.41	5.44	6.95

Note: a. Spain, Portugal, Yugoslavia, and Greece.
Source: UN ECE, *Economic Bulletin for Europe*, vol. 35, 1983.

The role of a demander of goods that are either non-existent or in short supply and a supplier of those that are in excess of domestic demand, i.e. that of a seller of surpluses, tells us nothing about the costs to the national economy of foreign trade. What is more, it dooms to failure — if planning theory in STEs were to be taken seriously — any attempt at achieving specialisation in manufactures. In the theoretical terms of the early STE model, surpluses in manufactured products in a rapidly industrialising economy would appear in different years in different product groups since investment indivisibilities and scale economies would each time affect the supply–demand relationship differently. Exports of surpluses are thus antithetical to export specialisation.

However, in practice, the requirements of the world market change the situation somewhat in this respect. By accepting some of the offered surpluses and rejecting others, it influences the selection of STEs' manufactured exportables. Given the STEs' inadequate supplies of higher-quality manufactures, the world market also affects the respective shares of commodities and manufactures in STE exports in favour of the former. STEs find it easier to sell homogeneous goods competing mainly on the basis of prices.

These 'corrections' of the central-planning model imposed by the world market have important consequences both for specialisation and, consequently, for export structure. STEs are to an extent *forced* to specialise in certain products (that is, if they are interested in importing from the world market — and we know already from section 5.1 that they increasingly are so). Thus, Polish ham or Hungarian salami may be accepted, but not, say, their soft drinks, and repeated rejections of the latter may increase export specialisation. By doing so, the impact of the world market also creates a more stable export structure that would otherwise have been much more volatile due to the changing composition of export surpluses.

However, there are other features of an STE that make specialisation more difficult than elsewhere. Consider the planning procedure itself. Central planners, having calculated the value of imports, subsequently calculate the volume of exports, making some assumptions about expected world prices. If planned surpluses turn out to be too small or partly not exportable, then in order to pay for imports, certain products for which there exists domestic demand are shifted to exports. These are quite often consumer goods which are regarded as 'non-priority' goods by central planners (on this shift see, *inter alia*, for the early period, Brown (1968); and more recently, Köves (1978) and Płowiec (1981)).

Permanent excess demand, however, whether for intermediate products and investment goods or for consumer goods, creates a situation in which central planners are interested in exporting *as little as possible*. Thus, if prices of exportables are expected to rise in a planning period, or turn out to be higher *ex post* (i.e. during the planning period), fewer goods need to be exported and *vice versa*.

This particular feature, i.e. negative price elasticity of exports,[8] may be illustrated graphically in the form of a downward-sloping export supply curve, as shown in Figure 5.2. If central planners expect prices of exportables to increase in the planning period, then they devote a smaller volume of surpluses to exports. If, on the other hand, they expect prices to change in the opposite direction, then the volume of exportables will have to be increased. Changing expectations may be reflected in Figure 5.2 by a downward movement along the supply curve S_{ste}. In each case, the planned value of exports will be the same to cover necessary imports. Moreover, central planners' behaviour is identical both *ex ante* and *ex post*. Unexpected price changes occurring during the planning period result in the same type of decisions. The issue of production costs of exportables does not enter the picture at all.

This is contrary to the behaviour of exporters from market economies in which the export supply curve is upward-sloping, the

Figure 5.2: Supply of exportables under a traditional centralised planning model (ste) and under market economy conditions (me), with stable, decreasing and increasing production costs (notated 1, 2 and 3 respectively) (small country assumption)

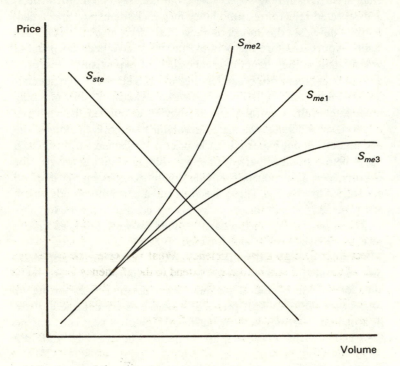

volume of exports being positively correlated with world price, i.e. it is positively elastic (under the small-country assumption). It is valid for exporters under the conditions of stable, increasing and decreasing production costs (as reflected in S_{me1}, S_{me2}, and S_{me3} supply curves respectively).

Negative price elasticity is the strongest argument for the thesis that under the early model of central planning, an export specialisation in manufactures was not possible, neither in theory nor, by and large, in practice. The question may be asked, however, whether the above situation can be described as trade-aversion; and if this is the case, whether trade aversion due to persistent excess demand on the domestic market has to lead to 'undertrading', i.e. a lower foreign trade/GDP ratio than the ratio that could be predicted from the population size and GNP *per capita* of a given STE. In my opinion this is not necessarily the case, even if, under the early model, central planners displayed an unwillingness to export that could be defined as export aversion, leading, hypothetically, to 'under-exporting', at the same time they displayed, due to systemic features, a very high propensity to import that forced them continuously to increase exports to achieve a trade balance.

In fact, if STEs 'undertraded' with the West in earlier years, it was probably more the result of extensive COCOM[9] embargoes on precisely these products that industrialising STEs were most interested in buying (raw materials, intermediate products and investment goods). In addition, even under these adverse conditions severe import controls at the central planner's level were often the last barrier to permanent pressure from below for more imports. With the change in the external environment on the one hand, and the growing needs of import substitution-oriented industrialisation on the other, the central planners had to give up their aversion to exports (Brown, 1968).

However, the disappearance of export aversion at the top did not change in the least the STEs' ability to specialise, and nor could it affect their foreign trade efficiency. What is worse, the corrective role of the world market did not extend to the efficiency issue. STEs may have been selling what they could sell on the world market (even if at sizeable discounts), but they still might have been incurring losses rather than gains from that trade.

Over time, the costs of such a role for foreign trade turned out to be painfully clear as more and more imports became necessary under the inward-oriented development strategy and had to be paid for with higher exports. These exports increasingly had to be *manufactured* exports, as STEs (except for the Soviet Union) one after another became net importers of raw materials. In consequence, the 1960s witnessed various attempts at increasing export efficiency (but not overall trade efficiency!). Inevitably, comparative advantage came into the picture.

Under the traditional STE foreign-trade model, gains from trade in terms of comparative advantage could be realised only by accident, since the well-known system-specific features did not allow central planners to learn which transactions were advantageous and which were not. In addition, where gains from the *existing allocation* of resources were realised only by accident, gains from the *reallocation* of resources would be beyond reach.

Thus, the 1960s began a long quest for export specialisation and efficiency, but this quest has been attempted under conditions of distorted domestic prices that were not playing their classical domestic scarcities-signalling role and under the unrealistic exchange rates that were not playing a world scarcities-signalling and domestic price-forming role. For these and other reasons, all East European STEs (perhaps with the exception of Hungary since 1980) find even now, after more than two decades, that they have not progressed very far since the beginning of the period. It is worth noting that the same situation exists with respect to modifications aimed at increasing overall efficiency of national economies, a question to which we will return somewhat later.

Some marginal modifications were nonetheless made. They introduced a degree of flexibility in the planning and implementation of both imports and exports (but especially of the latter) within the framework of their national economic plans. Mixed (quantity/value-type and value-type) export targets superseded, to a greater or smaller extent, pure quantity-type export targets of the early model with respect to manufactured exports. Furthermore, various performance incentives were introduced for producers and foreign trade enterprises, mainly tied to the implementation of export plans. However, these modifications could at best be described as attempts at partial optimisation.

A particular industrial ministry or a union of enterprises was given some latitude with respect to changes in product mix, but within a rather narrow range of products. The basis for the decision to change the exported product mix has become an *export efficiency calculus*. If some products showed better ratios than others, within the range of products exported by enterprises subordinated to a given administrative body, they were allocated for exports within the export quota determined for that body. The export efficiency calculus, based on specifically constructed coefficients, predominantly determined the amount of national currency units needed to earn one unit of foreign exchange. These attempts amounted to creating shadow exchange rates, with official exchange rates continuing to play a largely ornamental role.[10] Frequent revisions of these coefficients stemmed from the perceived needs to neutralise the effects of various distortions created by central planning.

This, however, has been next to impossible. A highly complicated set of subsidies, surtaxes, underpriced producers' goods, asset valuations and depreciation rates which are too low, underpriced imported inputs, etc., continuously distorts relative prices in STEs, while the permanent excess demand increases difficulties in differentiating between real and system-specific scarcities. Failed attempts to achieve specialisation in manufactures by STEs with respect to the world market could therefore easily be deduced from the history of revisions of various export efficiency coefficients across countries and over time.[11]

Given all the distortions, these coefficients have generally had one fatal flaw. The choices made on their basis could avoid gross distortions at the level of a narrow product group at best. Within that group, the similarity of equipment used, of raw material inputs, of semi-manufactures, parts and components, etc. gave some assurance that even if price distortions were serious, they were at least of a similar type. Thus, products could be ranked approximately in accordance with their export efficiency *within* that group. In the larger context, however, the choice of export specialisation has encountered difficulties of a different order of magnitude. A question whether products of a given broad (say, three-digit) ISIC product group should be exported or, on the contrary, should be imported and products of another broad product group should be exported instead, was largely left unanswered. Various procedures and methodologies of export specialisation choice, both with respect to the COMECON market and the world market, proposed in the East European literature, suffered from the similar flaw of being attempts at partial optimisation only in a sense outlined above (see, in particular, Guzek (1975); Guzek (1977); and Guzek and Winiecki (1980)).

On the other hand, attempts at optimisation at the overall foreign trade plan level, already undertaken in Poland in the 1960s with the assistance of econometric models, had some additional flaws, beside the distortions described above. The extent of optimisation was severely limited by the fact that the value of imports entered the model as an exogenous variable. Thus, the optimisation procedure aimed only at the choice of the least-cost exports (in terms of flawed export efficiency coefficients), given the value of imports. Thus, the choice still had to be made on the basis of distorted relative prices and largely unknown comparative advantages.

There have also been attempts to make STEs more export-oriented with respect to manufactures through the more or less arbitrary decisions as to which branches of industry ought to specialise in exports, but central planners discovered that export orientation of enterprises means something more than establishing large-capacity plants for export purposes (see, for example, the critique in Hrncir *et al.*, 1977). As a result, specialisation, decreed 'from above', so to say, did not bring satisfactory results. Leaving even aside the fundamental question (i.e. on what basis to decide whether to export products of one product group rather than those of another), the rationale of decisions has been further undermined by both the institutional features and the performance incentives of central planning.

Institutional features have been making it difficult to specialise in final products that require extensive production linkages between many enterprises usually subordinated to different unions of enterprises and industrial ministries. Given the prevalence of vertical, command-type linkages over horizontal, contractual ones, attempts to manufacture higher quality products (by world standards, of course) often turned out to be too complex to have been managed successfully. On the other hand, export incentives usually tended to reinforce the vertical fragmentation of industry under central planning, as suppliers of intermediate products, acting on the basis of their own micro-level rationality, were more interested in gaining bonuses for overfulfilling their own export plans than in supplying inputs to other enterprises' exports at no extra gain to themselves.

The introduction of export incentives ought not to be over-emphasised, though, since their impact has been marginal anyway. As has already been shown in the literature on the shift from import substitution to export orientation, it is not export incentives *per se*, but the balance between those inducing enterprises to sell at the domestic market and those inducing them to search for markets abroad, that matters.[12] On this point, moreover, there has never been any doubt with respect to central planning: the pull of the basic plan implementation-oriented (i.e. domestic economy-oriented) incentives has been overwhelming.

5.3 CAPITAL-INTENSIVE BIAS IN STEs' EXPORTS OR HOW TO MISREAD COMPARATIVE ADVANTAGE

In the preceding section I pointed out that under the traditional model of central planning, STEs were able to conform to comparative advantages in foreign trade only by accident, and even then they would not learn about it due to domestic distortions. However, yet another pattern of deviation from comparative advantage can be imagined where the export efficiency calculus yields answers that are often false, but in a systematic manner, i.e. consistently giving preference to exports of certain product groups. Under such circumstances the whole export structure may be biased towards these product groups.

It is easy to see how that could happen in STEs. Most of the price distortions common to STEs have a similar bias in the sense that they tend to make capital less costly than is actually the case. The two-tiered price system with investment goods priced lower than consumer goods, varying planned profit rates with lower rates in extracting and basic material-producing manufacturing industries, capital grants or low interest credits for investments, underpriced imported machinery, etc. — all these factors contribute towards making capital-intensive goods appear cheaper relative to labour-intensive ones. Distorted relative costs can be deduced, *inter alia*, from our earlier considerations on intra-industry structure, where it was shown that in 1963, heavy (meaning capital-intensive) industries had in reality much higher shares than those presented in official statistics when inputs at standard cost were calculated to obtain value added in the respective industries (see Chapter 4, section 4.3).

These underestimated costs did not disappear completely after the price realignments accompanying limited economic reforms in the 1960s (in Poland in the late 1950s), as may be seen from various statistics showing continuing profit rate differentials between heavy industries, such as, for example, iron and steel or electricity (to say nothing about mining) on the one hand, and light, consumer goods-producing industries on the other.[13] In addition, interest rates, usually too low in STEs and accompanied by credit rationing that traditionally prefers heavy industries, lower the real cost of investments and, consequently, result in a greater underestimation of capital costs in capital-intensive industries. It need hardly be added that capital grants only serve to reinforce the differential.

The above bias, which may lead to an increasing specialisation of STEs in capital-intensive goods, can be easily explained diagrammatically. In Figure 5.3 (adapted from Holzman, 1974), distorted information about costs indicates the ostensibly lower costs of international specialisation in capital-intensive goods. The distorted domestic price ratio is reflected by the slope of the curve P_d. A decision to increase production of capital-intensive goods will result in a change in the proportion of goods produced by a given STE. It is reflected in Figure 5.3 by a shift from the point A to the point D on the production possibility curve $P'P''$: an STE gains $A''D''$ capital-intensive goods in exchange for the loss of $D'A'$ of labour-intensive goods.

However, on the basis of undistorted information about domestic costs, a given economy ought to specialise in the production (and export) of labour-intensive goods. This choice is suggested by the

Figure 5.3: Costs of wrong specialisation choice under world prices (P_w) and under domestic prices (P_d). (Graphic presentation adapted from Holzman, 1974)

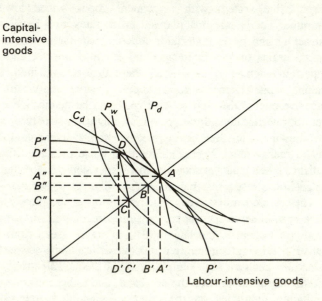

slope of the curve C_d, which reflects the real doemstic costs ratio of capital- and labour-intensive goods. The wrong choice of specialisation assures losses rather than gains from trade. A given economy will consume less after trade than before trade, regardless of whether it will trade at the domestic or world price ratio (reflected by the slope of the curve P_w). Losses will be smaller if trade is conducted at world prices rather than at domestic prices, given the smaller spread between the P_w and C_d curves than between the P_d and C_d curves.

The above diagrammatical analysis was run along the lines of the Heckscher–Ohlin factor proportions theory saying that, given the fact that products differ in factor requirements and countries differ in factor endowments, capital-abundant countries tend to specialise in and export capital-intensive goods to buy labour-intensive goods, while labour-abundant countries specialise in and export labour-intensive goods to import capital-intensive goods.[14] Thus, trade is based upon specialising in goods, demanding the more intensive use of a more abundant — and consequently cheaper — factor of production. One may expect that rapid industrialisation and the rise in GNP

150

per capita bring about changes in proportions of production factors. All East European STEs passed through such a period. The more abundant factor (labour) becomes scarcer and vice versa; the scarcer factor (capital) becomes more abundant. The said change is known in the Heckscher–Ohlin factor proportions theory as the factor reversal phenomenon. It has found its empirical confirmation, for example, with respect to Japan (Heller, 1976).

Usually, as the share of capital-intensive goods in industrial production increases, their share also increases, with a lag, in a given country's exports. There are, however, certain specific features of the process in the case of smaller STEs. These countries have increasingly become exporters of capital- and resource-intensive goods (characterised by the low degree of processing) to the West, i.e. to a more capital-abundant area. The process has taken place in spite of the fact that necessary inputs are largely imported (except for the Soviet Union). As comparative advantages do not stem from a domestic raw material base, around which capital-intensive production is usually being established, it is system-specific features that seem to be at work in the case of STEs.

It has long been suspected that STEs may have a biased export structure toward capital-intensive — and land-intensive — goods (Kindleberger, 1962). The few existing empirical studies did not, however, support theoretical considerations unambiguously in this respect. Thus, for example, Rosefielde (1973) found the USSR trade rational in Heckscher–Ohlin terms — that is, Soviet exports to LDCs were more capital-intensive and imports more labour-intensive, while exports to and imports from the West displayed opposite characteristics. On the other hand, a long-term trend towards greater overall capital intensity was found by the author in question, to the extent that by 1968, the Soviet Union was exporting to the West — the more capital-abundant area — more capital-intensive goods than it was importing from those countries.

Other studies, for example those on Polish foreign trade, yielded contradictory results. Studies following the established Leontief (1954) methodology and based on input-output tables (as, *inter alia*, the aforementioned Rosefielde (1973) study) did not in general find any distinctive capital-intensive bias in Polish exports to the world market (Finucane (1982) and Wyżnikiewicz (1982)). On the other hand, Balandynowicz *et al.* (1983), using a different methodology, came to the opposite conclusion. Analysing Polish trade in fuels, raw materials, and semi-manufactures, they found exports of these goods displaying higher capital requirements than imports measured in terms of import substitutes manufactured domestically.

This ambiguity has its historical underpinnings. At the beginning, STEs found themselves somewhere in between the mature industrialised Western MEs and little developed LDCs. Finding themselves in that intermediate position, they were almost automatically granted the appearance of Heckscher–Ohlin rationality. With such large differences in capital abundance (measured approximately by differences in GNP *per capita* between STEs and each group of countries respectively, they were almost bound to export more capital-intensive goods to less capital-abundant LDCs and less capital-intensive goods to the more capital-abundant West. However, the foregoing did not explain whether STEs did in fact export goods which were *too* capital-intensive to either group of countries taking capital-abundance differentials (i.e. GNP *per capita* differentials) into account. In other words, given the methodology and data generally used in empirical studies, the appearance of Heckscher–Ohlin rationality might have hidden substantial deviations from that rationality. The established methodology did not allow the problem in question to be addressed, however. Only in those cases like the Soviet one after 1968, when USSR exports to the West became *more* capital-intensive than imports therefrom, could excessive capital intensity of exports to that group of countries be ascertained.

There is yet another reason why empirical studies of the factor content of STEs' foreign trade may fail in giving unambiguous support to the above theoretically supported thesis. There is an important difference between import substitution-oriented LDCs and STEs with respect to the composition of exports. The former tend to produce more capital-intensive goods than is warranted by their level of capital abundance (approximately measured by GNP *per capita*). These more capital-intensive goods are sold on the heavily protected domestic market and in some part also abroad if they are subsidised enough to maintain price competitiveness on the world market.

Nonetheless, these LDCs suffer to a much smaller extent from the distortions of the domestic price structure and weak links between domestic and world market prices. Distorted as they were, comparative advantages have been known, both to governments and producers in import substitution-oriented LDCs. The same cannot be said about STEs, however, as shown in both this and the preceding section.

Consequently, exports by STEs, especially those without a rich resource base (that is, all except the Soviet Union), are much more varied with respect to their factor content. Both too capital-intensive goods (more typical for, say, the FRG or the United Kingdom), or too labour-intensive goods (more typical for, say, Malaysia, the Philippines or India), are exported from STEs to the West. As a result, *average* capital intensity in STEs may be about right for their level of capital abundance, but this situation may coexist with unprofitable or barely profitable exports of goods with respectively lower and higher capital intensity than that warranted by their level of capital abundance (assumed to be most competitive internationally according to the extended version of the Heckscher–Ohlin theory with a continuum of goods and more than two countries — see Krueger, 1977).[15]

Thus, approaches other than the established methodology have to be tried to support or reject a theoretically justifiable hypothesis on excess capital intensity of STE exports to the world market. For reasons that are obvious from the foregoing considerations, these approaches should analyse trade patterns at a more disaggregated level. At present, support from more detailed studies for the above hypothesis can be found only indirectly. Thus, for example, concentration indices for smaller STEs show a much greater dispersion of exports than those for the resource-rich Soviet Union or for the selected LDCs in the 1976–8 period (see Olechowski and Yeats, undated). In addition, on a product group by product group basis, both the Soviet Union and the smaller STEs demonstrate a high propensity to export such capital-intensive products as primary metals and bulk chemicals, that accounted for some 35–50 per cent of total manufactured exports to the West of the six smaller STEs and the Soviet Union respectively at the beginning of the present decade. Iron and steel provide a good example of deviations from the pattern of comparative advantage. All seven STEs in question display high revealed comparative advantage indices, i.e. those based on actual export figures,[16] regardless of whether they have to import iron ore, fuels or both. The said specialisation could be defended on the grounds that they display high transformation efficiency, i.e. add much value to the (largely imported) inputs. However, all indicators show that the efficiency is markedly *lower* in STEs, both in terms of transformation losses and less value that is added to the input in question (see, for example, Szpilewicz's (1979) comparison of Poland and Hungary with some industrial MEs in these respects).

These macro-level analyses are supported indirectly by micro-level ones, since they show that real cumulative costs of energy are often equal to more than half of the price obtained by Poland on the world market for exported steel products;[17] and the remaining half would have to cover all other costs as well as profits. Since this would be patently impossible, a Polish energy expert, Bojarski (1986), concluded that: 'The price system results in continuous and wide ranging subsidization of inefficient primary metal industry and bulk chemicals.' What he did not add was that it meant lower than average or outright losses from international trade — an outcome only to be expected when the trading pattern is not in accord with comparative advantage. In the same article, bulk chemicals did not fare any better in terms of energy costs relative to obtained export price. If anything, they were even worse, with some products barely paying for the energy used.[18] In the extreme case, World Bank experts found that, due to domestic price distortions, Romania was selling refined oil products for a price that was US$25 per ton *less* than the price of crude oil they were importing from the Middle East (Jackson, 1986).

Since other STEs also obtain lower than world market prices, even for standardised intermediate products (for chemicals, see OECD, 1980)[19] and, for system-specific reasons (see Part Two of this study), were also high-cost producers, their capital-intensive exports are also expected to be loss-makers (to an extent not known precisely, but almost certainly large). Sizeable shares of capital-intensive products in their exports result from distorted relative prices that hide the high real costs of both capital and natural resources. Some studies show STEs as countries that import inordinate amounts of natural resources, adding very little value to them (see Chapter 3), and exporting little processed goods, mainly in the form of intermediate inputs, to the world market (see Drabek (undated) for Czechoslovakia).

An alternative explanation of large shares of standardised intermediate inputs in STE exports to the world market has recently been advanced. It stresses the greater ability of these countries to manage the production of standardised goods that use as few inputs, and processes which are as simple, as possible. This preference is then supposed to be carried over directly into the field of foreign trade, in which the exporting of standardised goods is also easier to manage (Weiss, 1983).

Throughout this study, I have stressed the role of system-specific, including institutional, factors, but the suggested alternative does not seem very convincing. Firstly, it is not so much the alternative but a complement to the distorted relative-prices' explanation, since there is a high positive correlation between capital intensity and scale economies upon which such standardisation is based. Thus, an empirical evidence in the said study may be supportive for both, allegedly alternative, explanations.[20]

Secondly, it is not the case that central planners actually prefer to export standardised goods: their eternal aim is to be exporters of non-standardised goods, first and foremost machinery and equipment, to the world market as a measure of success of the socialist industrialisation. Year after year, they write into their export plans unrealistically high figures for machinery and equipment and year after year they are disappointed (if not in quantities exported, then in prices obtained, but usually in both). Standardised intermediate inputs (and consumer goods) for which there exists domestic demand enter the picture in larger than originally planned quantities when low quality, often technologically obsolete, machinery and equipment are rejected by the world market.

Thirdly, the alleged preference for the export of standardised goods is not carried over to intra-COMECON trade, where all STEs display machinery and equipment export shares between two and four times higher than those in their exports to the West. Obviously, it is the weak ability of STEs to export machinery and equipment, or more generally final products, *to the world market* that forces them to search continuously for alternatives, including standardised intermediate inputs, to fill gaps in export targets. Why STEs are unable to compete on an equal footing is another issue, to a large extent already addressed in the first and second parts of this study. Again, however, international trade theories are able to add to our understanding of the problem.

5.4. BURENSTAM-LINDER'S 'TRIAD', OR HOW TO SUCCEED IN EXPORTS WITHOUT THE DOMESTIC MARKET TEST

The particular problems of STEs can also, in my opinion, be explained in terms of yet another international trade theory. To begin with, let us stress the difference between the two categories of manufactures — intermediate and final products. Final products are often defined as differentiated products, differing in qualities or images created by advertising and, as such, being imperfect substitutes for each other (within a class of products). Except for the rare case of pure monopoly, final products are both imported and exported by MEs. The Swedish economist Staffan Burenstam-Linder

155

(1961) presented one of the most convincing explanations of international trade in these products.

Contrary to the basic premises of all supply-based trade theories, Burenstam-Linder stated that the more similar the levels of GNP *per capita* of countries and — at the same time — their factor proportions also, the greater will be the trade in final products between them. His reasoning, important for current purposes, runs as follows. A given market economy may achieve a comparative advantage only in the production of goods that are demanded domestically, for in the world of imperfect information, firms firstly perceive the existence of demand which is closest to them, i.e. domestic demand.

Only after they have successfully tested their products on the domestic market do they begin to think about exporting. However, given imperfect information (specifically, the high cost of its acquisition), they begin by exporting to countries with similar income levels. Similar income levels mean similar demand patterns and similar demand patterns mean more detailed (i.e. less costly) information about markets in these countries. Only at a later stage do they expand exports to other countries, with different income levels, in which demand for their products is smaller and export potential therefore lower. Subsequently, the volume of exports to third countries is also smaller.

According to Burenstam-Linder's explanation, each industrial market economy possesses a certain range of exportables determined by its domestic demand and not by *any* demand, but by one representative enough to generate a strong domestic productive and marketing base. Primary comparative advantages of a given economy stem from the skills gained in designing, producing, marketing, and servicing these goods domestically.

Burenstam-Linder's theory enables us to reveal important differences between the behaviour of exporters in Soviet-type and market economies. In the latter, it is the ability of producers to satisfy domestic demand which creates the foundations for export expansion, firstly, to countries with similar income levels and, later, to the rest of the world. In the former, however, the triad *domestic market —similar foreign markets—dissimilar foreign markets* does not exist.

The domestic market in STEs is a seller's market characterised by permanent excess demand. Under such conditions, producers may disregard any information flowing back from the market as to the qualities of their products. The test of the home market is thus missing, while the higher quality of exportables is exogenously enforced, as the very term 'production for exports' (meaning 'of higher quality') testifies.[21] However, it is at best a quality of workmanship that can be improved (at higher cost), not quality stemming from innovation in input characteristics, technological processes, better product design, etc.

As a result, representative demand, i.e. demand the satisfaction of which creates necessary skills for subsequent export expansion, does not exist in STEs. The quality of goods exported is at or above the level of home market-oriented goods, a feat by itself difficult to achieve. Moreover, given the anti-innovative bias of central planning, exported manufactures are well advanced along the product life cycle (an issue to which I return in the next chapter). As such, they compete on the basis of price only, and at the lower end of the quality spectrum at that.[22]

The above considerations may be presented graphically by adapting Burenstam-Linder's own diagram. In Figure 5.4, GNP *per capita* is shown on the abscissa and the quality range of produced goods on the ordinate. According to Burenstam-Linder's theory, a country III, with income *per capita* significantly lower than that of a country I, will export to the latter goods whose quality is represented by the *CD* section on the ordinate and will import goods of the quality represented by the *DE* section there. Both countries are market economies where the 'triad' discussed above is in existence.

Let us bring into the picture a Soviet-type economy (country II) with income *per capita* somewhere in between that of countries I and II, where the 'triad' does not exist. In spite of the higher *per capita* income than in country III, country II will only export goods of the quality represented by the *CD* section on the ordinate to country I and, possibly, goods of the quality higher than its regular quality range, represented by the *DD'* section there. If the quality of country III-exports to country I reflects the representative demand of the former, country II exports to the latter do not.

Incidentally, the realities of international trade seem to confirm the above interpretation of Burenstam-Linder's theory. To give but one example, Spain, in spite of lower *per capita* income than the GDR or Czechoslovakia, exports a much wider range of final products to industrialised MEs (and in greater volumes) than any of the STEs in question.

Burenstam-Linder's explanation is not the only demand-based one,[23] but no other seems to outline so clearly the role of domestic

Figure 5.4: An illustration of Burenstam-Linder's theory, adapted to conditions under which an STE (country II), in spite of a smaller difference in *per capita* GNP with respect to a market economy (country I) than the difference in this respect between the two market economies (countries I and III), trades less intensively with country I due to the lower quality range of its products than the quality range of country III

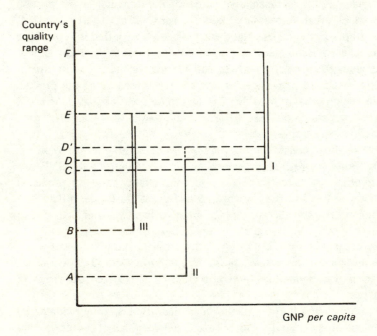

demand in laying foundations for future export expansion in market economies, and reveals — by contrast — the inherent weakness of STEs. By skipping the most important, domestic, phase of the Burenstam-Linder 'triad', STEs create at the very beginning a strong obstacle to successful exports of final products. The lack of a test on the domestic market will result in offering foreign buyers inferior products that often cannot be sold even at large discounts. The products are simply below the quality range of demand of industrialised MEs. In terms of Figure 5.4, they are below the quality range of country I (i.e. below point C on the ordinate).

Thus, contrary to certain doubts as to the validity of analysing STE performance in terms of the Burenstam-Linder theory (Holzman, 1979), it adds to our understanding of their weak position *vis-à-vis* the world market. Lack of competition, both assured institutionally and due to the permanence of excess demand, adversely affects quality; and the impact on quality is the strongest upon final, differentiated products. Without the primary selection process that goes with the domestic market test, the possibilities of failure on the world market increase dramatically.

Interestingly, exports to similar markets, the second in the chain of tests in Burenstam-Linder's triad, fail to do their job as well. The most similar markets are those of other STEs, but they also suffer from identical disabilities. With permanent excess demand, on the one hand, and without the representative demand on the other, they not only offer but also *accept* low-quality final products, whether machinery and equipment or consumer goods. Where almost anything produced can be sold, just like on the domestic market, exported final products do not meet any real test. Thus, there are more weak links in the chain. The test is on the world market and *only* there.

5.5. RECENT DEVELOPMENTS

The application of international trade theories added, then, to our knowledge of sources of STE underperformance on the world market. We can now see more easily why these countries cannot establish their patterns of comparative advantage. We know, as a result, why their trade must of necessity bring them fewer benefits than trade usually does. We also learned that the revealed comparative advantage pattern of STEs — as opposed to the largely unknown real one — brings them unidentified but serious losses, as far as their exports of capital- and resource-intensive goods are concerned. Finally, we understand why they encounter the greatest obstacles in their trade in final manufactured products.

The resultant situation is an unenviable one. STEs are exporting, for reasons of relative price distortions, more capital-intensive goods (primary metal products, bulk chemicals, cement, etc.) to the West than is warranted by the profitability of these exports. On the other hand, they are especially strongly constrained by system-specific features in exporting final manufactured products. To the extent that they succeed in exporting the latter, they do it at an often heavy discount, and in consequence, both types of exports more often than not bring lower benefits or outright losses to the national economy. There are still commodities to serve as dependable (if not necessarily very profitable . . .) foreign exchange earners, but a problem here is their availability. Except in the Soviet Union, they are increasingly scarce in Eastern Europe and they are everywhere increasingly costly.

This brings us back to the dynamic aspects of STE foreign trade, referred to in section 5.1 of this chapter. We know, then, that an import substitution-oriented strategy pursued by smaller STEs increases pressure for more imports and these needs can mainly be satisfied by imports from industrialised MEs. We also learned from Part Two of this study, however, that the increasingly distorted structure of the national economy — and that of industry itself — results in increasing costs in economic growth and a slowdown in structural change. Given the increasing cost of supplying STEs with ever higher imports, increasing problems with the external balance could be envisaged. The balance-of-payment problems of smaller East European countries since the mid-1970s and the crisis of the early 1980s are too vividly remembered to be discussed here. However, what I wished to stress in this respect was the long-term weakening of performance of the STEs as a contributing factor. The process of losing market shares in Western manufacturing imports, either absolutely or relatively — i.e. relative to LDCs — has been taking place with respect to STEs for quite a while.

Not only have shares been shrinking, but in addition the prices that STEs obtained on the world market for manufactures were decreasing relative to those obtained by other producers. It was most clearly visible with respect to engineering products. The results of comparisons of the so-called kilogram prices, i.e. prices in US$ per kilogram of engineering products, obtained by various countries and country grouping on the EEC market, are shown in Table 5.2. What is of particular interest is that it is not so much the fact that STEs obtained lower prices, since this was only to be expected (given lower quality, including technological sophistication, of their products), but that the prices were decreasing in relative terms. If STEs' prices were equal on average to half of the kilogram price obtained by the Western producers in 1965, they constituted only 45 per cent in 1970 and barely above one-third in 1980.

Obviously, kilogram prices are a pretty crude measure as far as relative position of a given country on a given market is concerned, but it is nonetheless conveying a lot of important information. Difference in kilogram prices tells us two things: firstly, it points to a difference in value added realised on a given market for a given product (product group) due to better quality, higher technological

Table 5.2: Average kilogram prices for engineering products obtained by selected countries and groups of countries on the EEC market relative to prices obtained there by Western MEs, 1965–80

	1965	1970	1975	1977	1980
World	0.99	0.99	0.98	0.98	1.00
Western MEs	1.00	1.00	1.00	1.00	1.00
United States	2.30	3.42	2.51	2.77	2.76
Japan	1.45	1.45	1.05	1.08	0.95
Switzerland	1.83	1.95	2.01	2.06	2.09
STEs	0.50	0.45	0.36	0.37	0.35
Bulgaria	0.32	0.39	0.35	0.33	0.30
Czechoslovakia	0.47	0.45	0.37	0.35	0.32
Hungary	0.76	0.71	0.51	0.52	0.47
GDR[a]	0.57	0.47	0.47	0.43	0.37
Poland	0.36	0.36	0.35	0.43	0.34
Romania	0.37	0.39	0.37	0.44	0.38
Soviet Union	0.46	0.43	0.29	0.27	0.29

Note: a. Excluding intra-German trade.
Source: Calculated from the statistics published in *Zahranicni obchod*, no. 2, 1983.

sophistication, etc; and secondly, it points to a different product structure in terms of the greater or smaller share of products with a higher value added. A kilogram price for such a large group of differentiated products as engineering products is determined by both quality and structural characteristics.

It is relatively unimportant to what extent either of these characteristics affected the kilogram price of STEs. What *is* important is the existence of the aforementioned differential and the fact that it has been increasing over time. It suggests that in spite of a decade of increased technological borrowing, quality changes with respect to existing products and/or the shift of the product structure towards new (more value-adding) products were slower in STEs than in the West — hence, the falling relative prices obtained by STEs.

Engineering is by far the most sophisticated industry and, consequently, problems in mastering its products and processes by underspecialised economies like STEs are commensurately greater. However, the relative decline in kilogram prices has also been visible in some other product groups.

The weakened performance of STEs with respect to manufactures both quantity-wise (shares in Western markets) and price-wise (widening price differentials) increased the role of commodities in

161

Table 5.3: Shares of manufactured goods in total STE trade with Western Europe, 1965–81 (%)

	1965	1977	1981
Bulgaria	36.7	66.0	34.3
Czechoslovakia	69.4	65.3	59.7
GDR[a]	77.0	74.7	44.9
Hungary	43.1	59.2	56.1
Poland	26.5	43.6	54.6[b]
Romania	15.3	56.6	44.4

Notes: a. Excluding trade with the Federal Republic of Germany that has, however, been even more oriented towards commodities (and standardised, low value-added intermediate manufactured products).
b. Poland's 1981 share has been overstated due to the sharp decline in the production of extractive industries and, consequently, exports of coal and other minerals.
Source: UN ECE, *Economic Bulletin for Europe*, vol. 37, 1985.

STE exports. Once again it turned out that STEs, under pressure of balance-of-payment considerations, are able rapidly to expand for the most part the export of food, raw materials and fuels. The share of manufactures in exports to the West decreased sharply and from already low levels at that.

Table 5.3 shows changing shares of manufactures over the 1965–80 period in exports to Western Europe. Whether rapidly, as in the case of Bulgaria, the GDR or Romania between 1977 and 1981, or less rapidly, as with Czechoslovakia and Hungary, the share of manufactures fell everywhere, except Poland. The latter case is atypical, however: all Polish exports to the West fell in absolute terms, but exports of mining products (particularly coal) fell much more heavily due to special circumstances of the period. After the introduction of martial law and, subsequently, its substitutes, exports of coal, etc.[24] increased sharply.

Just as with many other indicators of distortions under central planning, the Soviet Union, in spite of its gains from price realignments after both oil shocks, displayed similar signs of deteriorating performance. Even if the shrinking share of manufactures in its exports to the West could be explained by the rapid price increases of oil and natural gas, other developments could not. The fall in the share of Soviet exports in Western imports of manufactures between 1965 and 1980 was about the largest of all STEs. Only Bulgaria did worse in this respect, as may be seen from Table 5.1. In addition, with respect to kilogram prices to engineering goods, the USSR's decline was again about the largest of all STEs in relative terms (next to Hungary). In absolute terms, in 1980 the Soviet Union obtained the lowest prices of all STEs, equal to only 29 per cent of the kilogram price obtained by Western exporters (although in 1965, the Soviets were ahead of Bulgaria, Romania and Poland in this respect).

Once more the extent of the deterioration cannot be explained without recourse to historical rather than economic characteristics. With central planning being more deeply rooted in the Soviet Union and both political and economic systems sapping the vitality of its population for much longer, the Soviet ability to compete has been weakened to a considerably greater extent than in other STEs (in spite of the more favourable, or at least less disfavourable, impact of other factors).

While referring to the time factor and the accompanying deleterious effects of the Soviet-type system, the performance of East Germany and Czechoslovakia is worth noting as well. They were already well along the industrialisation path before the imposition of central planning; and since that time their performance relative to that of industrialised MEs has been in steady decline. In the foreign trade area it meant the decreasing shares of the Western market in manufactured goods (a decline from 0.63 to 0.47 per cent of Western manufactured imports for the GDR and from 0.48 to 0.33 per cent for Czechoslovakia between 1965 and 1980), the decline in the share of manufactures in total exports to the West (see Table 5.3), and, no less significantly, ever lower prices for the most sophisticated, i.e. engineering, goods, relative to those obtained by Western exporters. With respect to the latter indicator of declining performance, they ceased by 1980 to differ from other STEs any more. Thus, over time, the throttling impact of system- and policy-specific characteristics not only became stronger but also turned out to affect more developed STEs with greater severity.[25]

In conclusion, the exchange of STEs with the world market revealed steadily increasing import pressures generated by distortionary industrial growth under central planning and the markedly weakening ability to increase further exports of manufactures. The shift in the structure of manufacturing exports towards more value-adding products has been very slow. In fact, industrialised MEs have been effectuating that shift much more rapidly and the structural gap (as well as the quality gap) has been expanding. In times of increasing pressure for imports, STEs could count on exporting simple semi-manufactures and, first of all, commodities. However, since

163

exports of both types of goods have been limited by their sharply rising costs and/or declining availability, the external constraint upon the traditional economic growth pattern became stronger.

Since the peak of the balance-of-payment crisis there have been many official statements (and no less 'official' discussions) about the 'reorientation', i.e. the shift of trade away from the West and towards the COMECON partners. The possibilities of such reorientation are very limited, however. With the same system and strategy, STEs, not unexpectedly, have the same range of goods to offer (with the same type of negative quality characteristics). Their export structures to the West are more similar to each other than to those of other countries, as was shown in the painstakingly detailed study of Olechowski and Yeats (undated) on STEs' revealed comparative advantages. Once again, STEs displayed intra-group similarity which distinguished them from other countries.

All STEs not only sell the same range of goods in the West, but also buy the same range of goods there. The possibility of importing them from the other COMECON members is thus limited for reasons of unavailability (either permanent in the case of more sophisticated investment goods, or temporary in the case of intermediate products in short supply during the expansionary phase of the investment cycle). However, to the extent that STEs can substitute for industrialised MEs and decide to do so — mostly for reasons of convertible currency shortage — such substitution entails either continuation of or the increase in the technological gap (in the case of investment goods) or the decline in the quality of output (in the case of intermediate inputs).

Costs of intra-COMECON trading have been high and rising anyway. Our analysis of comparative advantages in section 5.2 above, explains why STEs were trading with the world market without knowing their own comparative advantages. However, at least they had the world prices to rely upon to learn about the real prices of their products. What they did not know were their own costs. In the case of intra-COMECON trade, even such partial guidance is not possible, since prices of *both* potential buyer *and* seller are distorted. The corrective role of the world market, imposing some specialisation on STEs through repeated rejections of certain offers, does not exist in intra-COMECON trade, either. With excess demand being the rule rather than the exception, almost everything can be sold there, no matter how substandard it is (the second test in Burenstam-Linder's 'triad' is missing: see the previous section).

The lack of knowledge about gains or losses that trade brings about has created some very peculiar defence mechanisms in intra-COMECON trade in the form of the bilateral balancing of trade flows, structural bilateralism (balancing trade by each product group), etc. The defence against losses is very weak, though, as best explained in a joke that the author heard over the years in at least three East European countries. A foreign trade organisation official comes back from a 'fraternal' (i.e. communist) country and reports to his boss about the highly profitable transaction he clinched there. 'I sold 500 dogs for 10,000 transferable roubles each', he boasts. 'Good', comments his boss, and then adds, remembering about balancing the trade: 'But what did you buy in return?' 'One thousand cats for 5,000 transferable roubles each', answers the official.

Trading without proper prices has over time been extended to *producing* for the other COMECON countries, also without proper prices. What passes as specialisation under the Soviet system is agreements on deliveries where quantities are agreed upon, with contributions of future buyers to the investment projects sometimes envisaged, but with prices being left to be agreed upon at the time of delivery. However, once projects are put into commission, producers are in a very vulnerable position *vis-à-vis* the COMECON buyers. Since their products, for reasons already explained in this study, are typically of low quality, technologically unsophisticated or downright obsolete, with generally unreliable after-sale servicing, they stand little chance of being sold outside COMECON. If their products cannot be absorbed by the domestic market, then they have to accept any price offered by COMECON buyers. That is why it is so difficult to establish real intra-industry subcontracting among the COMECON countries and such specialisation is usually pressed upon an unwilling industry by central planners and their political masters.[26] Without domestic prices reflecting domestic scarcities and exchange rates reflecting world market scarcities, no efficient specialisation, i.e. one bringing gains from trade, is possible.

Since internal patterns of comparative advantage remain largely unknown, each STE tries to establish new, technologically sophisticated industries in order to reap the alleged benefits of a higher level of economic development. However, since none is usually able to do it efficiently because of the system- and policy-specific reasons examined earlier, the result is a replication of the same industries throughout COMECON (as evidenced in Chapter 4).[27] An additional stimulus to inward-oriented development comes from the experience with deliveries of intermediate inputs from other COMECON countries that tend to be even less reliable than those from domestic suppliers.[28] As a result, there are not infrequent cases in which enterprises already involved in this peculiar sort of specialisation substitute domestic suppliers for those from other COMECON countries (see Csaba, 1983 and undated).

This author expects the costs of this sort of specialisation to have significantly increased over time for all COMECON trading partners. Greater numbers of such arrangements have raised their costs, since STEs' deviations from the (largely unknown) pattern of comparative advantage are not accidental but systematically biased towards highly capital-intensive and resource-intensive products (see above, section 5.3). In consequence, all STEs specialise to an (again, largely unknown) extent in products in which they possess comparative disadvantage.

The penalty for specialising in these products was lower for smaller STEs in the 1960s, i.e. in the era of falling relative prices of energy resources and some industrial raw materials. However, since the commodity price explosion of 1972–3 until at least the mid-1980s, the tables were turned and the costs of materials inputs for capital- and resource-intensive products in smaller STEs became substantially higher. The dynamics of price increases were slower due to the application of moving average prices in the intra-COMECON trading in commodities, but it was high nonetheless. Furthermore, the process of cost increases for importers was slower due to the willingness of the Soviet Union to run temporary surpluses on the balance-of-trade with other COMECON countries (that amounted to interest-free trade credits — see Marrese and Vanous, 1983).[29]

However, even with all the alleviating factors, smaller STEs have been facing increased costs of specialisation that also resulted from other developments. I stressed the increasing distortions that resulted from the expansion of underspecialised economies into the more sophisticated industries and products (see Part Two of this study). The peculiar intra-CMEA specialisation raised costs in two ways. Firstly, direct costs increased as STEs agreed to specialise in new products that they were at a competitive disadvantage to produce. Since the more sophisticated the product, the greater the costs of its production in underspecialised economies (see Chapter 4), expansion of such 'specialisation' must have increased production costs.

Secondly, indirect costs increased as STEs agreed to expand exports of goods whose production they were unable to master, and in consequence had to put into them high quality inputs imported from the West. According to both Polish and Hungarian data, the growth of imports used as inputs to exports has been higher in the 1970s than that of total imports and total exports (*Figyelo*, no. 1, 1982; Wojciechowski, 1981). Since the marginal cost of acquiring convertible currencies is very high in STEs, the costs of intra-COMECON specialisation increased as well. The latter, i.e. indirect costs, weighed more heavily on smaller STEs, especially in their trade with the Soviet Union, that takes about two-thirds of smaller countries' intra-COMECON manufactured exports. At the same time the cost of selling crude oil at below world market prices and running trade deficits raised the costs of intra-COMECON trading for the Soviet Union. With nobody satisfied, the peculiar specialisation of STEs became not only costlier but also more difficult to implement.

NOTES

1. Theoretical considerations in this chapter are based to a large extent on some earlier publications of the present author — see Winiecki (1983, 1984b, 1985b).
2. For an early interpretation of the inability of STEs to react flexibly to their partners' needs, see Stankovsky (1973).
3. Interestingly, fluctuations were also higher than the South–West trade in the 1960s (but not in the 1970s with their two oil-price shocks and other, more temporary, price realignments). See Winiecki (1984b).
4. On this point, see Stankovsky (1973).
5. They were on the increase in the Soviet Union, a large country, as well, although partly for different reasons (the unbelievably dismal results, even by East European standards, of Soviet collectivised agriculture).
6. In the following considerations, we equate the world market with the market of Western MEs, i.e. the dominant and most competitive part of the world market (the West constitutes over 60 per cent of world imports and over 80 per cent of world exports of manufactures).
7. That is, excluding China and (tradewise) unimportant STEs (Albania, North Korea, Vietnam, etc.).
8. Holzman, who analyses the said phenomenon in *ex post* terms only, also refers to the negative price elasticity of demand, but describes the demand curve as approaching the shape of a rectangular hyperbola (Holzman, 1974). He does not explain the divergence between his evaluation of the phenomenon and the proposed graphic presentation, however. On the negative price elasticity of STE exports, see also McAuley (1985).
9. COCOM is an abbreviation exclusively used to refer to a Western body, a co-ordinating committee controlling the flow of sensitive technology and goods to communist countries.
10. Unrealistically high exchange rates were to be taken by the rest of

the world as a measure of the strength of the socialist economy. Their role was patently non-economic.

11. For a history of that sort with respect to the Soviet Union, see, for example, Stouracova and Roubalova (1977); and with respect to Poland, see, for example, Dmowski and Foltyński (1982).

12. Besides the general literature on import substitution and export orientation, see also specific country studies by Westphal and Kim (1977) and Frank *et al.* (1978) on South Korea, and Fei *et al.* (1979) on Taiwan. See also an early comparative study by Balassa (1978).

13. It is interesting to see that these differentials tend to re-establish themselves after each price realignment, a phenomenon observed, *inter alia*, after Soviet price realignments in the mid-1960s and early 1980s. A similar pattern, however, could also be seen, for example, in Czechoslovakia, Poland and Hungary.

14. Under the set of strict preliminary assumptions.

15. A greater range of exported manufactures by STEs than by other import substitution-oriented economies — and including both more and less capital-intensive products than those that are in accordance with their comparative advantages — has been explained more systematically in Winiecki (1985b).

16. According to the formula

$$RCA_{ij} = (X_{ij}/X_{ti}) / (X_{jw}/X_{tw}),$$

where X_{ij} are exports of a product (or product group) j by country i, X_{ti} are total exports of country i, X_{jw} are exports of a product j by the whole world, and X_{tw} are total exports of the whole world. RCA indices have been calculated by Olechowski and Yeats (undated) for 127 manufactured products or product groups in East–West trade for the periods 1969–71 and 1976–8.

17. For example, for hot-rolled steel products, 57 per cent or for seamless tubes, 58 per cent (Bojarski (1986) for Poland).

18. For example, cumulative energy costs of methanol production in fact *exceeded* the prices obtained for the product, while for carbide energy costs were equal to 87 per cent of its world market price (ibid).

19. STEs at higher levels of economic development, i.e. Czechoslovakia and the GDR, sometimes obtained prices that were nearer to the world market prices (for bulk chemicals under consideration in the OECD study).

20. The evidence presented is in any case weaker than it is purported to be.

21. The very concept is contrary to the idea of export orientation: 'Expansion of such a production creates a dual economy, which may increase the backwardness of home market-oriented sectors and at the same time the home market will not contribute to the expansion of exports' (Kurowski, 1981).

22. It has been estimated econometrically that, for example, the price competition played a greater role in STE exports to the OECD area than did changes in the level of economic activity in the latter (Vanous, 1979).

23. See, for example, the cultural similarity explanation (Dreze (1960) and the variety hypothesis (Barker, 1974).

24. Even exports of meat, which the military, in an effort to buy the

population's favour, promised (after the 13 December 1981 coup) to discontinue, were renewed.

25. Goldmann and Kouba (1969) noted the falling relative prices of Czechoslovak machinery and equipment, although kilogram prices were still some two-thirds of Western prices at the time (i.e. in the early 1960s). It is obvious that the process started with the imposition of central planning upon otherwise efficient Czech industry.

26. In Eastern Europe the critique of this peculiar specialisation without proper prices is strongest in the Hungarian literature: see, for example, Drechsler *et al.* (1983) and Racz (1985).

27. On this, see again the Hungarian literature (Csaba (undated), Mosoczy (1983), as well as the authors referred to in the preceding footnote.

28. The case of spare parts is even more illustrative in terms of unreliability or long delivery times, because with domestic demand almost always much greater than supply, other COMECON country buyers are very far down the list of priorities of each country's producers.

29. This is not the right place to delve more deeply into the issue as to who subsidised whom, that gained a new lease on life with the below market prices for oil charged by the Soviet Union and the trade deficits that smaller STEs were nonetheless running with the USSR. It is worth noting, however, that the situation was different at different times. After the period of unilateral advantages for the Soviet Union in the Stalinist period came a period where terms of trade (rather than diktat) became important and the Soviet Union, as a commodity exporter, became a loser. With the change in the terms of trade for commodities in general and energy resources in particular, the USSR neither took full advantage with respect to price adjustments, nor did it press for immediate trade balancing (which would be impossible anyway). The above gave rise to the Vanous–Marrese concept of Soviet subsidies aiming at the maintenance of the inefficient Soviet-type system in smaller East European countries. Although conceptually right, it overstates the size of these subsidies in many ways (see, for example, Köves, 1983). Besides, another change is occurring at the time of writing, since the world market prices of oil are now lower than intra-COMECON prices, thus reversing the issue of the flow of benefits with respect to price level (but not necessarily that of trade balancing).

6

The Failure of Catching-up
Through Technology Imports

6.1. CENTRAL PLANNERS' EXPECTATIONS

We have already made it clear how and why the performance of STEs on the world market has been worsening over the years. However, while the international trade theories referred to in the preceding chapter assumed arm's-length trade, more elaborated forms of mutual involvement have also been taking place. Licensing and other deals, called 'industrial co-operation' in UN parlance, never gained much weight in East–West trade (some 5 per cent of total manufacturing exchange, i.e. some 2 per cent of total East–West trade:[1] see Bozyk and Guzek, 1976). Nonetheless since they were associated with the inflow of technology and capital to STEs — and later with increased imports — they became an important factor affecting the performance of STEs. Its impact is felt throughout these economies to the present, both domestically and in foreign trade.

The sources of the renewed interest of STE decision-makers in technology imports[2] have never been clearly spelled out, but they can be gleaned from numerous official statements. Cutting through a fog of official propaganda leaves us with only one real source. It should be remembered that economic growth rates in STEs fell markedly in the first half of the 1960s.[3] Modest economic reforms introduced in that decade improved the growth performance somewhat in the Soviet Union and some other countries, but reforms at the same time accelerated processes that communist leaderships regarded as dangerous to their position. As a result, reforms were

This chapter is adapted from an earlier publication by the author, 'Soviet-type economies' strategy for catching-up through technology imports — an anatomy of failure', *Technovation*, vol. 6/2 (June 1987). © Elsevier, Amsterdam.

Table 6.1: Kilogram Price Ratios in East–West Trade in Selected Engineering Products (STEs' export kilogram prices divided by STEs' import kilogram prices), 1965–8 and 1971–4

SITC	Products or products groups	1965–8	1971–4	
7125	Tractors	0.45	0.36	
7151	Machine tools (metal working)	0.39	0.28	
7152	Metal-working machinery	0.30	0.11	
7511	Textile machinery	0.75	0.81	(+)
7582	Printing machinery	0.57	0.47	
7185	Mineral, glass machinery	0.34	0.26	
7193	Handling equipment	0.53	0.34	
7195	Powered tools	0.68	0.40	
7197	Ball-bearings	0.75	0.67	
7198	Machinery and appliances (not elsewhere classified)	0.50	0.35	
7199	Parts and accessories (not elsewhere classified)	0.23	0.33	(+)
7221	Electric-power machinery	0.57	0.29	
7222	Electrical apparatus	0.43	0.42	
7231	Wire and cable	0.88	0.74	
7249	Telecommunications equipment	0.55	0.43	
7250	Domestic electrical equipment	0.79	0.80	(+)
7293	Valves, tubes, transistors	0.38	0.27	
7321	Cars	0.72	0.93	(+)
7323	Lorries and trucks	0.56	0.51	
7328	Chassis, bodies	1.02	0.80	
7350	Ships and boats	0.88	0.44	

Note: A (+) sign indicates higher prices obtained by STEs in 1971–4.
Sources: UN ECE, *Overall economic perspective for the ECE region up to 1990* (1978); own calculations.

'leached' (Poland, East Germany), reduced in scope at the outset (Hungary), or even stopped by the use of force (Czechoslovakia). Since that left the growth problem unsolved in the longer run, other factors stimulating economic growth had to be brought into play. Thus, with successful economic reforms implying 'too much political as well as economic upheaval . . . Party leaders opted for an alternative course of buying technological progress from abroad, especially from the West' (Cviic (1977), quoted in Zaleski and Wienert, 1980).[4]

Central planners and their political masters perceived in particular the existence of two barriers. The first was the *innovation barrier*. A further modernisation of their industries, or in the official STE parlance, 'intensive stage of economic growth', could be achieved, they believed, only with a more sophisticated technology than their research and development was able to deliver and their industry to introduce at sufficient speed. Moreover, smaller STEs felt increasingly strongly the impact of the rising costs of the import substitution-oriented strategy: rising import needs and falling

171

relative prices obtained by their decreasingly attractive manufactured products. Table 6.1 shows a marked turn for the worse in the case of the unit price ratios of the same engineering products exported to and imported from industrialised MEs between the late 1960s and early 1970s. It may be added that these rising costs have been noted in Eastern Europe much earlier (see, for example, Goldmann and Kouba, 1969).

The other barrier was an *investment barrier*. Central planners and their political masters believed that it is only the lack of sufficient resources that prevents them from completing all the capacity-increasing investment projects. In consequence, the resultant bottlenecks on the producer goods market (see Chapter 1) forced upon them costly delays in expanding their capacity to produce. Innovation aside, they saw, rather crudely, their economies as fitting into the one-gap model, while those who believed the lack of foreign exchange was another barrier saw STEs as fitting into the two-gap model of development economics[5]. Significantly, neither they nor politicians in developing countries pursuing import substitution saw any linkages between the existence of these gaps and system- and/or policy-specific features of their respective regimes.

Under the circumstances, Western technology and associated capital were regarded as able to overcome these barriers. Technology imports were to overcome the former, i.e., innovation barrier, while capital was to finance the machinery and equipment imports related to purchased technology to ensure the net increase in resources sufficient to complete the planned investment programme. Once completed, the new, expanded capacity, based on modern imported technology, would allow STEs to reach the 'intensive' stage of economic development.

Soviet and other East European decision-makers rightly regarded the early 1970s as a period of increased opportunities in this respect. Changes in the political and economic environment were seen as favourable for an extension of foreign economic policy beyond the arm's-length trade, because technology and capital imports had better prospects within the framework of *détente* (whatever its origins and definition). Moreover, the rapid increase in international liquidity created a buyer's capital market in the West and extended borrowing possibilities beyond government-to-government export credits.

However, if the international environment for *obtaining* resources was assessed realistically, the domestic environment for *using* the resources efficiently to overcome the perceived barriers were not. Marxist economic theory does not deal with the subject of resource transfer that benefits both the transferor and transferee. The political concept of 'brotherly assistance' (i.e. real or professed resource transfer from the Soviet Union) did not apply to the problem in question either. All in all, they had to rely on some vague generalisations drawn from the Western economic literature on the impact of foreign investment upon economic growth and the balance of payments and their changes over time, and, next, to try to adapt the above to the particular conditions of central planning. It is in the latter respect that they failed utterly.

Their expectations were strikingly simplistic. Firstly, they expected that net additions to domestic resources increase investments by the whole amount of additions and, in consequence, raise proportionately the rate of economic growth. The possibility of a disequilibrium threat to the consumer goods sector posed by the inflow of resources to the producer goods sector alone — and in an inward-oriented economy setting at that — was not considered at the time.[6] These problems were discovered *ex post* with the increasing disequilibria on the consumer goods market. What was not recognised until the very end, i.e. until the near-withdrawal from capital markets and balance-of-payments induced import cuts, was an inability to absorb extra resources by the STEs that were repeatedly thrown off the planned equilibrium growth path, even without such additional inflows.

Next, they expected that additional investment-increasing resources not only raise the economic growth rate, but also raise efficiency, since they would be associated with more productive and less input-using technologies. The question of how STEs were to accommodate the inflow of a more sophisticated imported technology, when less sophisticated domestic technology had been accommodated only with great delays and at higher than planned costs, was not seriously considered. Savings on time and domestic R and D resulting from technology imports were to materialise out of thin air in a fundamentally unchanged economic system (as we shall see below, especially in section 6.4 — even Hungary, with its most modified system, experienced identical problems).

The above simplistic views implied, however, even more 'simplisticism' than indicated above. Fixed assets under central planning are to a large extent seen as monuments of successful industrialisation. That they should be scrapped and superseded by more efficient ones if there is the *economic* rationale for such a change, is not a dominant factor in central planners' allocative decisions. Moreover, just like monuments, new capacities, once commissioned, are assumed to stay, while new resources are used to build new monuments (after all, there is so much excess demand, is there not? . . .) It is this curious thinking that generated a simplistic view that equated technology and associated capital imports with the once-and-for-all shift to a higher level of efficiency. Due to the *temporary* inflow of additional resources, the distance between STEs and industrialised MEs was to be reduced for the *indefinite* period (presumably forever). The ability of the system not only to absorb but to improve the imported technology (a more difficult task) was, again, not considered.[7]

Finally, no less simplistic were assessments of STEs' ability to pay for imported technology and capital. Thus, a new foreign economic policy was to result in a significant increase in exports of more processed manufactured products, i.e. those manufactured using Western machinery according to Western licensed technology. These products were supposed to generate enough convertible currencies to pay back the licence royalties, the interest on capital and the capital itself. For some, the improved export performance on the world market was also expected to continue indefinitely; and, once again, issues like the ability to absorb (and improve) new technology, the place of imported technology along the technological life cycle, the ability to deliver licensed products on time and at the expected cost and quality on the world market, etc., were not considered.

We stressed the lack of theory linking the increase in resources available with the *ability to use* increased resources under central planning. This deficiency was not regarded as crucial at the time (it is not even so regarded now: no authoritative scholarly literature about this linkage appeared in Eastern Europe). The decision to use imported technology and capital was a political one and, as such, needed only apologetic comments in the controlled press. Not surprisingly, such comments duly appeared all over Eastern Europe.[8]

The next section is a contribution to the missing theory of linkage referred to above. Such an analytical scheme can be used not only for 'postdictions', i.e. for predictions with respect to the known past, but also for predictions proper, i.e. for predicting the possibility of success in future STE attempts at technology imports (if undertaken without changing basic system-specific characteristics).

6.2. BARRIERS TO INNOVATION AND IMITATION AT THE MICRO LEVEL

The existence of strong barriers to innovation is an acknowledged feature of STEs. It is referred to in every textbook on comparative economic systems (see, for example, Grossman (1967) and Davies (1979)), as well as being dealt with in treatises on the subject (see, first of all, Grossman (1977) and Berliner (1976)). I did the same in explaining the preference for investment over innovation (Chapter 1, section 13), the low quality of STE products (section 15), the high resource intensity (Chapters 3 and 4), as well as the low and relatively declining sophistication of manufactures exported to the world market (Chapter 5, section 3).

If, however, barriers to innovation have been extensively analysed, the same cannot be said of barriers to *imitation*. The system-specific barriers to technology imports were even dealt with rather perfunctorily in a series of studies devoted to technology transfer commissioned by the OECD (Zaleski and Wienert (1980), Fallenbuchl (1983), Levcik and Skolka (1984)), as well as in recent articles on the subject (e.g. Hanson, 1982). Our subsequent considerations attempt to explain the impact of barriers to imported technology-based technical change. However, it is also important to be able to relate the impact of barriers to imitation to those to innovation, and I therefore considered them on a comparative basis, i.e. analysing the impact of barriers to both on technical change in STE industry.

The most neglected, in my view, is an analysis of barriers at the micro (that is, the enterprise) level. Although it is well recognised, for example, that the structure of incentives is strongly adverse to innovation, its impact (or impact of any other system-specific barrier for that matter) upon technical change should be evaluated *for each stage* of that change. Such step-by-step analysis has not been performed comprehensively for the impact of system-specific barriers upon innovation and it is simply non-existent for that on imitation.

In an attempt to fill the gap, I constructed an analytical scheme that specified all consecutive major stages in the process of technical change and related to each stage problems affecting that change. These problems were classified as those that affected domestic technology-based change, or imported technology-based change, or both — i.e. the classification took the source of technology into account. Furthermore, since the catching-up strategy through

175

Figure 6.1: The impact of barriers to technical change in STEs at the micro (i.e. enterprise) level

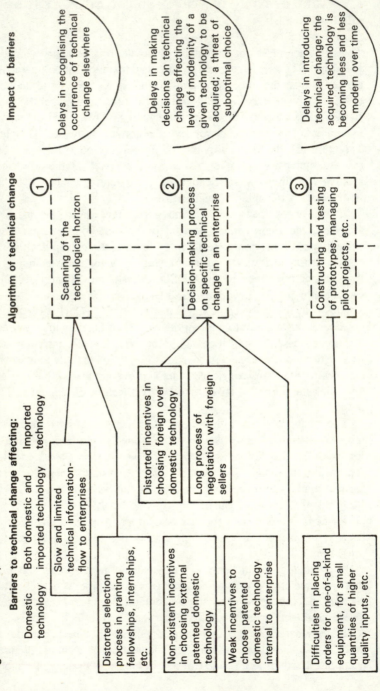

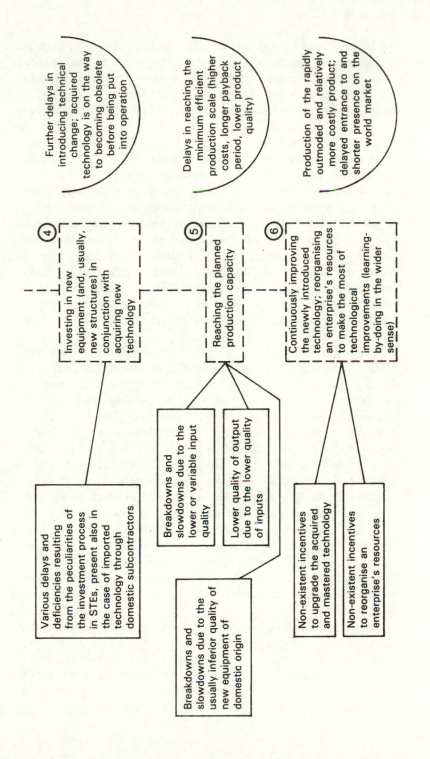

④ Investing in new equipment (and, usually, new structures) in conjunction with acquiring new technology

Various delays and deficiencies resulting from the peculiarities of the investment process in STEs, present also in the case of imported technology through domestic subcontractors

Further delays in introducing technical change; acquired technology is on the way to becoming obsolete before being put into operation

⑤ Reaching the planned production capacity

Breakdowns and slowdowns due to the lower or variable input quality

Lower quality of output due to the lower quality of inputs

Breakdowns and slowdowns due to the usually inferior quality of new equipment of domestic origin

Delays in reaching the minimum efficient production scale (higher costs, longer payback period, lower product quality)

⑥ Continuously improving the newly introduced technology; reorganising an enterprise's resources to make the most of technological improvements (learning-by-doing in the wider sense)

Non-existent incentives to upgrade the acquired and mastered technology

Non-existent incentives to reorganise an enterprise's resources

Production of the rapidly outmoded and relatively more costly product; delayed entrance to and shorter presence on the world market technology imports also entailed the upgrading and expansion of manufactured exports, the impact of system-specific barriers at each stage upon performance on the world market was also included in the scheme. The algorithm of technical change, the impact of barriers and consequences for the world market performance are shown schematically in Figure 6.1.

Applying the analytical scheme, we begin with the stage of *scanning the technological horizon*. Such scanning should be continuous, but in STEs the first problem is that at the enterprise level there is hardly any scanning at all. The departments of technology of the respective ministries to which enterprises are subordinated and the research institutes of these ministries are doing more in this respect, but their knowledge is completely unrelated to the interests of the enterprise (this bureaucratic divide is stressed in studies on science policy and innovation in STEs: see in particular Zaleski *et al.* (1969) and studies by Berliner and Grossman referred to earlier). In addition, the interests of enterprises are primarily those of the routine implementation of planned production targets without *any* change at all.

Thus, whatever little scanning is done in enterprises, it is not aimed at alerting the management on the need for technical change, since in the closed and shortage-plagued economies, such need does not exist. Underpaid and underappreciated engineers in STE enterprises[9] have not only very limited access to professional literature, conferences, fairs, etc., but very little incentive to follow technical developments abroad. Moreover, where low supply meets low demand, disequilibrium theory predicts equilibrium at a low level. In consequence, enterprise management not only does not want technical change, but does not even know much about what change is taking place elsewhere and, consequently, what the distance is in this respect between his enterprise and similar enterprises abroad. Thus, for example, a survey of Czechoslovak enterprises in the mid-1970s showed that the average manager knew little about productivity levels in his industry abroad and at least 20 per cent of managers knew *nothing* on the subject (quoted in Levcik and Skolka, 1984).

At first sight the deficient knowledge of the current state of the art abroad may seem to give an advantage to domestic over imported technology. In reality, however, the divide between bureaucratised research institutes and enterprises is so strong that the knowledge of domestic advancement in technology is not significantly greater in the latter. At the same time, ministerial bureaucrats who visit (a carefully chosen word) conferences and fairs much more frequently than scholars, and infinitely more frequently than enterprise engineers, at least familiarise themselves with foreign technical advancements. Since visits to, say, Hannover, Zürich or New York are more attractive than those to buildings a few blocks away from their own ministry, the disadvantage of foreign technology at that — more important than enterprise — level of decision-making is reduced.

Now assume that either at that or a higher level of the bureaucratic hierarchy, a decision has been made to upgrade the technical level of a given enterprise (or more rarely, enterprises). Thus, a search, i.e. a *decision-making process aimed at finding and acquiring a more productive technology* for a given enterprise has been instituted, taking place in the main outside the targeted enterprise. The term 'interested' was consciously avoided, because enterprise management is *not* interested in the change at all; and if it cannot avoid it, its main interest lies in convincing its superiors that new technology requires a new factory so that they can meet planned production targets without interference in the existing productive facilities. Thus, for example, in the already-quoted official Czechoslovak survey (Levcik and Skolka, 1984), a large majority of enterprise managers indicated that they did not want to introduce more modern products if it would entail discontinuing the production of any of the actually manufactured products. Since technical change is more often than not associated with production expansion rather than with rationalisation (greater output is ranked higher than cost reduction in the rank-order of plan targets), they may succeed even in cases where new investments in structures are superfluous.

Thus, enterprise management, acting as risk minimisers, prefers no new technology to new technology and, as a second line of defence, new technology in a new factory to new technology in the old one. However, if technological upgrading has already been decided at some higher level of the bureaucratic hierarchy, then barriers tend to be lower with respect to foreign technology.

For analytical reasons we need, however, yet another differentiation between domestic new technology external to a given enterprise, and one that is internal — i.e. one whose authors are engineers and/or other employees of that enterprise. In the case of the latter, there are at least weak incentives in the form of patent royalties if managers are co-authors (or if actual inventors were far-sighted enough to include them as co-authors).[10] Once the introduction of new technology cannot be avoided, one's own internal technology (if it exists) is better than a domestic but external one.

The incentives to choose imported technology (assuming that such an option is not foreclosed for balance-of-payments or political reasons) are nonetheless stronger than for 'own' domestic technology. Visiting foreign (nearly always Western)[11] enterprises, firstly within the framework of the search process and, next, as a part of the technology transfer, is certainly more lucrative. More importantly, the lure of foreign technology is much stronger for high-level bureaucrats from unions of enterprises, ministries, etc. It should also be noted that the latter are interested in the search process up to its conclusion, i.e. to signing a licence contract, but not in the transfer proper (since visits abroad would then concern different people).

One would not need to stretch the imagination very far to link the long licence negotiation periods with the interests of bureaucrats: officials who keep coming again and again, talking vaguely about the need of co-operation instead of sending their representatives to clinch the deal, obviously know what they are doing.[12] Certainly, there are other, probably more important, sources of long negotiation periods: planning procedures (the process of resource allocation for a given licence project), typical procrastination in making a binding decision (that stems from the unwillingness to bear the responsibility and needs of acquiring numerous approvals), the slowness in responding to the enquiries of Western partners (85 per cent of potential business deals of US companies fail at the stage of preliminary correspondence, even before face-to-face contact is established with an East European firm or institution),[13] and so on.

Altogether the search process that ends with the licence contract is very long by any standards, even those of import substitution-oriented LDCs. It is difficult to estimate just *how* long, since licences entail transfer of differing scale and complexity. Thus, in the case of Hungary we have estimates ranging from 1–3 years (*Business International: Eastern Europe*, 10 December 1976) to five years (Szatmary (1978) quoted in Poznanski, 1979). The last estimate seems to be surprisingly high when compared with the other, as well as with the experience of other countries.[14] For Poland, the average time was estimated to be no less than two years (Monkiewicz, 1983) and for Czechoslovakia 2–3 years (Levcik and Skolka, 1984). Perhaps Szatmary's estimates refer to the extreme, upper-range cases.

In consequence, the process of ageing of the targeted foreign technology already begins to take place at the search stage. Even if the technology is more productive than the competing domestic one, it already advances further along its life cycle by the time the licence deal is signed. Moreover, there is always a danger of suboptimal choice with the foreign technology involved, where the higher attractiveness of trips to one country over that to another may influence the choice of a supplier.[15]

What imported technology loses in terms of time elapsed during the search process, it makes up at the development stage. Inward licensing of the existing technology is able to reduce the time between the decision to come up with a new or improved product and actually developing a product. This textbook gain (see, for example, Lowe and Crawford, 1984) realised everywhere is particularly large in STEs, with their system-specific barriers to product or process development and their resultant problems with, for example, the ordering of a one-off piece of prototype equipment, small batches of higher quality parts, components for prototypes, higher quality inputs for test runs, etc.[16] Thus, only barriers to domestic technology are registered at the stage in question.

The fourth stage entails investing in new equipment and usually also in new structures. We did not single out in our analysis the impact of the investment barrier because it was meant to be analysed in conjunction with the innovation/imitation barrier exactly at this stage. Usually, borrowed capital (if not dissipated through general import support) was tied to particular technology import projects. In consequence, a comparison of problems encountered simultaneously by domestic and imported technology *and* capital can be put into sharper focus.

In theory, licence-related investment projects enjoy central planners' priority, but in economies in which shortage is pervasive, all priorities are *relative*. It means that priority projects are supposed to face lower barriers with respect to supplies and construction capacities than non-priority projects. In reality, even this was not always the case. The cyclical (see Chapter 1, section 1.3) over-expansion of investments may create (and did create) such serious supply and capacity bottlenecks that it may affect (and, again, did affect) priority projects, including licence-related ones. However, it is not so much the typical investment cycle-related problems that affect the *relative* position of imported technology- (and capital-) based projects *vis-à-vis* domestic technology- (and capital-) based ones.[17] It is rather the new and higher requirements with respect to domestic construction enterprises, the suppliers of auxiliary domestically produced equipment and the producers of building

181

materials that were more important. Even turn-key projects entail some domestic inputs, to say nothing of less comprehensive deals. All projects are affected to a greater or smaller degree. In consequence, even a relative priority may not be enough and imported technology- (and capital-) related projects are in some cases completed with as long or longer delays as those based on domestic technology. (Domestic capital, as we see, is involved in both types of projects.)

The time needed for putting the project into commission may often be as long as four to six years (for examples, see Levcik and Skolka (1984) for Czechoslovakia, and Monkiewicz (1983) for Poland). The average is of course much shorter. Various sources put that of Czechoslovakia within 1–2 years' range (Nyers (1977) and Levcik and Skolka (1984)). For Hungary, Nyers (1977) showed again a much shorter project completion time (21–17 months between 1972 and 1975) than Szatmary. Polish estimates differed significantly, ranging between 2 and 3½ years in this particular respect (but not in others).[18]

Thus, by the time the imported technology-based project is put into commission in an STE, the targeted technology is already quite advanced along its life cycle and well on the road towards becoming obsolete. However, the problem of ageing does not stop here: it spills over to the stage of *reaching the planned production capacity* and at that (usually last) stage of the life of the licence deal, they sometimes become perennial, since planned capacity is not reached at all. At that stage, barriers to imported technology are stronger than they are to domestic technology. The latter 'only' suffer from the usual weakness, i.e. inferior quality of domestic machinery and equipment and resultant breakdowns or slowdowns in their use. It is, however, better adapted to manufacturing from the low and/or variable quality of material inputs.

This is not the case with respect to imported technology. The input quality requirements are higher and the tolerance of its variability is markedly smaller. Consequently, machinery breakdowns occur frequently once domestic (or other STE) inputs are substituted for the imported ones. Delays in reaching the planned capacity are very often an outcome: for example, according to the Soviet Central Statistical Office, in 126 (66 per cent) out of some 200 surveyed cases, planned production capacity based on imported machinery and equipment was not reached on schedule.[19]

Another outcome is lower than planned quality of the licence-based product. The ironic term 'Bulgarisation', used to describe the pronounced decline in quality once foreign specialists running the trial runs and imported inputs used for these runs were no longer present, is an indicator of the problem. In addition, although the lower quality may still be high enough (or higher than that of comparable domestic products) for the domestic market, it may not be high enough for exports, especially exports to the Western supplier of technology as a payment in resultant products.[20]

Thus, in the foreign trade area, of greatest interest here, both delays in reaching planned capacity and lower quality result in stretching the period of repayment. If the former problem cannot be remedied without increasing the level of sophistication of various suppliers and suppliers' suppliers (that is, of domestic manufacturing *as a whole*), the latter can be remedied by increasing the import content of the licensed product. This is, however, as smaller STEs learned at the threshold of the 1980s, a temporary remedy only. If raising the sophistication level cannot occur (for system-specific reasons — see Part Two), then the recoupment period not only lengthens but forces the domestic producer to face the alternative: either to become permanently dependent on imported inputs or lower the quality of licensed products and further decrease their exportability (already low due to delays in entering the world market and the resultant ageing of a product). Judging from the recent experience, East European STEs chose each option in turn: firstly, increasing import of inputs and, next, cutting imports under the balance-of-payments pressure and opting for lower quality instead.[21] More on that will be said in the final section of this chapter.

The extent of delays in reaching capacity does not differ strikingly among analysts of Hungarian experience in this respect, i.e. the country for which such data are most widely available. The target capacity is reached within 1–3 years (Juhasz, n.d.), 2–3 years (Nyers, 1977) or about two years (Szatmary, 1978, whose estimates do not differ this time from those of others). No comparable estimates exist for other STEs.[22]

Thus, imported technology, whether new products or new technological processes, has been absorbed on the average for at least six years if search, investment and capacity-reaching stages are added together. Now, the technology sold to another firm is rarely the freshly introduced one. Adding those six years to the age of technology at the time it is targeted by STE buyers, we arrive at its approximate position along technology's life cycle. If we accept what Juhasz (undated) takes as a norm for Hungary, that imported technologies are applied (i.e. used at a minimum efficient scale — JW) some eight years after their first appearance abroad, we see that the absorption period is equal to some three-quarters of that lag.[23] Out of this three-quarters, a major part may be ascribed to the system-specific weaknesses of STEs. The imported technologies they buy may still allow them to turn out products superior to those on the domestic market, but with respect to world market exportability they are in a disadvantageous competitive position (see section 6.4, below). The by now oft-repeated Holzman (1979) phrase that bad innovators are also bad imitators found its theoretical, system-specific underpinnings, as well as some scattered but fairly convincing evidence.

Nonetheless, given the extremely long periods in the case of domestic innovation, the use of technology imports may still bring benefits in the form of the reduced lag between the best practice technology and that used in STEs. Hungarian sources estimate the gap reduction to be about 2–3 years (Juhasz (undated) and Nyers (1977)). In addition, there are some difficult-to-estimate savings in domestic R and D, but at the same time substantial convertible currency costs. The latter tend to become even bigger with the inability of an STE to follow up the absorption with the upgrading of imported technology.

6.3. WHY THE DECREASE IN THE TECHNOLOGICAL GAP (IF ACHIEVED) IS ONLY TEMPORARY

A sixth stage in Figure 6.1, i.e. upgrading new technology that is coupled with the continuously improved utilisation of all resources at hand, deserves separate treatment, since it goes a long way towards explaining the permanence of the technological gap existing between industrialised MEs and STEs. Furthermore, by going beyond technical change proper, it links the gap more explicitly to system-specific features. Barriers at that last — and lasting — stage affect both domestic and imported technology-based technical change.

The term 'technical change' is used here for reasons of convenience only, since only a part — and not always a larger part — of the effects of technical change can be ascribed to technical change proper. The literature of the last few years stresses more insistently than that of the not-so-distant past the impact of organisational change. Technical change yields the highest effects only when it is integrated into a more efficient use of *all* resources: labour, fixed capital, raw materials and intermediate inputs. The latter is, let us say, an important source of higher performance *per se*, i.e. without accompanying technical change. That effect known in the literature as *learning by doing* (Arrow, 1962) is however to a decreasing extent realised in the physical hardware production. Increasingly, sources of improved performance lie in the upstream (designing, differentiating, testing, etc.) and downstream activities (packaging, transportation, advertising, feeding back information from consumers, etc.). The continuous restructuring of all activities ensures improved performance (see, for example, Eliasson, 1976).

It is this particular organisational (or more properly, *entrepreneurial*) change that allowed a steel mill in Horndal, Sweden, to raise productivity by 2 per cent per annum for 15 consecutive years without new investments, except for the replacements of the physically used-up equipment (Lundberg, 1961). A similar example was found recently in Sweden where another steel mill was increasing productivity by 3.7 per cent annually without new investments (Carlsson, 1981).

The 'Horndal effect', understood here as learning-by-doing applied to all enterprise activities, is also substantial in the case of the organisational changes accompanying technical change. In such cases, more interesting within the framework of the chapter, productivity gains due to the former are often not lower than those resultant from the introduction of new technology. Carlsson (1981), referring to his earlier studies, points to the productivity differentials between aggregate productivity increases and those made possible by the introduction of new technologies (on the basis of assessments by best-practice firms). In 14 cases from several industries, possible gains over the 1955–75 period from technical change ranged between 20–30 to 60–70 per cent of aggregate productivity increases.[24] For manufacturing as a whole, the contribution of technical change accounted for 47 per cent of aggregate productivity growth, with the balance attributed to the continuous restructuring of all activities of enterprises.

The organisational (or entrepreneurial) imperative, to continuously restructure enterprise activities stems, first of all, from the constant preoccupation with profitability, attainable by reducing inputs per unit of output. This is stimulated, in turn, by the need to survive in an environment of competing firms, both domestic and foreign, and changing tastes of consumers. It is a system, i.e. *market*

185

system-specific environment, completely foreign to STEs.

Enterprises under central planning have no incentives whatsoever to upgrade the absorbed technology. Nor are incentives much stronger in the case of organisational changes, whether accompanying technological upgrading or not.[25] The preference for routine is as strong in the case of old as in the case of new technology. It is, perhaps, even stronger in the case of the latter, since after extra effort in absorbing the new technology, everybody in the enterprise is looking towards an uninterrupted routine (for some time at least).[26]

There is no competition, or at best no competition to speak of (as in the case of Hungary). Nothing can force enterprises to improve their performance through technological upgrading and/or continuous organisational restructuring. System-specific excess demand also acts discouragingly in this respect, although it is not the all-important factor, as some STE decision-makers and some Marxist economists often suggest. In those (rare) cases of excess supply, enterprises continued to produce unneeded goods due to their 'soft' budget constraint and the resultant immunity from financial failure. The only visible effect was an increase in inventories (while costs were borne by the population through other channels).

However, permanent excess demand has other deleterious effects on technical change. The literature on the subject shows convincingly that the most numerous and successful innovations are those that stem from market demand, i.e. where an idea originates from beyond the technical group (see, for example, Gerstenfeld (1977) and the authors quoted therein). Since under central planning there is not much feedback from the market, and whatever little exists can be safely disregarded, the innovative activity of STE enterprises is deprived of its strongest stimulus.

Not only are enterprises not interested in improving the licensed technology but they are not even pressed very strongly to do so by central planners, whose main concern seems to be a one-off rise in productive efficiency effectuated through particular technology imports rather than one of continuous improvements in this respect. Thus, there is not much interaction between the domestic R and D and licence-based technology transfer. The former in fact has its own rigid five-year plans that have to be implemented. Besides, just like investment funds, they are spread over too many projects (out of which nine out of ten should be abandoned at one time or another, since only a miniscule proportion of all development projects turn into successful innovations).[27]

According to Monkiewicz (1983), R and D funds for upgrading the imported technology were very limited: in 1977, for example, they amounted to barely 1.4 per cent and in 1978 to 1.9 per cent of total R and D expenditures. This is in sharp contrast to the experience of the most successful technology importer, Japan, where imported technology and firms' R and D formed integral parts of the same process of technological upgrading. In the early 1960s, one-third of the firms' R and D was related to imported technology (see Winiecki (1979) and authors quoted therein). I have no approximately comparable figures for other STEs, but at least the literature on Hungary is full of references to the highly unsatisfactory R and D support for imported technology (see, for example, Dezsenyi-Gueuliette (1983), Juhasz (undated) and Kardos (1985)).

Cases from other STEs support the foregoing. Thus, for example, some Soviet authors long ago expressed concern that not enough was done to upgrade automotive technology and related equipment imported to produce Lada–Zhiguli cars (see sources quoted in Zaleski and Wienert, 1980). In consequence, the Russians recently had to repeat the operation, again buying both technology and equipment in the West. Thus, the distance reduced at one point tends to increase again over time; and a more general acceleration of technical change — also visible in the automotive industry — may result in an *increased* lag rather than the return of the *status quo ante*. This concerns the industry as a whole even more, since the Soviet Union is not able to find resources to upgrade *all* products of its overgrown and underspecialised industry in this way. In addition, what is too costly for the Soviet Union is all the more so for smaller East European countries, which are even more handicapped due to their small size by the twofold underspecialisation of STEs (see Chapter 3 on the subject).

Would more spending solve the problem in question, however? In the opinion of this writer the answer must be in the negative. Barriers to innovate at this upgrading stage of the technical change algorithm are as much system-specific as they are at all earlier stages, and without changing an environment which is hostile to innovation, the effects would only be marginally positive at best. What is more, the increased spending would be very problematic, not only due to the usual budget constraint (much stronger at the present troubled time!), but also due to the already high level of resources involved, in terms of both R and D funds and personnel. This level is generally *higher* than in the most innovative industrialised MEs. Estimates for both are set out in Table 6.2.

Table 6.2: Inputs for technological change in the East and West: the R and D share in GDP expenditures, and scientists and engineers in R and D establishments and in total employment as a percentage of total employment (excluding agriculture) at the end of the 1970s

	R and D as a percentage of GDP in 1979	R and D personnel as a percentage of: total employment	Scientists and engineers as a percentage of: excluding agriculture
East European STEs			
Bulgaria	1.7 (1977)[b]	1.5	8.2
Czechoslovakia	2.9 (1978)[b]	1.8	5.4[c]
Hungary	2.5 (1978)[b]	1.4	9.3
GDR	—	2.2	6.3
Poland	1.6 (1978)[b]	1.4	6.9[d]
Romania	—	0.7	—
Soviet Union	3.4 (1977)[b]	—	11.6
Western MEs			
Canada	0.9	0.5	7.6
Finland	—	0.8	9.3
France	1.8	1.3	9.2
FRG	2.3	1.0	5.3[d]
Italy	0.8	0.5	7.0
Japan	2.0	1.4	11.5
Sweden	1.9	1.0	—
United Kingdom	2.2 (1978)	—	—
United States	2.4	0.8	3.2

Notes: a. R and D personnel and scientists and engineers around 1977; total employment in 1975.
  b. Estimated from NMP data according to the UN ECE methodology.
  c. Scientists and engineers in 1973.
  d. Scientists and engineers in 1970.
Sources: *Yearbook of international statistics* (1981); Giersch and Wolter (1983); own calculations.

Since STEs did not achieve much with the resources higher than those used by MEs, there is no reason to expect that any further increase of resources would materially alter the outcome if the other factor, i.e. the environment for innovation (and imitation), is highly adverse.[28]

When pressed by their superiors, enterprises would come up with small incremental technical improvements that are more easily designed, tested and introduced. Soviet sources demonstrate the foregoing beyond any reasonable doubt by complaining, for example, about the low productivity effects of new machinery that ranged between 5 and 20 per cent at the end of the 1970s (*Planovoye Khozyaistvo*, no. 7, 1979). On another occasion, a deputy chairman of the Soviet Price Commission (Goskomtsen SSSR) pointed out that the economic effects of new technology are generally overestimated in the reports of respective producers by some 30–50 per cent, and in some cases they are even several times higher than those obtained in reality (*Planovoye Khozyaistvo*, no. 8, 1979). These are typical pseudo-innovations generated for the purpose of claiming higher prices before the Price Commission and achieving higher profits as a result (see above, section 6.1 and Chapter 1, section 1.5). Incidentally, they also help to implement other plan targets, this time those pertaining to the plan of technical progress.

Interestingly, according to the same Price Commission's deputy chairman, users of the said machinery quite often confirm the overestimated economic effects presented by producers, since they are not interested in economies realised through the installation of new equipment (*Planovoye Khozyaistvo*, no. 8, 1979). There is another reason for their behaviour, however. Just as trade organisations on the consumer goods market do not exercise their rights to fine their suppliers for underdeliveries, changes in assortment, lower quality, etc., for fear of losing their supplies next time, which are irreplaceable on the seller's market, so the users of machinery do not want to incur the wrath of their suppliers on the seller's market for producer goods.

Finally, we point out that the R and D establishment, just like enterprise management and workers, is also interested first and foremost in small incremental technological improvements. These are more likely to be realised within the planned period and, as such, put at a smaller risk the plan-related premium and/or bonuses. With such attitudes prevailing for the same system-specific reasons in both areas, the catching-up is obviously impossible and even reductions in the existing technological gap are only temporary.[29] Worse still, they seem to be dependent on recurrent injections of imported technology which STEs can decreasingly afford, given the high cost of importing technology by bad innovators who are also bad imitators.

The situation was no better on the export side. In Figure 6.1 we stressed the export effects of the time lag that increased from one stage of technical change to another, independent of whether the technology in question was of a domestic or an imported origin. In the following step-by-step evaluation I pointed out the delays that affected the position of applied (in this case imported) technology in its life cycle, since the absorption process by itself added some six years to the age of that technology. If the technology was 2–4 years old at the time it was targeted by an STE; then export expansion began in earnest when it was 8–10 years old, i.e. when it was near the end of its life cycle.

Thus, the position of an STE as an exporter of manufactures did not improve materially. The product based on a given imported technology became standardised long ago and at that time was already at the lower end of the quality range of similar products. Again, an STE competed on the world market on the basis of low price alone, even if with a different product. In the case of buy-back arrangements, STEs had (an) assured market(s) for a specified time and quantity of output, but beyond that they were dependent on the willingness of the licensor to continue to order the product. There were quite a few cases of such continuous exports, but even if STE supplies were flowing smoothly (which was not often the case . . .), the ability of the licensor to sell the aged product, even at the lower end of the market and at a suitable discount, was not infinite. With the high rate of product renewal, the time has to come sooner or later (and usually sooner) when the product can no longer be sold at *any* discount. Its world market life cycle (in contrast to the domestic STE life cycle) has ended.

The impact of system-specific barriers upon the imitation process in terms of STE export performance can thus be explained in terms of product life cycle theory.[30] According to Vernon (1966), innovating high-income countries manufacture new products for which there exists domestic demand alone. As production volume increases and technologies become more standardised (and prices fall), the demand for these products appears in other high-income countries and they begin to be exported from an innovative country. When products mature and technologies become fully standardised, the trade flow is reversed (at least partially). Other countries catch up with the innovating country, either through direct foreign investment, licensing or indigenous effort, and, having lower labour costs, begin to manufacture these products themselves, exporting mature products to the innovating country.

The difference across countries with respect to their ability to catch up are as follows. Leaders in that race, generally MEs, of which Japan is the best example, are not only absorbing technologies but also upgrading them. Thus, the distance between an innovating country (originally the United States) and the leaders catching up decreases as they move up the technological ladder. The latter display greater demand for new products than laggards in the race and are already able to manufacture them at the stage of standardising

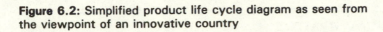

Figure 6.2: Simplified product life cycle diagram as seen from the viewpoint of an innovative country

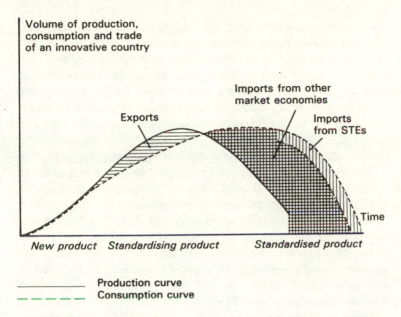

Volume of production, consumption and trade of an innovative country

Imports from other market economies

Exports

Imports from STEs

Time

New product   Standardising product   Standardised product

——————— Production curve
— — — — — Consumption curve

or still new products. In fact, some of these countries become innovating countries in their own right, launching new products that pass through life cycles of their own.

Laggards, including all STEs, are sooner or later able to absorb new technologies but are unable to move any further. Thus, they continually stay at the final stage of the cycle, i.e. they manufacture these products when they are mature and they do not move up the ladder (or, if they do, they progress a notch or two and then fall back to their earlier place or lower). Given the system-specific problems of technology absorption, whether of domestic or imported origin, they begin to manufacture and export these products in the later part of the final phase of the product life cycle, as graphically displayed in Figure 6.2. As with the least qualified on the labour market which, according to the well-known saying, are the last to be hired and the first to be fired, STEs as marginal suppliers of manufactures on the world market go through similar cycles; and if they sometimes happen to stay in the game longer, it is due to their willingness to sell at a loss to earn badly needed convertible currency (with obvious effects for the living standards of their citizens).

6.4. PAYING MORE AND EARNING LESS: COSTS OF A FAILED STRATEGY

There is not much consistent and comparable data, or even many analytical studies using such data, with respect to the costs of the catching-up strategy. Besides the usual paucity of published data on most STEs, the problem is compounded by the near impossibility of drawing even an approximate balance-sheet for such a strategy under the specific conditions of central planning. Firstly, domestic currency costs cannot be added to convertible currency costs, and secondly, these costs cannot always be identified in the case of the second- and third-order consequences of technology imports.

The latter also makes it nearly impossible to draw a balance sheet limited to convertible currency alone. To be more precise, we refer to Table 6.3, showing the costs of new licences and licence-related imports of goods by Czechoslovakia and Poland in the 1970s. However, the latter are the *direct* costs of a licensee, i.e. the costs of buying machinery and equipment needed to produce licensed products or apply licensed technology and the cost of raw material and intermediate inputs to licensed products not produced domestically (or in other STEs).

However, these imports are in the case of STEs only a part of the total licence-related imports and may even be a small part at that. Licensed products usually set higher requirements for domestic subcontractors and suppliers of inputs. Higher requirements are then set for subsubcontractors, and the resultant ripple effect may have several rounds. It should be remembered that if enterprises have little incentive to raise technological sophistication through licensing, there are literally none for their suppliers. The latter bear only costs (extra effort to produce better materials, parts, etc., with all the attendant threats to plan implementation-related premiums and bonuses) and reap no accompanying benefits (extra bonuses, trips abroad to licensors' plants) which sweeten the bitter pill of having to go beyond the routine.

Their defensive actions bring about various outcomes that invariably raise convertible currency costs and/or lower respective earnings. Thus, for example, if suppliers in a command economy cannot refuse supplying the licensee, they themselves apply for imports of machinery and equipment and/or better quality materials with which to produce the required inputs to licence-based products. Now if they get what they asked for, *indirect* licence-related imports (unaccounted for in analysing inward licensing by STEs) increase

Table 6.3: The Costs of New Licences Purchased and Direct Licence-Related Imports for Czechoslovakia (in millions of crowns)[a] and for Poland (in millions of *deviza zloty*)[b]

	Czechoslovakia			Poland		
	New licences purchased	Direct licence-related imports	3 : 2	New licences purchased	Direct licence-related imports	6 : 5
1	2	3	4	5	6	7
1970	93.3	261.5	2.8	6.6	—	—
1971	—	—	—	200.0	500.0[c]	2.5
1972	153.3	—	—	174.5	700.0[c]	4.0
1973	15.4	—	—	193.4	953.0	4.9
1974	37.7	—	—	400.0	1565.0	3.9
1975	36.3	738.2	20.4	491.0	2091.0	4.3
1976	87.8	1503.4	17.1	532.7	2659.0	5.0
1977	114.9	782.7	6.8	57.3	3185.0	55.6
1978	68.2	419.0	6.1	100.7	2196.0	21.8
1979	44.5	619.7	13.9	(182.6)[d]	2710.0	14.8
1980	67.0	1023.7	15.3	176.3	2165.0	12.3
1981	21.7	450.0	20.7	—	—	—
Total	440.4	5536.7	12.6	2152.3	1872.4	8.7
	(1975–81)			(1971–80)		

Notes: a. US $1 was equal to 4 Polish *deviza zlotys* up to 1970, 3.68 in 1972, 3.32 in 1973–8, 3.09 in 1979 and 3.06 *deviza zlotys* in 1980.
      b. US $1 was equal to 7.20 Czechoslovak crowns up to 1971, 6.6 in 1972, 5.86 in 1973–4, 5.70 in 1975, 5.58 in 1976, 5.77 in 1977, 5.43 in 1978, 5.32 in 1979, 5.38 in 1980, and 5.89 crowns in 1981.
      c. Estimated by Monkiewicz (1983).
      d. Estimated from *Życie Gospodarcze*, nos. 16 and 21, 1980, and Monkiewicz (1983).
Sources: Costs from Levcik and Skolka (1984), Monkiewicz (1983), and the journal quoted above; exchange rates from statistical yearbooks.

and so do convertible currency costs. If they do not, they do their 'average' (rather than their best . . .) to turn out the required inputs with the existing equipment and materials. Consequently, the quality of the licensed product declines, exports fetch a lower per unit price or even become unsaleable, and convertible currency earnings fall. Again, the same may be the case of subcontractors. Yet another — and no less costly — outcome is when no domestic subcontractor can be found for some inputs and they have to be purchased abroad (nine times out of ten in the West),[31] over and above the originally planned imports.

Various Hungarian and Polish sources stress the high import intensity of licence-related output in general and its export-oriented part in particular (Poznanski (1979), Juhasz (undated), Monkiewicz (1983), Dezsenyi-Gueuliette (1983)). This is the outcome of the impact of system-specific features upon import intensity. A high import-intensity cannot be inferred, however, from direct licence-related imports of goods. In Poland between 1971 and 1980, for example, these imports were equal to over 18.7 billion *deviza zlotys* (about US$ 5½ billion). This represented 4.7 per cent of total Polish imports for the period in question and almost 12 per cent of imports from the West. It was much less for Czechoslovakia over the period 1975–81, where direct licence-related imports were equal to over 5½ billion crowns (about US$0.8 billion) — that is, as little as 1.1 per cent of total Czechoslovak imports and about 3.5 per cent of imports from the West. Nonetheless, if total, direct *and* indirect (the latter being unknown but considerable) licence-related imports are taken into consideration, the convertible currency burden may turn out to be considerable.

The burden is additionally large, given the final product fascination — to use Bognar's (1978) term — of STEs. In the context of technology imports, this fascination reveals itself through a relatively larger share of final products in total licence purchases. In MEs, inward-licensing is a microeconomic endeavour based on market considerations, while in STEs it is primarily a macroeconomic one, at least as far as the choice of industry and product is concerned. Moreover, since the matter of prestige weighs heavily upon the minds of central planners and their political masters, the choice of a product may be based upon its role as a status symbol, i.e. a symbol of the achieved level of economic development.[32] However, since the twofold underspecialisation of STEs (see Chapter 3) makes them less efficient than the economic development indicator (GNP *per capita*) would suggest, they usually encounter greater problems in absorbing the technology than MEs at a comparable level of development. Subsequently, they have to import a lot more investment goods, materials, parts, etc. than originally envisaged to produce so wide a range of licence-based products.

Since the development pattern of STEs based upon the extreme variant of the import substitution strategy generally requires high and rising levels of imports (see Chapter 5, section 5.1), the catching-up strategy puts an additional — and often quite heavy — burden upon STEs' performance in this respect. It may have contributed to the rising overall import intensity of STEs. The data for Czechoslovakia, Hungary and Poland in Table 6.4 predominantly

Table 6.4: Intermediate Imports as a percentage of final outputs in Czechoslovakia, Hungary and Poland, 1960–80

	Czechoslovakia	Hungary	Poland
1960	—	11.7	11.6
1965	16.3[a]	16.6	13.6
1970	—	19.5	15.1
1971	—	21.3	15.4
1972	—	20.1	15.9
1973	17.7	20.5	17.6
1974	—	27.2	17.7
1975	—	27.6	17.8
1976	—	23.4[b]	18.3
1977	21.2	—	17.2
1978	—	—	17.2
1979	—	—	17.6
1980	—	26.8	17.4

Notes: a. 1967.
    b. Change of accounting principles.
Sources: Orlicek (1980) for Czechoslovakia; Conference on Input–Output Methods and Applications, Heviz, Hungary (1981) for Hungary; and Wojciechowski (1981) for Poland.

indicate the accelerating import intensity in the 1970s (as well as attempts to stem the tide somewhat at the end of the decade).

Now, not only were the convertible currency costs of licence-based output larger in reality than those calculated on the basis of direct licence-based imports, but convertible currency earnings from export of licensed products in the West were also smaller than planned. Such an outcome was only to be expected on the basis of our considerations in sections 6.2 and 6.3. On the one hand, a very long absorption period delayed STEs' entry into the world market with licence-based products; and on the other, weak or non-existent technology upgrading activities reduced the period in which they were able to recoup the convertible currency costs of licensing deals, i.e. until unchanging products ended their life cycle on the world market.[33]

In reality the situation was even worse. The low reliability of domestic subcontractors (referred to frequently in the literature on the subject — see, for example, Dorosz (1979), Poznanski (1979), Juhasz (undated), Wojciechowski (1981), Dezsenyi-Gueuliette (1983), Monkiewicz (1983) and Kardos (1985) generated higher demand for last minute imports, or, if these could not be obtained, small-scale (and high-cost!) production of some inputs at the licensee's enterprise. Delivery delays resulted in earnings-reducing fines or dissolved contracts. No less (if not more) costly was the reduced willingness of Western partners in complex licensing deals to continue to market STE-produced goods beyond the period stipulated in the buy-back arrangements. Alternatively, last minute imports affected the convertible currency balance on the other side of the ledger. Both convertible currency and the overall balance sheet suffered in such cases.

Thus, intermediate imports for licence-based exports were rising faster than exports of licensed products. Again, as in the case of the rising overall import intensity of STEs, intermediate imports for exports of licensed products became an additional burden put upon the already-rising import intensity of exports of STEs (for an explanation of the latter, see Chapter 5). Certain data for Hungary indicate that imports for export purposes have been rising faster than exports themselves, thus reducing net export earnings. If Hungarian exports, calculated at current prices, rose by 179 per cent between 1970 and 1979, then imports required for exports rose by 239 per cent, reducing the net earnings from 75 to 69 per cent of total export earnings. Significantly, imported inputs rose faster than exports, both with respect to exports to the world market and to other STEs (see *Figyelo*, 6 January 1982).

This is a point often stressed by Hungarian economists who underline the fact that rouble exports need not only more rouble imports but more dollar imports. The point is usually missed by Western analysts who see the more obvious subsidised oil prices (see in particular Marrese and Vanous, 1983) but do not see the flow of convertible currencies embodied in Western inputs to Eastern manufactures exported predominantly to the Soviet Union and, to a much smaller extent, to other smaller STEs. By East European standards, these costs are anything but small. According to the present author's assessments, dollar inputs might have cost as much as US$350–500 million annually for Hungarian rouble exports to the Soviet Union alone. It is obvious that exports of licensed products to other STEs contributed to the process described above and, conversely, increased licence-related convertible currency imports.

The foregoing showed the difference between what may be called a normal pattern of absorption of imported technology and that of STEs. While most MEs spend much more on licences relative to R and D and GDP expenditures, their licence-related imports are much smaller. Not constrained by the quality gap (see Chapter 1, section 1.5 and Chapter 5, section 5.3), the latter countries import only those inputs whose domestic production is more costly than imports.

Thus, STEs, with their high convertible currency (and total) costs of inward licensing, are destined to remain low-level users of licences as a means of raising the level of technological sophistication of their products.

Thus, comments about Poland in the 1970s having tried to absorb *too much* imported technology made by Hanson (1982) and Fallenbuchl (1983) are put in the proper framework. For system-specifically constrained Poland, the level of technology imports in the decade of the 1970s, although still much lower relative to R and D and GDP expenditures than in MEs, generated too great a level of disturbance due to the high domestic costs of absorption and an adverse impact upon the foreign trade balance.

It is within the same framework that mistakes in the choice of imported technology should be considered. Mistaken choice in itself is a highly ambiguous notion. Only when related to the environment for technical change as determined by the level of economic development and/or system-specific features do mistaken choices gain in relevance. Now only in very rare cases did Poland buy technology that remained at the frontiers of the technological advances of the day. (The same was true with respect to other STEs as well). Accordingly, development level-determined mistakes were also very rare. It is, then, the error of not taking into account the adverse effects of system-specific features upon technical change through licensing which formed the bulk of the mistaken choices.

Poland's performance with respect to the absorption of licence-based technology was not shown to be different from that of other STEs for which some data exist (see above, section 6.2). Interestingly, even the level of technology imports by Poland was not much higher than that of Hungary, whether measured in relation to R and D expenditures or to other indicators (cf. Monkiewicz (1983) and Kardos (1985)). What mattered was that Poland tied licensed imports with the purchase of turn-key plants and other large-scale investment projects much more often than Hungary (and other smaller STEs). It was these overambitious plans that affected both internal and external equilibria in Poland to a larger extent than elsewhere.

Furthermore, licence-related convertible currency costs exceeded licence-related earnings. Data for Poland presented in Monkiewicz (1983), even if they refer to an extreme case, are worth quoting in this respect. If only direct licence-related imports[34] are taken into account, total export earnings from licence-based products[35] were lower for the whole 1971–80 period than licence-related imports. It

197

should also be noted that only a part of these exports went to the convertible currency area. The remainder (in many cases more than half of the total) went to other STEs. Monkiewicz estimates that convertible currency exports covered as little as 55 per cent of the direct licence-related imports. Adding the indirect licence-related imports would make the picture radically worse.

Again, according to Monkiewicz, none of the 50 licence-related projects checked on by the Comptroller's Office[36] in 1980 yielded planned production and financial effects. It is the latter result that speaks eloquently about the failure of the catching-up strategy with respect to STEs' ability to raise significantly the export of manufactured products through technology and related capital imports. Not only did licensed production not become a bigger convertible currency earner, but it was not in most cases able to earn the amount of convertible currencies spent on royalties, as well as on licence-related machinery and inputs. In addition, it is not only Poland that was unsuccessful in this respect. The literature on Hungary also refers to higher than planned costs and lower than planned earnings realised on the world market (see, for example, Dezsenyi-Gueuliette (1983) and Kardos (1985)). The overall performance of STEs in manufactured exports to MEs also allows the judgement to be extended to all countries in question.

Graphically, a convertible currency flow pattern for a licensing deal for an STE enterprise, i.e. at the microeconomic level, can be contrasted with that of textbook (Lowe and Crawford, 1984) cash-flow patterns under an own R and D-based product strategy and licensing deal-based strategy for an ME enterprise (see Figure 6.3). Comparability is, however, limited by the non-additive character of domestic currency and convertible currency flows in all STEs. Given the distorted domestic relative prices and weak or non-existent linkage between domestic and world market prices, total cash flow under central planning (whether modified or not) is impossible to calculate.

Thus, only convertible currency flow was taken into account in the stylised STE enterprise. The stylised STE enterprise curve shows higher costs of absorption than an ME enterprise choosing the same licensing option at the beginning of the period as well as an increase in convertible currency imports towards the end of the product life cycle due to the convertible currency costs of maintenance and parts for the ageing imported equipment. It may be safely assumed that overall cash flow was also much less advantageous in the case of an STE enterprise, since both domestic costs were

Figure 6.3: Stylised cash flow of a licensed product (continuous line) or own R and D-based product (broken line) in an ME firm, and convertible currency flow of a licensed product at an STE enterprise level (cash flow patterns for an ME firm taken from Lowe and Crawford, 1984)

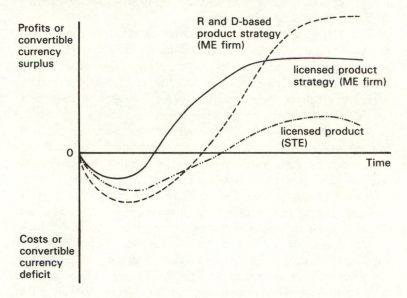

usually higher than planned and high marginal costs of foreign exchange at least suggested lower profits. Factors and goods price distortions make it impossible to draw a precise balance.

With the support from licence-based production being rather weak, the share of six smaller STEs in Western imports of manufactures continued to shrink in the 1970s, although at a slower rate than in the period 1965–70: 1965 — 1.56 per cent, 1970 — 1.48 per cent, and 1981 — 1.46 per cent. In addition, the USSR share fell in both periods according to the same pattern: 1965 — 0.84 per cent, 1970 — 0.56 per cent, and 1981 — 0.51 per cent. However, there has been a difference within the 1970–81 period between STEs that used licensing deals more intensively (Hungary, Poland, Romania and the Soviet Union) and the remaining ones. STEs belonging to the first group increased their shares between 1970 and 1977, but lost all or part of the gains in the second part, i.e. 1977–81, of the period. It may be assumed that as long as imported inputs were flowing in demanded quantities to STEs, the exportability of certain products, among them also licence-based ones, was high enough to ensure a

199

slight increase in their shares. However, the import reductions that began in the late 1970s decreased the flow of high quality and sophisticated inputs from the West and — accordingly — also the exportability of STE products to the West.[37] In contrast to the foregoing, less intensive users of licensing deals found their shares shrinking throughout the period.

The difference between the patterns suggests that increases in exports are dependent upon preceding increases in imports; and if Hungarian experience is any guide (see above), they depend upon *faster* increases in imports. It means that the price of exporting manufactures to the West is on the increase. No catching-up process can be inferred from such a performance.

Even more telling is the case of engineering exports. Engineering industries received the lion's share of licences bought by East European countries: from over one-half to two-thirds of the number of licences (and even more in terms of royalty payments).[38] Yet in spite of that infusion, STEs' share in Western engineering imports fell from 1.4 per cent in 1970 to 1.0 per cent in 1983, while at the same time less developed countries increased their share from 1.4 to 7.7 per cent, that is, more than five times. The decline cannot be explained, then, by the lower economic growth of importing countries or other exogenous barriers to STE export expansion.

What is more, STEs were not only selling less to the West at the end of the period in question, but were also *selling for less*. According to Table 5.3 (see Chapter 5), all exported engineering products obtained on the EEC market by seven STEs together were on average equal to 45 per cent of the same price obtained by Western MEs in 1970, but only 35 per cent in 1980.

So much for the expected improved export performance. Nor were other STEs' expectations fulfilled — i.e. those of higher economic growth rates and higher efficiency levels which would both decrease the income-level gap relative to the West and allow STEs to achieve the long-desired 'intensive' stage of economic growth. Economic growth did to some extent accelerate, fuelled by capital (and technology) imports, but it was a short-term phenomenon. When capital began to dry up and STEs, already more unstable due to their greater technology absorption efforts, had to cut imports, economic growth decelerated sharply to the lowest levels in the whole history of the Soviet economic system.[39]

It is more difficult to evaluate changes in the distance between STEs and Western MEs with respect to such an elusive concept as efficiency. There has been some scattered evidence that imported technologies did close the technological gap somewhat: for example, a Hungarian source (Juhasz, undated) puts the gains at 2–3 years. It should be remembered, however, that these were *temporary* gains. When the inflow of imported technology slowed down towards the end of the 1970s, the technological gap may have begun to increase again, given the weak upgrading capabilities of STEs (see above, section 6.3). The distance may now be even greater than it was before the start of the catching-up strategy. Besides, a decreased technological distance is not always translated into a decreased *economic* distance, especially in the case of STEs. The high domestic and import costs of technology absorption and lower prices obtained for licence-based products on the world market underline the difference.

More rigorously, my own studies on investment cycles under central planning (see Chapter 1, sections 1.3 and 1.4 in the first part of the study) showed, however, an *increasing* dependence of STEs' economic growth upon capital inputs. The addition of the recent 1978–83 period to the earlier 1961–77 period increased the coefficient of determination in the regressions of net material product growth rates on investment growth rates in all seven STEs. Other studies show more directly increasing capital/output ratios (see in particular the UN ECE studies in the recent *Economic surveys of Europe*). Consequently, an 'intensive' stage of economic growth is even further away than in the past. The catching-up strategy has failed here as well.

If technology-imports coupled with capital imports have failed, is the much stressed 'technical progress' through domestic and/or pooled COMECON resources able to change matters for the better? I have already pointed to the hostile environment to technical change at the macro and micro levels under central planning, regardless of the source of technology. Reversing the Holzman dictum, without fundamental changes in the Soviet system, bad imitators are bound to remain bad innovators.

NOTES

1. In itself some 4–5 per cent of world trade at the time (now somewhat less).
2. The expansion of Soviet industry in the 1930s was heavily based upon imported technology (see, for example, Köves, 1976).
3. Czechoslovakia even went through regular recession with negative

growth rates. The fact that it happened at the time of accelerated economic growth in the West added insult to injury in this case.

4. I do not intend to pursue here the fascinating subject of why, how, and when economic reforms in STEs fail. It is so important that it deserves separate treatment. Nonetheless, it is worth noting that the reforms are stopped much before they are able to threaten the system. At their last stage, however, i.e. one during which the trend is (often sharply) reversed, they do threaten the rules of distribution of incomes and goods based upon loyalty to political masters. The above points to the need to look more closely not only at the 'whys' and 'hows', but also at the 'whens', since it is the much neglected 'whens' that suggest some important 'whys' for the failure.

5. The third gap (i.e. the innovation gap) was a specific 'property' of STEs since the type of disincentives to it are in most respects unique.

6. And we know already from Part One, the consumer goods market has continually been in the state of excess demand.

7. Or — contrary to fact — assumed to exist.

8. It is ironic that more sophisticated apologetics in scholarly guise began to appear only later, when the failure of the policy they were supposed to underpin had already become visible, i.e. toward the end of the 1970s.

9. STE statistics show, for example, the constantly falling relative earnings of engineers compared with those of industrial workers for the Soviet Union and Poland (the ratio is barely above 1.0 for the former and already below it for the latter) or continuous equality of both for the GDR and Bulgaria. As far as underappreciation is concerned, a hostile environment for creativity, professional competence and knowledge in Yugoslavia, well described in Cengic (1984), applies very well to typical STEs.

10. To soften their future resistance to its application by sharing the royalties with them.

11. This was the case of Hungary in 1971–5 (see Nyers, 1977) and Poland in 1971–80 (Monkiewicz, 1983).

12. Another funny story heard by this author in the late 1970s concerns an eager young man who was accidentally sent to India (his superiors were either ill or travelling to more exciting places) to continue negotiations on a deal. The young man went there, cleared minor ambiguities and concluded the deal. Having returned to Warsaw, very proud of himself, he was met with a frosty reception by his superiors. Later, his colleagues explained that he killed a goose laying golden eggs (meaning trips abroad with per diems in convertible currencies). His position became so unbearable that he decided to quit the job.

13. Information learned at the Graduate School of Business, New York University in 1978.

14. At least two years are mentioned as a norm in an assessment by *Business International: Eastern Europe*, 31 October 1975.

15. Even excluding the cases of possible corruption.

16. The long lead times needed to include them in the plan, the unwillingness of would-be suppliers to engage in non-routine production, and delays in deliveries after the producer has been found (since it is for him the least important part of his production plan).

17. They have played a much greater role in the case of Poland due to the runaway investment boom (see Monkiewicz, 1983). However, *Business*

International: Eastern Europe, 2 May 1975, quoted a Czechoslovak State Bank survey showing that out of 16 billion crowns' worth of imported machinery, some 6 billion had not as yet been installed.

18. Although it is difficult to estimate to what extent they were the consequence of the larger size of too many projects that entailed massive capital infusion (see Zaleski and Wienert, 1980), i.e. were policy- rather than system-specific weaknesses.

19. The extent of delays was not mentioned, however. See the article by Isajew, the first deputy of the Soviet Gosplan (*Planovoye Khozyaistvo*, no. 9, 1973).

20. For examples from Poland, see Monkiewicz (1983).

21. An intermediate option has sometimes been chosen, i.e. that of dual quality, with imported inputs used only for exports (or even for Western exports only), while inferior domestic inputs are used for the domestic market . . .

22. Estimates for Poland for the 1960s show longer periods for reaching target capacities (Monkiewicz, 1983). None are given for the 1970s.

23. In another place, Juhasz (undated) writes, however, on the average time-lag of ten years for imported know-how based products.

24. With outliers excluded.

25. At best they have incentives marginally to reduce organisational slack to improve performance to some extent, to exceed planned output targets when all else (i.e. increases in input volume, imaginative reporting, etc.) fails.

26. In the aforementioned Czechoslovak survey of 1976 (Levcik and Skolka, 1984), 65 per cent of surveyed enterprise managers regarded their output profile as remaining stable for more than five years.

27. See, for example, the classic study of Booz, Allen and Hamilton, Inc. (1965).

28. The Polish analyst Balcerowicz (1984) applies the same approach to determine what he calls the innovative dynamism of a national economy.

29. For example, Gomulka (1982) sees the STEs as being handicapped by the Soviet system to the extent that they are unable to make any further significant gains in decreasing the gap, and, without the change in the system, have to accept the gap as more or less permanent. With respect to the past, Davies (1977) maintained that there was no evidence of a decrease in the technological gap between the Soviet Union and the West in the preceding 15–20 years.

30. There is more on this in Winiecki (1985b).

31. See, for example, Monkiewicz (1983) for the case of Poland.

32. It is in this sense that Wiles's (1977) remark on an STE as a technological Potemkin village may be understood.

33. Such products could and did continue to be sold on the closed domestic market or on the no less closed markets of other STEs, but their role as hard currency earners definitely ended.

34. Including licence royalties.

35. Including the value of licensed inputs in other exported products.

36. The Supreme Chamber of Control in Polish terminology.

37. All data after UN ECE, *Economic Bulletin for Europe* (1983). For more details, see Table 5.1 in the preceding chapter.

38. With respect to the former, various national and UN sources present enough data, while data in value terms are for Hungary (80 per cent for 1972–5; see Nyers, 1977).

39. The fact that the Soviet Union, whose terms of trade *improved* sharply in the 1973–82 period, experienced a similar pattern of deceleration suggests that other factors, those of long-term systemic decline, have also been at work.

Conclusion

What have we learned, then, from this study of distortions in the Soviet-type economies? What has this study added to existing knowledge on the subject? Generalising the arguments of the consecutive chapters of the book, the following conclusions seem to be most significant.

The first conclusion is that deviations from what is regarded as normal within the framework of Western economic rationality result in efficiency-reducing distortions, generating the type of output growth that to quite a large extent feeds upon itself, including the fruits of 'imaginative reporting' in output growth figures, and entailing an inordinate amount of plain waste. This study has concentrated on distortions in, and the resultant self-reinforcing distortionary pattern of, economic growth. At the same time, higher output growth figures, courtesy of imaginative reporting and usually treated as anecdotal, have been integrated systematically into the analytical framework of the book. Plain waste accompanying economic activity in STEs has only been referred to where necessary, since I regard it as a rather well recognised and described by-product of the Soviet system.

My second conclusion is that deviations which turn into distortions are almost exclusively system-specific. In some cases, the sources of distortions are supplemented, however, by policy-specific ones. Each type of source tends to reinforce rather then moderate the adverse impact of the other. The twofold underspecialisation of STEs is the most telling but not the only case of the mutually reinforcing impact of system- and policy-specific sources. It is the logic (or the illogic, as many — including this author — would have it) of the system that more often than not dictates policy choices.[1]

The third conclusion is that, given their common sources, distortions in the Soviet-type economy tend to be mutually interrelated. The Soviet system — the primordial source — affects most strongly the dynamics of these economies, i.e. the quantity and price changes (including hidden price changes). A new type of uncertainty and quality problem is an accompanying by-product of the distorted macroeconomics of central planning. However, as we have seen in Part Two, the dynamics directly distort output and employment structures in Eastern Europe, apart from those system- and policy-specific features that indirectly affect structures and their change over time through twofold underspecialisation. Distortions of the dynamics and structure adversely affect, in turn, the structure of exports and — more generally — the overall performance of STEs on world markets. On the feedback principle, the dead weight of the distorted structure affects the macroeconomic balance as well.

My fourth conclusion is that within the framework of the system in question and the pursued industrialisation strategy, it is the industrial sector that not only becomes the most distorted sphere, but also exerts a distortionary influence upon other sectors, especially services. Compared with the well-recognised and described distortions of the collectivised agricultural sector in STEs, distortions in the industrial sector of these countries have a much stronger impact upon the performance of all sectors and areas of economic activity. In addition, the latter affect first and foremost the structure of output. The term 'growth feeding upon itself' — another well-recognised feature of the Soviet system — is inseparable from the distortionary growth of the industrial sector. Moreover, distortions in collectivised agriculture — although a systemic constant, so to speak — tend to decrease to some extent over time. The same cannot be said about distortions in industry that, although also present from the early days of central planning, tend to *increase* over time.[2]

This directly leads us to the fifth conclusion on the increasingly adverse consequences of the distortions analysed in this study. The evidence can be found in the book. A stronger association of economic growth with the very process of investing rather than with production from new capacity shows the increasingly distorted dynamics of the Soviet system; the increasingly inflated share of industry indicates a similar situation with respect to its structure; and the falling relative prices of exported manufactures and their shrinking shares in competitive Western markets stress directly or indirectly the same theme with respect to foreign trade performance. The said evidence supports theoretical considerations that explain, especially in parts Two and Three, why only increasing distortions are to be expected.

The sixth and final conclusion that the author found significant enough to be presented here is that increasing distortions are associated with higher levels of economic development (approximately equal to higher levels of GNP *per capita*). Since the higher the level of sophistication of products and industries, the greater are the distortions observed therein, it is easier after reading this book to answer the question as to why Czechoslovakia and East Germany were the main losers. The former is a clear-cut case of the impact of the system. One of the five leading heavy-industry centres in the world at the turn of the twentieth century, Czechoslovakia found its relative position constantly being eroded after the imposition of central planning. One after another West European country — countries that were either at the same or on a lower rung of the ladder, as far as GNP *per capita* is concerned — left Czechoslovakia behind with respect to competitive position at the international scale and, consequently, with regard to living standards internally. Austria, and more recently Italy, achieved this with respect to both,[3] and Spain and Ireland with respect to the former (and both are also in the process of bypassing it with respect to the latter). With the experience of the last half a dozen years, Czechoslovakia is clearly being left behind by the first wave of non-European competitors, with consequences for relative living standards at some point in the future.[4]

Next, the fact that the GDR as a separate state had greater adjustment difficulties than the Federal Republic could explain the reversal of the relative standards-of-living position between East and West Germany in the first 10–15 years after the war; but only system- and policy-specific features can explain why the gap in living standards has been on the increase since 1960. Moreover, as a prelude to this, the GDR's international competitive position has also been weakening.[5]

Now, shifting our focus of attention from conclusions on the past and present to their consequences for the future of STEs, it may safely be said that they augur badly for both the living standards of East European consumers and the traditional economic growth pattern preferred by central planners and their political masters. It is obvious that, given the preference of the ruling communist elites, living standards are the first to suffer. Their stagnation or decline has already been taking place for some time, as pointed out by many Western area specialists. I have also dealt elsewhere with its causes, symptoms and effects (see Winiecki, 1984c, 1986c). A joke circulating in Poland during the late Gierek era — 'When will it be better? It already was!' — is nowadays repeated all over Eastern Europe (and probably as far as Khabarovsk and Vladivostok . . .). It is highly probable that the modest living standards reached in STEs by the mid-1970s will long be remembered as a golden period in the history of the Soviet system.

However, and this is significant in the wider context as well, distortions in STEs are also going to affect increasingly the traditional economic growth pattern of these economies. Some Western specialists long ago questioned the ability of an STE to perform efficiently and produce an ever-widening range of more and more value-adding products along the lines of contemporary market economies (Kuznets, 1971b). However, they did not at the time question STEs' ability to grow along the lines of the traditional pattern of economic growth. The last 5–10 years have changed opinion in this respect, and the future is going to put even greater constraints upon the economic growth that does not bring much prosperity, but does need substantial resources to produce whatever is to be produced.

A first constraint pertains to investments.[6] Although investments in the 1981–5 FYP exceeded planned targets (plans provided for even greater cut-backs in some cases), absolute growth rates were either low or negative. With net material product officially growing within the 2–4 per cent range (and even less in reality),[7] no East European country could sustain for long yet another large-scale investment expansion. Any such programme would sharply curtail already stagnant or falling consumption and — on the feedback principle — result in either the eruption of discontent or a further decline in the quantity and quality of the labour supply (see Chapter 1, section 5, and Winiecki, 1985d).

A second constraint, pertaining to material inputs, is strongly associated with the first. Because of the lack of sufficiently large investments, STEs are unable to expand further the already inflated extractive industries subsector and, as a result, to expand the supply of domestic material inputs. On the other hand, their weak competitive position on world markets constrains their ability to obtain these inputs through foreign trade. The resource-rich Soviet Union is in a better situation as far as reserves are concerned, but in turn the constraint on investment expansion is stronger, given the relatively low accessibility of these reserves. At the same time, the falling prices of fuels and raw materials constrain somewhat the world market option. The foreign exchange constraint will not be as strong as in smaller STEs, however.

With little possibility of expanding the supply of factors rapidly (labour supply has also been increasing very slowly for some time) and material inputs, it is improvements in the *quality* of factors that may be seen as the main source of acceleration of economic growth — and of a much desired 'intensive' variety at that. However, neither the oft-repeated official declarations about the 'leading role of technical progress', nor even the increased resources allocated to R and D, are going to lead to much change. The role of technical change has been stressed in STEs since the early 1960s, without much being achieved, and these economies already allocate more resources to R and D, as well as employ more engineers than highly industrialised Western MEs.[8] Thus, a third constraint is not the inability to increase R and D inputs, but to increase their *outputs*, i.e. innovations, in a hostile systemic environment.

A fourth constraint concerns structural change. Rapid economic growth in the past was mainly the result of two major shifts: firstly, the shift from lower productivity agriculture to higher (although not impressively high) productivity industry; and secondly, an above average growth rate of heavy industries enjoying economies of scale. However, a further shift of labour away from agriculture is constrained by the inefficiency of collectivised agriculture, while the stage of structural change into which STEs have entered (or are trying to enter) is characterised by the shrinking share of scale economies-based industries and the expansion of those based upon flexibility, quality and innovation, i.e. characteristics antithetical to central planning.[9]

A fifth and final constraint relates to participation in the international division of labour — yet another qualitative source of accelerated economic growth. I explained in my earlier articles,[10] however, and above in Part Three, that STEs are system-specifically constrained in their ability to specialise in manufactured products. Data produced in Chapters 5 and 6 highlighted their deteriorating competitive position on the world market, while theoretical considerations suggest decreasing (and in some cases negative) returns from manufactured exports. At the same time, the increased share of commodities,[11] often exported in spite of existing domestic demand, points to *despecialisation* rather than specialisation as the direction of change.

Without fundamental reforms, the aforementioned constraints will affect all STEs, regardless of chosen policies and introduced marginal systemic modifications. The STEs are quite obviously off course, as far as their development path is concerned.[12] That feeling of being off course, being unable to find the right path, sometimes shows through the more or less cautious utterances of Hungarian and Polish scholars. However, that feeling spills over into the more popular media rather than scholarly presentations.

It is not, however, that the right answers to the questions of remedies are unknown, but that, given the interests of the ruling communist elites, they are largely disregarded. Obviously, the feeling of getting lost is not yet prevalent within the elites; and where it is so, the dislike of real change is — at least for the time being — stronger than the (simultaneously felt) necessity to reduce the increasingly strong impact of distortions upon the economy (and, let it be added, society). These conflicting desires may generate many scenarios aimed at keeping the past going a little longer. What is more, the probability that these scenarios will materialise in the not too distant future is much greater than that of scenarios of fundamental change. However, the former may either accelerate or slow down the decline somewhat, but they will be unable to change the course . . . But this is a different story, beyond the purview of this study (the author tried to outline both types of scenarios, as well as the determinants of fundamental change in Winiecki, 1986d).

NOTES

1. Although it is outside the purview of this book, post-1956 Hungary is the only country in Eastern Europe where persistent attempts were made to reduce the adverse impact of the Soviet system upon the economy and society. The system-specific modifications were only marginally (if at all) effective, but policy effects have been visible both before and after various phases of these modifications (see Winiecki, 1986d). Thus, for example, the ratio of growth rates of producer and consumer goods has been different in Hungary compared with other STEs (see Winiecki (1985c, 1986a) and Chapter 1, above).

2. It is worth noting that if some partial modifications of the system in the agricultural sector in STEs tend to be long-lasting, the same cannot be said about those in the industrial sector. No lasting change and commensurate lasting improvement in performance can be observed in STEs' industrial sector. This failure of industrial reforms, again outside the purview of the book, is linked to the role of the industrial sector in the control of society and the appropriation of benefits from the Soviet system by the ruling communist elites and their supporters (see Winiecki, 1986d).

3. To say nothing of Japan.

4. That point may not be far off in the case of Singapore.

5. Although at a slower rate than that of Czechoslovakia (see Chapter 5).

6. The following few pages are based on Winiecki (1986d).

7. See Part One of this study.

8. See Chapter 6, section 6.3, Table 6.2.

9. See Winiecki (1984c, 1986c) and above, Chapter 1, section 1.5 and Chapter 3, section 3.3.

10. See Winiecki (1983, 1985b).

11. See Chapter 5, section 5.4, Table 5.3.

12. The fact of being off the development path is even more striking if we extend the field to other walks of life, e.g. demographic trends with their rising infant mortality, sharp rise in the mortality of working men, and

overall decrease of life expectancy in most STEs. The same may be observed with respect to the degradation of the environment. Already now southern Poland, the Czech part of Czechoslovakia and East Germany together constitute what is the most polluted area in the world; and matters are quickly getting worse there and elsewhere in Eastern Europe (the six smaller countries of Eastern Europe already emit, for example, almost twice as much sulphur dioxide as the more industrialised EEC countries).

Bibliography

Allen, G. C. (1967) *The structure of industry in Britain: a study in economic change*, Longman, London

Arrow, K. (1962) 'The economic implications of learning by doing', *Review of Economic Studies*

Askanas, B. and Laski, K. (1985) 'Consumer prices and private consumption in Poland and Austria', *Journal of Comparative Economics*, vol. 9, no. 2

Asselain, J. C. (1981) 'Mythe ou réalité de l'epargne forcés dans les pays socialistes' in M. Lavigne (ed.), *Travail et monnaie en système socialiste* Economica, Paris

Aukrust, O. (1970) 'A model of the price and income distribution', *Review of Income and Wealth*, series 16, no. 1

Bajt, A. (1971) 'Investment cycles in European socialist economies: review article', *Journal of Economic Literature*, vol 9, no. 1

Balandynowicz, H.W., *et al.* (1983) 'An analysis of energy-capital and foreign-exchange intensity of fuels, raw materials and semi-manufactures exported and imported by Poland in the year 1980', mimeograph, prepared for the Institute of Economics, Polish Academy of Sciences (in Polish)

Balassa, B. (1978) 'Export incentives and export performance in developing countries: a comparative analysis, *Weltwirtschaftliches Archiv*, Band 114, Heft 1

——— *et al.* (1971) *The structure of protection in developing countries*, Johns Hopkins University Press, Baltimore

Balcerowicz, L. (1984) 'Economic system and technical innovation' in *Innovations in the national economy*, Polish Economists' Society, Bialystok, November, mimeo. (in Polish)

Barker, T.S. (1974) 'The variety hypothesis as an explanation of international trade', Seminar Paper, Institute for International Economic Studies, Stockholm University, no. 41

Barro, R. and Grossman, H. (1974) 'Suppressed inflation and the supply multiplier', *Review of Economic Studies*, vol. 41

Bauer, R. *et al.* (1972) *Political economy of socialism*, PWN Publishers, Warsaw (in Polish)

Bauer, T. (1978) 'Investment cycles in planned economies', *Acta Oeconomica*, vol. 21, no.3

Baumol, W.J. (1967) 'Macroeconomics of unbalanced growth: the anatomy of urban crisis', *American Economic Review*, vol. 57, no. 3

Beksiak, J. (1966) 'Inflation in a socialist economy', *Ekonomista*, no. 1 (in Polish)

——— (1982) *Policy change in the economy*, PWN Publishers, Warsaw (in Polish)

——— and Libura, U. (1974) *Equilibrium in the socialist economy*, PWN Publishers, Warsaw (in Polish)

Belovic, A. (1982) 'Trends in economic effectiveness of investments in

CMEA countries in the 1970s and at the beginning of the 1980s', *Politicka Ekonomie*, vol. 30 (in Slovakian)

Berliner, J.S. (1952) 'The informal organisation of the Soviet firm', *Quarterly Journal of Economics*, vol. 66

—— (1956) 'A problem in Soviet business administration', *Administrative Science Quarterly*

—— (1957) *Factory and manager in the USSR*, Harvard University Press, Cambridge, Mass.

—— (1976) *The innovation decision in Soviet industry*, MIT Press, Cambridge, Mass.

Bobek, J. (1975a) 'Change in the growth rate of production of consumer and investment goods in the economic development process', *Gospodarka Planowa*, no. 5 (in Polish)

—— (1975b) 'Similarities and differences in the growth rate of production of consumer and investment goods — over time and across countries', *Gospodarka Planowa*, no. 6 (in Polish)

Bognar, J. (1978) 'A new foreign trade strategy', *New Hungarian Quarterly*, vol. 19, no. 70

Bojarski, W. (1986) 'Energy constraint or doctrinal constraint?' *Życie Gospodarcze*, no. 1

Boot, P. (1983) 'Continuity and change in the planning system of the German Democratic Republic', *Soviet Studies*, vol. 35, no. 3

Booz, Allen and Hamilton, Inc. (1965) *The management of new products*, 4th edn, New York

Bornstein, M. (1976) 'Soviet price policy in the 1970s' in *Soviet economy in a new perspective. Studies prepared for the use of the Joint Economic Committee, US Congress*

Bozyk, P. and Guzek, M. (1976) 'The commodity structure of East–West trade' in F. Nemtschak (ed.), *World economy and East–West trade*, Springer Verlag, Vienna

Bozyk, P. and Wojciechowski, B. (1971) *Polish foreign trade 1945–1969*, PWE Publishers, Warsaw

Brody, A., (1983) 'About investment cycles and their attenuation', *Acta Oeconomica*, vol. 31, nos. 1–2

Brown, A.A. (1968) 'Towards a theory of centrally planned foreign trade' in A.A. Brown and E. Neuberger (eds), *International trade and central planning. An analysis of economic interactions*, University of California Press, Berkeley

Brzeski, A. (1979) 'Commerce Est–Ouest: un estimation des possibilités et des gains', *Revue d'Études Comparatives Est–Ouest*, vol. 10, no. 4

Burenstam-Linder, S. (1961) *An essay on trade and transformation*, Almqvist and Wiksells, Uppsala

Carlsson, B. (1981) 'The content of productivity growth in Swedish manufacturing', *Research Policy*, vol. 10, no. 4

Cengic, D. (1984) 'Social frame of innovation — the example of Yugoslavia', Third Workshop on Capitalist and Socialist Organisation, Helsinki, 29–31 August (mimeo)

Chenery, H.B. (1960) 'Patterns of industrial growth', *American Economic Review*, vol. 50, no. 3

—— (1977) 'Transitional growth and world industrialization' in B. Ohlin *et al.* (eds), *The international allocation of economic activity*, Macmillan, London

────── (1982) 'Industrialization and growth. The experience of large countries', *World Bank Staff Working Papers*, Washington, D.C., no. 539

────── and Syrquin, M. (1975) *Patterns of development 1950–1970*, Oxford University Press, London

Chenery, H.B. and Taylor, L. (1968) 'Development patterns: among countries and over time', *Review of Economics and Statistics*, vol. 50, no. 4

Chenery, H.B. and Watanabe, T. (1958) 'International comparisons of the structure of production', *Econometrica*, vol. 26, no. 4

Clarke, R.A. (1983) 'The study of Soviet-type economies: some trends and conclusions', *Soviet Studies*, vol. 35, no. 4

Csaba, L. (1983a) *Economic mechanism in the GDR and in Czechoslovakia*, Hungarian Scientific Council for World Economy, Budapest

────── (1983b) 'New features of the Hungarian economic mechanism in the mid-eighties', *New Hungarian Quarterly*, vol. 24, no. 90

────── (1985) 'Three studies on the CMEA', *Trends in the World Economy Series*, Budapest, no. 52

────── (undated) 'COMECON perspectives for the 1980s' (mimeo)

Csikos-Nagy, B. (1975) *Socialist price theory and price policy*, Akademiai Kiado, Budapest

────── and Racz, L. (1983) 'Rise of the price level and its factors in Hungary', *Acta Oeconomica*, vol. 30, no. 2

Culbertson, W.P., Jr. and Amacher, R.C. (1978) 'Inflation in the planned economies: some estimates for Eastern Europe', *Southern Economic Journal*, vol. 45

Cviic, C. (1977) 'COMECON and East-West Trade Policies' in *COMECON: Progress and prospects, Colloquium*, Directorate of Economic Affairs, NATO, Brussels (quoted in Zaleski and Wienert, 1980)

Dahlstedt, R. (1980) 'Cyclical fluctuation under central planning: an inquiry into the nature and causes of cyclical fluctuation in the Soviet economy', Helsinki School of Economics

Davies, R.W. (1977) 'The technological level of Soviet industry an overview' in R. Amman, J.M. Cooper and R.W. Davies (eds), *The Technological Level of Soviet Industry*, Yale University Press, New Haven

────── (1979) 'Economic planning in the USSR' in M. Bornstein (ed.), *Comparative economic systems: models and cases*, Irwin, Homewood, Ill.

Dezsenyi-Gueuliette, A. (1983) 'The utilization and assimilation in Hungary of advanced technology imported from the West', *Soviet Studies*, vol. 35, no. 2

Dmowski, Z., and Foltyński, Z. (1982) *Economics of foreign trade*, PWN Publishers, Warsaw (in Polish)

Dolejsi, B. (1979) 'Labor productivity, wages and the satisfaction of needs of the population, *Politicka Economie*, vol. 27, no. 6 (in Czech)

Dorosz, A. (1979) *Aims and scope of capital imports by a socialist country*, Main School of Planning and Statistics Publ., Warsaw (in Polish)

Drabek, Z. (undated) 'The Heckscher–Ohlin model and centrally-planned foreign trade', mimeograph, School of Economics, University College of Buckingham

Drechsler, L. *et al.* (1983) 'Production cooperations among CMEA countries: aims and realities', *Acta Oeconomica*, vol 30, no. 2

Drecin, J. (1971) 'Investment equilibrium: mechanisms of control and decisions', *Acta Oeconomica*, vol. 7, nos. 3–4

—— and Tar, J. (1978) 'Investment experience during the 1976–1980 Five-Year Plan in Hungary', *Acta Oeconomica*, vol. 21, no. 3

Drewnowski, J. (ed.) (1982) *Crisis in the East European Economy*, Croom Helm, London

Dreze, J. (1960) 'Quelques reflexions sereines sur l'adaptation de l'industrie Belge au Marché Commun', *Travaux de la Société Royale d'Économie Politique de Belgique*, no. 275

Dunajewski, H. (1979) 'Evaluation de la pression inflationniste en Pologne dans les années 1960–1975, *Revue d'Études Comparatives Est–Ouest*, vol. 10, no. 3

Dyker, D.A. (1982) 'A note on the investment ratio in Eastern Europe', *Soviet Studies*, vol. 34, no. 1

Edgren, G. *et al.* (1969) 'Wages, growth and the distribution of income', *Swedish Journal of Economics*, vol. 71, no. 3

Eliasson, G. (1976) *Business economic planning — theory, planning and comparison*, Wiley, New York

Ericson, J. (1983) 'A difficulty with the "Command" allocation mechanism', *Journal of Economic Theory*, vol. 31, no. 1

Fallenbuchl, Z. (1983) *East–West technology transfer. Study of Poland 1971–1980*, OECD, Paris

Farrel, J. (1975) 'Bank control of the wage fund in Poland: 1950–1970', *Soviet Studies*, vol. 27

Fei, J. *et al.* (1979) *Growth with equity: the case of Taiwan*, Oxford University Press, London

Fink, G (1981) *Preisverzerrungen und Unterschiede in der Produktionsstruktur zwischen Osterreich und Ungarn*, Springer Verlag, Wien–New York

Finucane, B.P. (1982) 'Foreign trade rationality in a centrally planned economy: an empirical study of Polish international trade, 1966–1977', unpublished doctoral dissertation, University of Pittsburgh

Frank, Ch.R., Jr., Kim, K.S. and Westphal, L.E. (1978) *Foreign trade regimes and economic development: South Korea*, Columbia University Press for NBER, New York

Gerstenfeld, A. (1977) *Innovation: a study of technological policy*, University Press of America, Washington, D.C.

Giersch, H. and Wolter, F. (1983) 'Towards an explanation of the productivity slowdown: an acceleration–deceleration hypothesis', *Economic Journal*, vol. 93

Goldmann, J. (1964) 'Fluctuations and trend in the rate of economic growth in some socialist countries, *Economics of Planning*, vol. 4, no. 2

—— and Kouba, K. (1969) *Economic Growth in Czechoslovakia*, Academia, Praha

Gomulka, S. (1982) 'The Polish crisis: will it spread and what will be the outcome?', in J. Drewnowski (ed.), *Crisis in the East European Economy*, Croom Helm, London

Greskovits, B. (1985) 'Some thoughts on Hungarian development policy', Paper elaborated for the Polish–Hungarian Round Table Seminar, Gardony, 23–5 April

Grossman, G. (1963) 'Notes for a theory of the command economy', *Soviet Studies*, vol. 15, no. 2

—— (1967) *Economic systems*, Englewood Cliffs, NJ

—— (1977) 'Price control, incentives, and innovation in the Soviet economy' in A. Abouchar (ed.), *The socialist price mechanism*, Duke University Press, Durham, NC

Guzek, M. (1975) *Methods of programming international specialization of production in CMEA*, PWE Publishers, Warsaw (in Polish)

—— (ed.) (1977) 'An operational model of CMEA international prices. An interpretation of a quantitative simulation', Papers of the Economic Academy, Poznań (in Polish)

Guzek, M. and Winiecki, J. (1980) 'Structural changes in the world economy and foreign economic policies: East and West'. Paper prepared for the Dutch–Polish seminar on structural change, Tilburg, 29 September–1 October (mimeo.)

Hanson, P. (1982) 'The end of import-led growth?', *Journal of Comparative Economics*, no. 2, June

Heller, P.S. (1976) 'Factor endowment change and comparative advantage. The case of Japan 1956–1969', *Review of Economics and Statistics*, vol. 58, no. 3

Holzman, F.D. (1956) 'Financing Soviet development' in *Capital formation and economic growth*, Princeton University Press (for NBER), Princeton

—— (1960) 'Soviet inflationary pressures, 1928–1957: causes and cures', *Quarterly Journal of Economics*, vol. 74, no. 2

—— (1974) *Foreign trade under central planning*, Harvard University Press, Cambridge, Mass.

—— (1979) 'Some systemic factors contributing to the convertible currency shortages of centrally planned economies', *American Economic Review*, vol. 69, no. 2

Howard, D.H. (1976) 'A note on hidden inflation in the Soviet Union', *Soviet Studies*, vol. 28, no. 4

Hrncir, M. *et al.* (1977) 'External economic relations in a planned economy', *Czechoslovak Economic Papers*, vol. 17

Jackson, M. (1986) 'Romania's debt crisis: its causes and consequences' in Joint Economic Committee, US Congress, *East European economies: growth in the 1980s, vol. 3*, Washington, DC

Jansen, P. (1982) *Das Inflationsproblem in der Zentralverwaltungswirtschaft*, Fischer Verlag, Stuttgart

Javorka, E. (1973) 'Prices and incomes, Budapest' (in Hungarian), quoted in *Abstracts of Hungarian Economic Literature*, vol. 3, no. 6

Juhasz, J. (undated) 'General questions of the adaptation of the most advanced technical achievements in Hungary, conclusions and recommendations', Budapest (mimeo.)

Jurek-Stepień, S. (1982) 'Characteristics of the engineering industry' in J.

Lisikiewicz (ed.), *Structural changes in industry*, PWE Publishers, Warsaw (in Polish)

Kalecki, M. (1969) *Introduction to the theory of growth in a socialist economy*, Blackwell, Oxford

Kardos, P. (1985) *Hungary targets for licensing*, LES Nouvelles, March

Karlik, E. and Kormnov, J. (1980) 'Concentration and specialisation of production in CMEA countries', *Voprosy Ekonomiki*, no. 8 (in Russian)

Katselineboigen, A. (1977) 'Disguised inflation in the Soviet Union' in A. Abouchar (ed.), *The socialist price mechanism*, Duke University Press, Durham

Kemme, D.M. and Winiecki, J. (1984) 'Disequilibrium in centrally planned economies', Working Papers in Economics, University of North Carolina at Greensboro, August (mimeo.)

Khachaturov, T.S. (1975) *The Soviet economy at the present stage of development*, Mysl Publishers, Moscow (in Russian)

—— (1979) 'Ways of increasing the effectiveness of investments', *Voprosy Ekonomiki*, no. 7 (in Russian)

Kindleberger, Ch. P. (1962) *Foreign trade and the national economy*, Yale University Press, New Haven

Klacek, J., Klaus V. (1970) 'Inflationary gap on the consumer goods market', *Czechoslovak Economic Papers*, vol. 12

Klaus, V. (1979) 'Irregularities in households' consumer expenditures in the 1970s', *Politicka Ekonomies*, no. 5 (in Czech)

Klvacova, E. (1982) 'Goal-oriented programmes of the development of science and the future structure of the Czechoslovak economy', *Politicka Ekonomie*, vol. 30, no. 9 (in Czech)

Konnik, J.J. (1963) *Course of political economy, vol. 2*, Ekonomizdat, Moscow (in Russian)

Kornai, J. (1971) *Anti-equilibrium*, North-Holland, Amsterdam

—— (1972) *Rush versus harmonic growth*, North-Holland, Amsterdam

—— (1979) 'Resource-constrained versus demand-constrained systems', *Econometrica*, vol. 47, no. 4

—— (1980) *Economics of shortage*, North-Holland, Amsterdam

—— (1982) *Growth, shortage and efficiency*, Blackwell, Oxford

Köves, A. (1976) 'Chapters from the history of East–West relations', *Acta Oeconomica*, vol. 17, no. 2

—— (1978) 'Socialist economy and world economy', *Acta Oeconomica*, vol. 21, no. 4

—— (1983) ' "Implicit subsidies" and some issues of economic relations within the CMEA (Remarks on analyses made by Michael Marrese and Jan Vanous)', *Acta Oeconomica*, vol. 31, nos. 1–2

Kowalska, R., Michalski, R. and Rosati, D. (1977) *Planning and forecasting of foreign trade*, SGPiS, Warsaw (in Polish)

Krawczyk, K. (ed.) (1981) *Economic reforms: proposals, tendencies, main strands of discussion*, PWE Publishers, Warsaw (in Polish)

Krencik, W. (1959) 'The impact of assortment change policies on the income of population', *Studia Ekonomiczne*, vol. 1 (in Polish)

Krueger, A.O. (1977) 'Growth, distortions, and patterns of trade among many countries', *Princeton Studies in International Finance*, Princeton University, no. 40

────── (1982) 'Comparative advantage and development policy twenty years later', *Working Paper, Industrial Institute for Economic and Social Research*, Stockholm, no. 65

Kucharski, M. (1969) *Money, national income, growth proportions*, PWN Publishers, Warsaw (in Polish)

────── (1983) 'Proportions, efficiency, incomes, equilibrium, part I and II; *Zycie Gospodarcze*, nos. 11 and 12 (in Polish)

Kurowski, L. (1981) 'International competitiveness of a national economy and domestic decision-making' in J. Sołdaczuk (ed.), *Economic management. Essays in honour of the memory of Professor Paweł Sulmicki*, PWE, Warsaw (in Polish)

Kuznets, S. (1930) *Secular movements in production and prices*, Houghton Miffin, Boston

────── (1966) *Modern economic growth: rate, structure and spread*, Yale University Press, New Haven

────── (1971a) *Economic growth of nations. Total output and production structure*, Harvard University Press, Cambridge, Mass.

────── (1971b) 'Notes on stage of economic growth as a system determinant' in A. Eckstein (ed.), *Comparison of economic systems. Theoretical and methodological approaches*, University of California Press, Berkeley

Laski, K. (1979) 'The problems of inflation in socialist countries', *Eastern European Economics*, vol. 17, no. 4

Leontief, W. (1954) 'Domestic production and foreign trade: the American capital position re-examined', *Economia Internazionale*, vol. 7

Levcik, F. and Skolka, J. (1984) *East–West technology transfer. Study of Czechoslovakia*, OECD, Paris

Libura, U. (1979) *Consumption and the explanation of the production possibilities in a socialist economy*, PWN Publishers, Warsaw (in Polish)

Lipowski, A. (1981) 'Limitations of price controls', *Oeconomica Polona*, no. 2

Little, I.D. *et al.* (1970) *Industry and trade in some developing countries. A comparative study*, Oxford University Press, London

Lokshin, R. (1981) 'Value and structure of the retail trade', *Voprosy Ekonomiki*, no. 10 (in Russian)

Lowe, J. and Crawford, N. (1984) *Innovation and technology transfer for the growing firm*, Pergamon Press, Oxford

Lundberg, E. (1961) *Productivity and profitability*, SNS Publishers, Stockholm (in Swedish)

McAuley, A. (1985) *Les déterminants du taux de change dans une économie planifiée. Un rapport preparé pour le Congrès International des economistes de langue française*, Budapest 27–9 mai

Maciejewski W. and Zajchowski, J. (1982) 'Problems in analysing plan execution' in W. Maciejewski (ed.), *Informational problems of planning*, PWE Publishers, Warsaw (in Polish)

Maizels, A. (1963) *Industrial growth and world trade*, Cambridge University Press, Cambridge

Major, I. (1983) 'Tensions in transportation and the development level of transport in some socialist countries', *Acta Oeconomica*, vol. 30, no. 2

Marciniak, S. (1970) *Structure of production and the dynamics of growth*, PWN Publishers, Warsaw (in Polish)
—— (1984) 'Economic structure of Poland (directions and methods of change)', Paper presented at the conference on 'Criteria, Methods of Control, and Directions of Structural Change', Warsaw (in Polish)

Marrese, M. and Vanous, J. (1983) *Soviet subsidization of trade with Eastern Europe: a Soviet perspective*, University of California, Berkeley

Monkiewicz, J. (1983) *Licences: Myths and the reality*, Trade Unions Publishers, Warsaw (in Polish)

Mosoczy, R. (1983) 'Possibilities and trends in the development of international cooperation in the 1980s', *Acta Oeconomica*, vol. 30, nos. 3–4

Nove, A. (1969) *An economic history of the USSR*, Allan Lane, London
—— (1977) *The Soviet economic system*, Allan Lane, London
—— (1982) 'Soviet economic performance: a comment on Wiles and Ellman' in J. Drewnowski (ed.), *Crisis in the East European economy*, Croom Helm, London
—— (1985) 'A note on errors and their causes', *Soviet Studies*, vol. 37, no. 2

Nyers, J. (1977) 'Foreign licenses and know-hows in Hungary 1971–1975', *Acta Oeconomica*, vol. 18, no. 2

OECD (1980) *East–West trade in chemicals* (Paris)

Ofer, G. (1973) *The service sector in Soviet economic growth. A comparative study*, Harvard University Press, Cambridge, Mass.

Ohlin, B. *et al.* (eds) (1977) *The International Allocation of Economic Activity*, Macmillan, London

Okólski, M. (forthcoming) *Modernization and reproduction of the population: the Polish syndrome*, KiW Publishers, Warsaw
—— and Winiecki, J. (1984) 'Structural change and adaptation: on reintegrating planned economies into the world economies', *Konjunkturpolitik*, vol. 30, nos. 2–3

Olechowski, A. and Yeats, A. (undated) 'An analysis of the revealed comparative advantage of the socialist countries of Europe: implications for current economic policies and future trading patterns', Geneva (mimeo)

Orlicek, Z. (1980) 'Utilisation of imports in the national economy and particularly in export-oriented production (with illustrations from the Czechoslovak economy)', *Politicka Ekonomie*, vol. 28, no. 11 (in Czech)

Pajestka, J. (1975) *Determinants of progress. Factors and interdependencies of a country's socio-economic development*, PWE, Warsaw (in Polish)

Paretti, V. and Bloch, G. (1956) 'Industrial production in Western Europe and the United States', *Banca Nazionale del Lavoro Quarterly Review*, no. 39

Pasinetti, L.L. (1981) *Structural change and economic growth*, Cambridge University Press, Cambridge

Peknik, M. (1983) 'Aspects of the effectiveness of industrial investments in state investment plans', *Planove Hospodarstvi*, no. 5 (in Czech)

Pickersgill, J. (1976) 'Soviet household saving behaviour', *Review of Economics and Statistics*, vol. 58

──── (1980) 'Recent evidence on Soviet household behaviour', *Review of Economics and Statistics*, vol. 62

Pindak, F. (1983) 'Inflation under central planning', *Jahrbuch der Wirtschaft Osteuropas*, vol. 8-II

Piotrowska, M. (1982) 'The cross-sectional analysis of the industrialisation process of capitalist countries', *Prace Naukowe Wrocław School of Economics*, no. 209 (in Polish)

Płowiec, U. (1981) *Functioning of foreign trade and intensive growth*, PWE, Warsaw (in Polish)

Plyshevsky, B.P. (ed.) (1972) *Effectiveness of investments. Issues in theory and practice*, Ekonomika Publishers, Moscow (in Russian)

Porket, J.L. (1984) 'The shortage, use and reserves of labour in the Soviet Union', *Osteuropa-Wirtschaft*, vol. 29, no. 1

Portes, R. (1974) 'Macroeconomic equilibrium under central planning', *Institute for International Economic Studies, University of Stockholm, Seminar Paper*, no. 40

──── (1977) 'The control of inflation: lessons from East-European experience', *Economica*, vol. 44, no. 2

──── (1979) 'Internal and external balance in a centrally planned economy', *Journal of Comparative Economics*, vol. 3

──── (1981) 'Macroeconomic equilibrium and disequilibrium in centrally planned economies', *Economic Inquiry*, vol. 19, October

──── (undated) 'The theory and measurement of macroeconomic disequilibrium in centrally planned economies' (mimeo)

──── and Winter, D. (1977) 'The supply of consumption goods in centrally planned economies', *Journal of Comparative Economics*, vol. 1, no. 4

──── and Winter, D. (1978) 'The demand for money and for consumption goods in centrally planned economies', *Review of Economics and Statistics*, vol. 60, no. 1

──── (1980) 'Disequilibrium estimates for consumption goods markets in centrally planned economies', *Review of Economic Studies*, vol. 47

Poznanski, K. (1979) 'Research activity and licensing policy in Hungary in the 1970s', Warsaw (mimeo)

Pryor, F. (1977) 'Some costs and benefits of markets: an empirical study', *Quarterly Journal of Economics*, vol. 91

Racz, M. (1985) 'Inter-country relations at the microeconomic level: the intra-CMEA and the Hungarian experience', *Trends in the World Economy Series*, Budapest, no. 51

Rosefielde, S. (1973) *Soviet international trade in H-O perspective*, Lexington Books, Lexington, Mass.

Rostow, W.W. (1960) *The stages of economic growth*, Cambridge University Press, Cambridge

──── (1961) *Politics and the stages of economic growth*, Cambridge University Press, Cambridge

──── (1978) *The world economy. History and prospect*, Macmillan, London

Sakai, S. (1956) *The theory of structural change of national economy*, The Science Council of Japan, Tokyo

Schroeder, G. and Severin, B. (1976) 'Soviet consumption and incomes policies in perspective' in *Soviet economy in a new perspective. Studies prepared for the use of the Joint Economic Committee*, US Congress

Shen, T.Y. (1984) 'The estimation of X-inefficiency in eighteen countries', *Review of Economics and Statistics*, vol. 66, no. 1

Skolka, J.V. (1977) 'Unbalanced productivity growth and the growth of public services', *Journal of Public Economics*, vol. 7

Sokołowski, K. (1978) *Inflation*, Toruń University, Toruń (in Polish)

Soos, K.A. (1983) 'The problem of time lags in the short-term control of macroeconomic processes', *Acta Oeconomica*, vol. 30, nos. 3–4

——— (1985) 'Planification impérative, régulation financière, "grand orientations" et campagnes', *Revue d'Eetudes Comparatives Est–Ouest*, vol. 16, no. 2

Srejn, Z. and Novotny, V. (1980) 'The development of the investment rate in the Czechoslovak economy', *East European Economics*, vol. 18, no. 4

Stankovsky, J. (1973) 'Determinant factors of East–West trade', *Soviet and East European Foreign Trade*, vol. IX, no. 2

Stojkov, I. (1983) 'Certain dependencies and regularities in the development of the investment processes in Bulgaria', *Statistika*, vol. 30, no. 1 (in Bulgarian)

Stouracova, J. and Roubalova, L. (1977) 'A contribution of Soviet economists with respect to the effectiveness of foreign economic relations', *Politicka Ekonomie*, no. 3 (in Czech)

Streeten, P. (1962) 'Wages, prices and productivity', *Kyklos*, vol. 15, fasc. 4

Szatmary, T. (1978) mimeo. (in Hungarian), quoted in Poznanski (1979)

Szpilewicz, A. (1979) *Resources for the future*, 'Poland 2000' Committee, Warsaw (in Polish)

——— (1984) 'What will we be forging in 20 years?', *Przeglad Techniczny*, no. 38 (in Polish)

——— (1985) 'Fuel and energy policy, 1986–1990', *Przeglad Techniczny*, no. 33 (in Polish)

Timmermann, V. (1983) 'Contributions of economic science to solving the problems of developing countries', *Economics*, vol. 27

Tuitz, G. (1983) 'Structural change and productivity. Development in manufacturing industries of the European centrally planned economics', *Forschungsberichte, The Vienna Institute for Comparative Economic Studies*, no. 85

Ueno, H. (1976–7) 'Conception and evaluation of Japanese industrial policy', *Japanese Economic Studies*, vol. 5, Winter

United Nations, (1977) *Structure and change in European industry*, New York

——— (1971, 1980, 1983–5) *Economic Bulletin for Europe*

United Nations Economic Commission for Europe (1969; 1980–5) *Economic survey of Europe, Part I: Structural trends and prospects in the European economy*, 1980–5 issues

——— (1978) 'Overall economic perspective for the ECE region up to 1990', UN ECE, Geneva, ECE/EC. AD./17, 17 March (mimeo)

US Congress, Joint Economic Committee (1982) *USSR: Measures of economic growth and development, 1950–1980*, Studies prepared for the use of the JEC

Vanous, J. (1979) 'An econometric model of world trade of member countries of the Council of Mutual Economic Assistance', Unpublished PhD dissertation, Yale University

Varga, W. (1980) 'Industrial structure and structural change in the FRG, Austria, Poland and Hungary and their influence on productivity, 1960–1972', *Eastern European Economics*, vol. 18

Vernon, R. (1966) 'International investment and international trade in the product cycle', *Quarterly Journal of Economics*, vol. 80, no. 2

Wakar, A. (ed.) (1959) *An outline of the theory of socialist economy*, PWN Publishers, Warsaw (in Polish)

Watanabe, T. (1969) 'Approached to the problem of intercountry comparison of input–output relations: a survey and suggestions for further research', in *International comparisons of intercountry data*, UN, New York

Weiss, F.D. (1983) 'West Germany's trade with the East: hypotheses and perspectives', *Kieler Studien*, Nr. 179, Kiel

Westphal, L.E. and Kim, K.S. (1977) 'Industrial policy and development in Korea', *World Bank Staff Working Paper*, Washington, D.C., no. 263

Wiles, P.J.D. (1977) *Economic institutions compared*, Blackwell, Oxford

——— (1983) 'Soviet inflation, 1982', *Jahrbuch der Wirtschaft Osteuropas*, vol. 8-II

Winiecki, J. (1978) 'Sources of inflation in Western economies. Some theoretical considerations', *Maandschrift Economie*, nos. 11–12

——— (1979) 'Japan's imports and exports of technology policy', *Studies in Comparative International Development*, vol. XIV, nos. 3–4, Fall–Winter

——— (1982) 'Investment cycles and an excess demand inflation in planned economies: sources and processes, *Acta Oeconomica*, vol. 28, nos. 1–2

——— (1983) Central planning and export orientation, *Oeconomica Polona*, no. 3–4

——— (1984a) 'What next in [Polish] Economic Reform?', May (mimeo) (in Polish)

——— (1984b) 'Permanent problems of disequilibria and shortage in centrally planned economies', *Skandinaviska Enskilda Banken Quarterly Review*, no. 3

——— (1984c) 'Economic trends and prospects in comparative perspective: East', October (mimeo)

——— (1984d) 'The overgrown industrial sector in Soviet-type economies: explanations, evidence, consequences', mimeograph, Warsaw (later published in *Comparative Economic Studies*, vol. 28, no. 4, 1987)

——— (1985a) 'Portes *ante portas*: a critique of the revisionist interpretation of inflation under central planning', *Comparative Economic Studies*, vol. 27, no. 2

——— (1985b) 'Central planning and export orientation in manufactures. Theoretical considerations on the impact of system-specific features on specialization', *Economic Notes*, vol. 14, no. 2

——— (1985c) 'Inflation under central planning: sources, processes and manifestations', *Konjunkturpolitik*, vol. 31, no. 3

—— (1985d) 'Heckscher–Ohlin N × M × 2 model: notes on policy effects and cross-theoretical compatibilities', Warsaw (mimeo)

—— (1986a) 'Distorted macroeconomics of central planning, an approach to theory and evidence', *Banca Nazionale del Lavoro Quarterly Review*, no. 157

—— (1986b) 'Production structures in planned economies: world trends and institutional factors, *Ekonomista*, no. 1 (in Polish)

—— (1986c) 'Are Soviet-type economies entering the era of long-term decline?' *Soviet Studies*, no. 3

—— (1986d) 'Soviet-type economies: considerations for the future', *Soviet Studies*, no. 4

—— (1986e) *Inflation under market and plan*, PWN Publishers (in Polish)

Winiecki, E.D. and Winiecki, J. (1987) 'Manufacturing structures in CPEs: patterns of change and institutional factors', *Jahrbuch der Wirtschaft Osteuropas*, vol. 12-I

Wojciechowski, B. (1981) 'Import intensity of production. Branch-level analysis', Institute of Foreign Trade, Warsaw (mimeo) (in Polish)

Wyżnikiewicz, B. (1982) 'Factor price ratios in Polish foreign trade', *Central Statistical Office Studies*, Warsaw, vol. 125 (in Polish)

Zaleski, E. and Wienert, H. (1980) *Technology transfer between East and West*, OECD, Paris

Zaleski, E. *et al.* (1969) *Science policy in the USSR*, OECD, Paris

Index

toward capital-intensive goods 148–54; and exports of sophisticated goods to COMECON countries 166–7; and import needs for export goods 191–2, 196

Crawford, Nick 181, 198–9

credits, Western 170–4

Csaba, Laszlo 8, 77, 166, 169n27

Csikos-Nagy, Bela 34, 45–6

Culbertston, William P. 55

Czechoslovakia *see* most developed STEs

Dahlstedt, Roy 16, 36n29

Davies, R.W. 130n11, 175, 203n29

Dezsenyi-Gueuliette, Agota 37n39, 187, 194–5, 198

disequilibrium theory, applications to STEs 3, 55, 61

Dmowski, Zygmunt 168n11

doctored plan fulfilment reports *see* economic growth, enterprises, incentives

do-it-yourself bias *see* production and employment structures, enterprises

Dolejsi, B. 59, 68n29

Dorosz, Andrzej 195

Drabek, Zdenek 154

Drechsler, L. 169n26

Drecin, J. 19

Drewnowski, Jan 69n35

Dreze, J.H. 168n23

Dubcek, Alexander 54

Dunajewski, Henri 53

Dyker, David A. 36n82

East Germany *see* most developed STEs

economic growth 4, 6–8, 11–12, 15, 26, 46–51, 53, 90, 92–6
  and economic reforms 170–1
  and structural distortions 90, 92–6

import constrained 140
'intensive' growth 171–2
maximisation strategy 11–12, 15
partly fictitious due to doctored reports 4, 46–51
'rush' growth 4, 6–7

economic reforms, Western credits as a substitute of 170–1

Edgren, Gosta 67n6

Eliasson, Gunnar 85

enterprises 4–6, 10–13, 17–19, 42–7, 75–6, 136, 138, 146–8, 175–90, 192–3
  and barriers to innovation and imitation 175–90
  and exports 146–8, 183
  and goals similarity of managers and workers 42–3
  and uncertainty of supplies 5–6, 11, 77
  as suppliers of inputs to exported goods 148, 192–3
  do-it-yourself bias of 75–6
  incentives to doctor plan fulfilment reports 4, 11–12, 52
  incentives to plan fulfilment 4, 17, 77
  interactions with central planners 4–5, 11–13, 18–19, 47
  see also central planners, incentives

excess demand 3–10, 16–21, 24, 38–9, 55, 60–1, 90–3, 136–41, 145, 156, 174, 186, 192–7
  and distorted production structure 90–3
  and technological obsolescence 186
  endogenous to the system 8, 15
  for imports 136–41, 145, 183, 192–7